Slimming
Recipe Book

By the Experts of Slimming Magazine

Foreword by Patience Bulkeley

COLLINS

Slimming Magazine contributors:
Editors: Sybil Greatbatch and Glynis McGuinness
Home Economists: Helen Mott and Victoria Anthony
Nutritionist: Nigel Dickie, BSc, PhD
Editor of Slimming Magazine: Patience Bulkeley

First published in 1984
by William Collins Sons & Co Ltd
London · Glasgow · Sydney
Auckland · Johannesburg

© Slimming Magazine, S.M. Publications Ltd 1984

Designed by Sackville Design Group Ltd
32-34 Great Titchfield Street, London W1P 7AD
Art director: Al Rockall
Editor: Heather Thomas

ISBN pb 0 00 411944 4
ISBN hb 0 00 411943 6

Printed and bound by South China Printing Co, Hong Kong

Contents

Foreword

by Patience Bulkeley

Editor, *Slimming Magazine*

We work to a very basic recipe rule on *Slimming Magazine:* if *we* wouldn't want to prepare it, cook it and eat it, then we don't put it into print! If a dish doesn't make good sense to us, we certainly aren't going to serve it up to you. That is why, in this first complete collection of our recipes, you will *not* find instructions for making, for instance, a low-calorie Christmas pudding.

Yes, there is such a creation. We can still hear unenticing echoes of its ingredients — rather a lot of grated carrot, we remember — being solemnly recited on some radio programme by an obviously well-meaning woman. But, without wishing to be unkind to her or to carrots, we have to say that it is *this* kind of concept that gives weight control a bad name.

What gets you slim and ensures that you stay in shape, you see, isn't what you eat once a year or even once a month. The odd brief blow-out now and then, if you feel the urge, is not going to turn you into a Michelin madam. The true key to a lithely slim shape — the sort of figure it's a joy to face in a full-length mirror — lies in what you eat day in, day out. So, when surplus weight is a problem, the secret of getting slim for ever lies in systematically improving all the nitty-gritty little habits that make up your personal daily eating pattern.

If what's been 'normal' for you up till now has made you overweight, it means accepting that you have to find — to some extent, anyway — a *new* norm. It means inspecting your total everyday food intake with a nutritionally aware and calorie-conscious eye. For the sake of your general health as well as your figure, it means making all kinds of little switches and substitutions which, singly, may scarcely seem worth bothering about — but they do eventually add up to better health and *effortless* weight control.

The really good news is that a lot of these little improvements are practically painless. Once you realise, for instance, that swapping your usual whole milk for the skimmed sort halves your milky calories without cutting your calcium, then it is an *easy* new habit to acquire. And we are utterly against unnecessary suffering of any sort!

This very special recipe book will get you used to cooking with much less fat, cutting sugar and upping fibre. These are things which many doctors nowadays urge *everybody* to do, whether or not a weight problem is present. So you have here an ideal basis for healthy eating, whether you are catering for one, for two or a whole family.

If you do have surplus weight to lose, though, then these recipes and the whole eating philosophy they express can play a big fat role in keeping you slim. Just as important, this kind of cooking will make sure that you stay that way. And the best news of all? You'll *enjoy* it!

Introduction

If you had been trying to lose weight and protect your health 20 years ago, you would have said a virtuous 'no' or 'very little, please' to any food labelled with the dreaded word carbohydrate and have cut right down on starchy foods like bread and potatoes. Probably you thought that these were the most fattening foods — even the only fattening foods, the real baddies for weight and health. While those animal protein foods, such as meat and cheese, were the golden goodies that helped your health and made you slim.

Have a look at that 1960s 'perfect' meal in our picture on page 10 and observe that its so-called virtuous steak, salad and cheese add up to a hefty 1,025 calories. No wonder so many people found weight loss slow on old low-carbohydrate diets. Even more worrying in the light of today's nutritional knowledge, the 1960s meal puts a heavy emphasis on foods that are not only calorie-laden in themselves but are now also known to be actually bad for health if they are eaten in too-generous amounts.

To be specific, that steak and salad meal is horrendously high in fat. No less than 71 per cent of all those calories it supplies come from the fat in the milk, oily salad dressing, butter, cheese and steak (even lean meat contains fat). Fat is not just calorie-loaded; it is now strongly suspected of being directly implicated in heart disease and other serious conditions.

Perhaps the most interesting thing about the 1960s perfect meal is what is missing. Apart from the meagre starch-reduced crispbreads, there is not a starchy food in sight, not even one humble potato. Now we know better. Nutritionists have confirmed that starchy carbohydrate foods, such as potatoes, wholegrain breads and cereals, are invaluable sources of vitamins, minerals and dietary fibre. They are extremely good for our health, and because of their fibre content they have built-in benefits for a slimmer.

Today's advice for a healthy diet is summed up as: eat far less fat, less fat-supplying animal foods (such as red meat, full-cream milk and cheese) and eat less salt (you can use a potassium chloride salt substitute in any of the recipes in this book). Eat more fruit, more vegetables, more cereals and wholegrain breads and only a moderate amount of animal foods, ideally those with a low-fat content, such as poultry, fish and skimmed milk. Now have a look at the perfect 1980s meal (page 11) and see how this advice works in practice. Chicken, vegetables, fresh fruit make a balanced meal that is very low in fat, adequate in protein, high in vitamins, minerals and dietary fibre — ideal for a slimmer.

Do you need to slim?

Check the charts below which are a guide to your ideal weight. You could easily be a little more or less than the figures given and be at your personal best weight. You are aiming at a flesh layer that looks good and feels non-flabby. For practical purposes, forget about 'big bones' and wrist, hand or shoe measurements as a firm indication of frame size. Consider instead your skeleton's spread. Neat and narrow body 'scaffolding' will call for less cladding than would a rangier bone structure. If you are more than 2 stone/12 kilos overweight, you may have to reassess your ideal weight target as you get slimmer. Many a long-time 'big girl' often discovers that her flab had been concealing a much smaller frame than she had imagined.

How to lose excess weight

You can use the recipes in this book to construct slimming menus using either of the following very successful methods. The first is the classic method of counting calories.

Counting your calories

A calorie is a unit of energy. Most drinks and all foods contain calories, and these energy units are literally burned up by the body as fuel both for its maintenance and for movement.

If you eat more calories than your body uses, it will store them as fat. If you eat fewer calories than your body burns up, it will call on its fat reserves to make up the difference and you will lose weight. If you keep your calorie intake in balance with the calories your body burns, then you will maintain your weight.

The perfect 1960s meal
A meal considered nutritionally marvellous in 1960 centred on a great big steak with oil-dressed salad alongside — salt to taste, too. It was felt that crispbreads, butter and a hunk of Cheddar cheese were much better for you than a pudding. To drink, there was a big glass of creamy milk. The total calories for the meal amount to 1,025, and no thought was given then to fats and fibre. This 'perfect' meal contained 30.5 fat units and a very low 3 grams fibre — a tenth of the minimum daily amount now recommended.

IF YOU ARE A WOMAN				IF YOU ARE A MAN			
4-ft-10	1.47m	7-st-8	48kg	5-ft-1	1.55m	8-st-11	56kg
4-ft-11	1.50m	7-st-11	49.5kg	5-ft-2	1.57m	9-st-1	57.5kg
5-ft-0	1.52m	8-st-0	51kg	5-ft-3	1.60m	9-st-4	59kg
5-ft-1	1.55m	8-st-3	52.5kg	5-ft-4	1.63m	9-st-7	60.5kg
5-ft-2	1.57m	8-st-7	54kg	5-ft-5	1.65m	9-st-10	62kg
5-ft-3	1.60m	8-st-9	55kg	5-ft-6	1.68m	10-st-1	64kg
5-ft-4	1.63m	8-st-12	56.5kg	5-ft-7	1.70m	10-st-5	66kg
5-ft-5	1.65m	9-st-1	57.5kg	5-ft-8	1.73m	10-st-9	67.5kg
5-ft-6	1.68m	9-st-8	61kg	5-ft-9	1.75m	10-st-13	69.5kg
5-ft-7	1.70m	9-st-9	61.5kg	5-ft-10	1.78m	11-st-4	72kg
5-ft-8	1.73m	9-st-12	62.5kg	5-ft-11	1.80m	11-st-8	73.5kg
5-ft-9	1.75m	10-st-2	64.5kg	6-ft-0	1.83m	11-st-12	75.5kg
5-ft-10	1.78m	10-st-5	66kg	6-ft-1	1.85m	12-st-3	77.5kg
5-ft-11	1.80m	10-st-10	68kg	6-ft-2	1.88m	12-st-8	80kg
6-ft-0	1.83m	11-st-0	70kg	6-ft-3	1.90m	13-st-0	82.5kg

Heights are minus footwear; but these
medium-frame weights include
an allowance of 2 to 3lb
(about 1kg) for light clothing.

The perfect 1980s meal

The 1980s emphasis is on diets low in fat, and high in fibre. This meal contains 19 grams fibre, 3.5 fat units. Concern with protein intake is now considered misplaced, so the big steak becomes a smaller and much less fatty chicken breast. There is a baked potato (with a low-fat dressing), sweetcorn and broad beans, which are all good fibre sources. To drink, there is a glass of no-fat tomato juice. To follow, the fruit salad plus ice-cream meets a sweet craving at low calorie cost. The meal's total is, in fact, a very moderate 635 calories.

Are you getting enough fibre?

Experts estimate that you should eat between 30 and 45 grams fibre a day, whether or not you have surplus weight to shed. These four groups show just how much fibre that means:

1 40g/1½oz toasted bran cereal (8.5 grams fibre), 25g/1oz dried dates with stones (2.1 grams), 4 bran crispbreads (4.4 grams), 1 medium apple (2.7 grams), 1 baked 200g/7oz potato (4.9 grams), 115g/4oz carrots (3.2 grams), 115g/4oz peas (8.8 grams). Total: 34.69 grams fibre; 570 calories.

2 Two small slices wholemeal bread (4.8 grams fibre), 40g/1½oz All Bran (12.0 grams), 1 medium pear (2.4grams), 25g/1oz dried apricots (6.8 grams) and 115g/4oz frozen peas (8.8 grams). Total: 34.8 grams fibre; 375 calories.

3 *Fibre foods for the sweeter tooth: 40g/1½oz bran flakes (6.3 grams), 25g/1oz dried apricots (6.8 grams), 30ml/2 level tablespoons sultanas (1.4 grams), 15ml/1 level tablespoon bran (1.2 grams), 1 medium orange (3.4 grams), 4 small slices wholemeal bread (9.6 grams), 150g/5oz can baked beans in tomato sauce (10.5 grams). Total: 39.2 grams fibre; 625 calories.*

4 *40g/1½oz crunchy bran cereal (11.6grams), 2 slices wholemeal bread (6 grams), 115g/4oz spinach, boiled and drained (6.8 grams) 115g/4oz sweetcorn, boiled and drained (5.2 grams), 1 baked 200g/7oz potato (4.9 grams), 1 medium pear eaten with skin (2.4 grams). Total: 36.9 grams fibre; 575 calories.*

The Top Twenty

These are top of the calorie charts and each food shown supplies at least 130 calories per 25g/1oz. However, it is not the calories-per-ounce figure alone which determines whether the food is potentially highly fattening or just moderately fattening. The amount normally eaten is equally important. All the foods pictured carry a 'go easy' warning, but the ones to pick out as the greatest potential dangers to your diet are those with not only a high calorie-per-ounce rating, but also a comparatively heavy average-portion weight, too.

1 Cooking oil
255 calories per 25g/1oz; 120 calories in a 15ml tablespoon, 40 calories in a 5ml teaspoon.

2 Lard
253 calories for the 25g/1oz shown.

3 Butter and margarine
210 calories per 25g/1oz; 50 calories in the quantity spread on a small slice of bread.

4 Peanut butter
177 calories per 25g/1oz; 85 calories' worth spread on this small slice of bread.

5 Peanuts
162 calories per 25g/1oz roasted and salted. Just over 300 calories in this small packet. With the exception of chestnuts, all nuts are very high in calories.

6 Crisps
150 calories per 25g/1oz — but note there is less than this in an average small packet — 140 calories.

7 Cheese straws
170 calories per 25g/1oz — around 100 calories in the six shown.

8 Chocolate cake
155 calories per 25g/1oz; nearly 400 in this portion.

9 Pastry
150 calories per 25g/1oz in baked shortcrust. And 305 in the pastry alone in this average portion of apple pie.

10 Sausage rolls
130 calories per 25g/1oz and these two drum up a staggering 845 calorie total.

11 Shortbread biscuits
These two small ones together weigh 25g/1oz and come to 145 calories.

12 Chocolate
This charts 150 calories per 25g/1oz — this bar costs 390 calories.

13 Pâté
Up to 135 calories per 25g/1oz. A weighty 640 calories in the portion shown.

14 Cream cheese
There's 25g/1oz spread on this crispbread: 125 calories.

15 Double cream
This rates 127 calories per 25g/1oz and there's that much on top of this trifle.

16 Hard cheese
Between 115 and 135 calories for 25g/1oz; about 400 calories in this portion of Gruyère.

17 Bockwurst sausage
180 calories per 25g/1oz and 625 calories in these two sausages.

18 Clotted cream
165 calories for 25g/1oz — the quantity on top of this scone.

19 Mayonnaise
205 calories for the 25g/1oz portion shown.

20 Salami
160 calories per 25g/1oz, but this 40g/1½oz portion weighs pretty light at 240 calories.

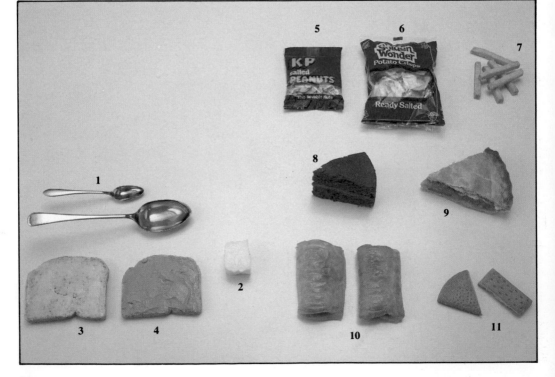

It is estimated that the average woman burns up about 2,000 calories daily; and the average man from 2,500 to 3,000 calories a day. This means that if a woman is overweight and cuts her calorie intake down to 1,500 a day, she will be calling up about 500 calories-worth of fat from her reserves each day. Roughly speaking, about 3,500 calories 'called-up' means 0.5kg/1lb of surplus weight lost. As a general rule, for various reasons, the more overweight you are the faster you will shed weight when you start dieting. We suggest you start at 1,500 calories a day (that's the *maximum* allowance) if you have 19kg/3st or more to lose. But most dieters find the 6kg/1st difficult to shift, and it may be necessary to cut down to 1,200 or a strict 1,000 calories a day in order to shed the final stubborn pounds. Women who have only a few surplus pounds to lose may also need to keep to 1,000 calories a day to ensure weight loss. Men can add 250 calories to these figures, dieting on a minimum of 1,250 calories a day — up to 1,750.

If you are in good health, it is not necessary to get your doctor's permission to go on a properly designed diet of 1,000 calories daily or more: if you follow one of the menu plans in the next chapter, you will be getting all the nutrients you require and you will see how you can construct your own nutritionally balanced menus.

Calorie-counting remains the classic slimming method because it has the great advantage of flexibility. Within a sensible framework, you can eat literally anything you like and still lose weight, provided you do not exceed your overall calorie total for each day.

The Low-Fat Diet

The nutritional principles on which the low-fat diet is based are good ones to follow for your health's sake even if you do not have a surplus weight problem. But they will lead to sure and speedy weight loss, too — because, by cutting fats, you will automatically cut the highest-calorie foods you normally consume. Ounce for ounce, fats from any source — animal or vegetable — provide double the calories of even the highest-calorie carbohydrate foods such as flour or sugar. Just 25g/1oz butter or margarine costs 210 calories. Corn, cooking or olive oil is even higher: 255 calories. Compare these figures with the cost of 25g/1oz sugar at 112 calories or the cost of plain boiled or baked potatoes at a mere 24 calories for 25g/1oz, and you can see why fats are the most fattening foods of all. Fats are so disproportionately high in calories that if you were simply to cut all the obvious fats right out of your daily diet from now on, you would greatly reduce your overall calorie intake. It is not, however, quite as straight-forward as this. Although butter, margarine, lard and cooking oils are easily identifiable as fats, many foods contain large amounts of 'invisible' fats. We are not just talking of manufactured foods: you might be surprised to know just how much 'invisible' fat is to be found in a pint of whole milk, a hunk of cheese or a juicy steak. There is, for instance, as much unseen ofat in cheese as in chocolate. It is these unseen fats as well as the readily identifiable ones that make such a high-calorie contribution to everyday eating.

The greatest contribution to the low-fat

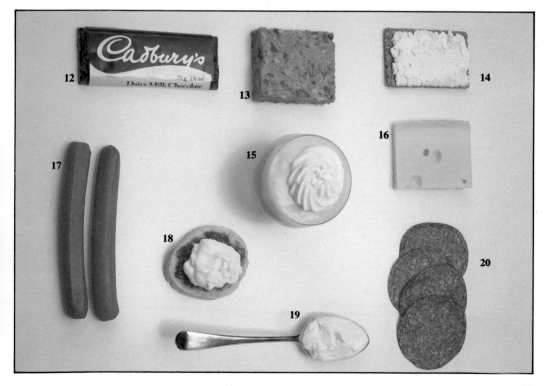

The Bottom Twenty

These foods are bottom of the calorie charts which means you can eat them by the barrrowful — that is, unless you cook them with any high-calorie additions.

1 Rhubarb
2 calories per 25g/1oz raw but a wolf in sheep's clothing unless you are happy to use artificial sweetener when you stew. Most people add 115g/4oz sugar to a pound of rhubarb bringing the total to 480 calories.

2 Apricots
7 calories per 25g/1oz when fresh weighed with stones, but dried apricots work out higher at 52 calories for the same amount — 10 calories in a dried apricot. The Apricot Snow is just 120 calories a portion (recipe page 108).

3 Tomatoes
4 calories per 25g/1oz raw. There are 8 calories in a fresh average tomato and 60 calories when it is sliced and fried.

4 Aubergine
4 calories per 25g/1oz raw, aubergine sheds all its calorie advantage when fried. A 25g/1oz slice fried is 60 calories. Half a stuffed aubergine need only come to 195 calories (see recipe page 87).

5 Celery
2 calories per 25g/1oz. Only 1 calorie in the piece of celery shown, but 65 calories in the cream cheese filling.

6 Chicory
3 calories per 25g/1oz. Only 10 calories in this whole chicory heart.

7 Carrots
6 calories per 25g/1oz. Only 12 calories in an average carrot.

8 Gherkins
5 calories per 25g/1oz. Less than 2 calories in a small gherkin; 3 calories in a large one.

9 Melon
*4 calories per 25g/1oz for a yellow or
honeydew melon with skin and 24 calories
in an average 175g/6oz portion. The ogen
melon is 5 calories per 25g/1oz but is still
only 60 calories for this very generous 350g/
12oz portion.*

10 Lemon
*4 calories per 25g/1oz. Just 20 calories in a
whole lemon.*

11 Onions
*7 calories per 25g/1oz raw. Only 5 calories
in a pickled onion and 20 calories in an
average whole onion — but a hefty 100
calories in the 25g/1oz fried portion.*

12 Radishes
*4 calories per 25g/1oz; count 2 calories for
each radish.*

13 Courgettes
*4 calories per 25g/1oz and about 10 calories
in an average boiled helping. But please
note the substantial 55 calories in the fried
courgette serving.*

14 Watercress
*4 calories per 25g/1oz — that's the amount
shown here.*

2

3

7

11

10

12

14

15 Cucumber
3 calories per 25g/1oz — that's the seven slices shown.
16 Lettuce
3 calories per 25g/1oz; only 15 calories in the whole lettuce.
17 Strawberries and raspberries
7 calories per 25g/1oz. Only 30 calories in the portion of strawberries shown. Sugar adds just 17 calories per 5ml teaspoon, but double cream adds another 127 calories for the 25g/1oz topping.
18 Mushrooms
4 calories per 25g/1oz when raw. Fried whole button mushrooms increase to 40 calories; sliced and fried buttons to 50 calories. Flat

mushrooms fried whole total 60 calories; sliced and fried they add up to 75 calories.
19 Gooseberries
5 calories per 25g/1oz for cooking gooseberries, but it took 40g/1½oz sugar to give this 175g/6oz portion of stewed gooseberries a sweet taste — brings the total to 200 calories. Ripe dessert gooseberries, eaten raw are 10 calories per 25g/1oz.
20 Grapefruit
At 3 calories an ounce, grapefruit is an ideal low-calorie fruit. It's pretty silly to use canned sweetened grapefruit when this average portion supplies 60 calories in comparison to only 20 calories for the medium fresh grapefruit half.

dieting concept, pioneered by *Slimming*, was made when the magazine's nutritionists devised the fat unit method of counting the fat in foods. Each food is given a fat unit rating from 0 upwards. You are allowed up to 10 fat units a day and in this way you should achieve a good weight loss. Not only will you shed weight, but by eating far less fat you will also be following one of the major guidelines for healthy eating now earnestly recommended by world health authorities. The correlation between high fat consumption and obesity and obesity-linked diseases has long caused medical and scientific concern.

All the recipes in this book are given a fat unit count. To follow a low-fat diet, just make sure you choose no more than 10 fat units a day. You do need a little fat in your diet, so do not go below 7 fat units a day. If you eat anything in addition to the meals you choose, you must also count in their fat units. Basic foods are listed in the chart at the back of this book. You can pile up your plate with as many vegetables and eat as much fruit as you wish. Fruit and vegetables, with the exception of avocado pears, contain virtually no fat and can be eaten freely on a low-fat diet.

Why eating more fibre can help you slim

Dietary fibre occurs naturally in unrefined cereals and in fruits and vegetables. Composed of cellulose and other substances whose benefits are gradually being explored and revealed by nutritional research, it is really the residue of plant cell walls: the 'packaging' that surrounds all the other nutritional elements such as protein, vitamins and minerals.

A diet rich in fibre offers very real advantages on both health and weight grounds. Its first plus from a slimming viewpoint is that high-fibre foods also happen to be the kind that fill you up and are, therefore, extra satisfying to eat. Very often, they are more 'chewy'. It does not take long for a fibre-free glass of milk or piece of cheese to slip down, for example; in fact, it has often gone so fast you hardly noticed eating it. You cannot say that about a juicy apple or a bowl of crunchy bran flakes. Foods like these give added enjoyment to your meals — and, because you have to eat them slowly, you savour them more fully.

The next plus is that you feel fuller on less food. High-fibre foods fill the stomach more effectively than the same calorific quantity of any other food. Furthermore, fibre-rich foods take longer to digest than fibre-free foods do. This means that, if your diet contains an adequate amount of fibre, you should never feel uncomfortably hungry while you are slimming.

The last plus — but by no means the least

One way of increasing the fibre in your diet is to substitute brown rice for white. Whereas boiled white rice has only 0.1 grams fibre per 25g/1oz, brown rice has 0.4 grams for the same weight

— is that there is considerable evidence that fibre-rich foods are less fully digested than others. Dietary fibre passes straight through the body. This means that not all the calories you have actually eaten are utilised by the body. To give you an example, let us suppose you have enjoyed a serving of a fibre-rich food like sweetcorn. Some of that sweetcorn will pass straight through your system un-digested; so that though you have eaten, say, 70 calories' worth, your body has not used all of them.

All fibre in fibrous foods passes through the body undigested and it serves a very valuable function in doing so. On its way, it collects other waste matter and helps it pass through the intestines and bowel more easily and quickly. There is evidence that this keeps the whole digestive system much healthier and reduces the risk of such 'modern' diseases as diverticulitis and bowel cancer. Intensive research into all aspects of fibre is continuing, but one fact to emerge is that the exact nature of dietary fibre varies a little from plant to plant. While the overall benefits of a high-fibre diet are ever more widely appreciated, nutritionists now believe that different fibre-forms vary in their specific health benefits and functions. This is why it is best for you to obtain your fibre from as many different sources as possible.

Whether you are limiting your overall calorie intake by directly counting calories or indirectly controlling them by means of a low-fat diet, you should also make sure you are eating a reasonable amount of fibre. Ideally, you should consume between 30 and 45 grams of fibre each day. Each recipe in this book has been fibre-counted for you, and fibre figures are given for basic foods in the chart at the back of the book.

Choosing a balanced diet

What is the perfect way to eat? Nutritional scientists tend to be a little reticent about this question, mainly because they realise that much is still unknown or not yet proved. However, from what current research tells us, a perfect diet should be low in fat, salt and sugar, and high in fibre, and provide a good mix of foods to ensure that all essential vitamins and minerals are included.

If you eat a varied healthy diet it is not necessary to add extra vitamins or minerals in the form of pills or potions that you can buy from chemists or health stores. All the things you need should be reaching you in the ordinary food you eat. In order to survive, your body needs carbohydrates, a small amount of fat, proteins, vitamins, minerals, as well as oxygen and water. It gets oxygen out of the air; all other items come from your food and drink. Without any of these essentials the body cannot function properly. But you do not benefit more by taking in more water than you need to satisfy your thirst, and it will certainly not do you any good to take in more vitamins or minerals than you need — in fact, in some instances it could do you harm.

The average person in the West has little difficulty in getting all the essential nutrients from our varied diet. When you are planning a slimming diet, though, it makes sense to check that you are choosing the best

These tasty-looking dishes add up to 1,500 calories — a perfectly balanced menu for a day of healthy eating. They are 1 Cottage Cheese, Ham and Gherkin Crispbreads — just top 2 crispbreads with 28g/1oz lean chopped ham and 2 chopped gherkins mixed with 50g/2oz cottage cheese. This totals 150 calories/2 fat units/0.8 grams fibre; 2 Bran Cereal with Banana and Apricots (recipe page 71); 3 Speedy Pilchard Pizza (recipe page 40); 4 Liver and Orange Parcel (recipe page 24); and 5 Strawberries and Yoghurt (see page 27 for ingredients)

selection of meals to make up a good nutritionally balanced diet. At the end of a slimming campaign you should feel fitter and more energetic as well as looking the best you can.

Protein

The body is mainly made up of water, protein and fat; and as the tissues of the body are constantly undergoing repair, it is essential that we eat some protein to replenish supplies. All protein is composed of a number of basic units called amino acids and most of these can be made by the body itself; the remainder, termed essential amino acids, must be provided ready-made in the diet. Proteins not only come from meat, fish and dairy products but also from some vegetables and pulses, beans being a particularly useful source. At one time, protein from animal sources was thought to be superior to vegetable protein, but that idea has now been discounted. Also in recent years the recommended amount of protein required has been reduced from previous estimates. It is now recommended that 380 grams protein a week is sufficient for the average woman, and some leading nutritionists believe that 280 grams is adequate. On a daily basis it makes sense to have meals each day that provide about 55 grams protein in total. Here is a selection of recipes to show you how this works in practice. Each recipe will, of course, supply a whole range of nutrients and we tell you about the most important ones and how they contribute to your diet in the introduction to each recipe.

21

Baked Beans and Bacon on Toast

There are 12 grams protein in a 225g/8oz can of baked beans; the bacon contributes 6 grams protein and the slice of wholemeal bread 4 grams. The protein total for the whole meal is 22 grams. This recipe will also contribute some iron, calcium and B vitamins. Both bread and bacon are good sources of vitamin B1 — the vitamin that is essential for metabolising carbohydrate in the body. Together with the B1 contained in the baked beans, this recipe will supply about 45 per cent of your daily B1 requirement.

2 rashers streaky bacon
225g/8oz can baked beans in tomato sauce
Dash Worcestershire sauce
1 large slice wholemeal bread, 40g/1½oz

Grill the bacon until crisp, then break into small pieces. Heat the baked beans, then stir in the bacon and Worcestershire sauce. Toast the bread and serve the beans on toast.

Serves 1/350 calories
2.5 fat units/20.4 grams fibre per portion

Bean Stuffed Potato
(see picture page 22)

The small 150g/5oz can of baked beans supplies 7 grams protein, and the red kidney beans in this recipe contribute another 6 grams. There are also 4 grams of protein in the potato bringing the total up to 17 grams for the meal. This meal also supplies iron, vitamin C and a range of B vitamins.

200g/7oz potato
150g/5oz can baked beans in tomato sauce
75g/3oz cooked or canned red kidney beans,
  drained
Dash Worcestershire sauce
Dash Tabasco or chilli sauce

Scrub and prick the potato, then bake in its jacket at 20°C/400°F/gas mark 6, or until soft when pinched — about 1 hour. Mix together the baked beans, red kidney beans, Worcestershire sauce and Tabasco or chilli sauce. Heat through. Make a cut along the top of the potato and carefully open out to make a hollow. Pile the beans on top and serve.

Serves 1/355 calories
0 fat units/22.3 grams fibre

Rice Salad with Chicken

The chicken in this meal supplies 14 grams protein, the peas 4.8 grams and the brown rice 4.3 grams. This brings the meal total up to 23 grams. This meal will also supply some vitamin C, plus iron and A and B vitamins.

50g/2oz long-grain brown rice
75g/3oz frozen peas
30ml/2 tablespoons oil-free French dressing
1 stick celery
75g/3oz white grapes
50g/2oz cooked chicken

Boil the rice and peas separately until tender. Drain, rinse in cold water and drain again. Mix with the oil-free French dressing. Chop the celery. Halve and pip the grapes. Discard the skin from the chicken and cut the flesh into small bite-sized pieces. Mix the celery, grapes and chicken with the peas and rice.

Serves 1/390 calories
1.5 fat units/10.7 grams fibre per portion

Prawn and Corn Chowder

The prawns come to 13 grams protein; the sweetcorn to 4 grams. There is also 5 grams protein in the milk and 2 grams in the potato and onion. The total for the meal is 24 grams. Milk contains almost all the vitamins and minerals we need in a healthy diet. Skimmed milk usually loses its vitamin A and D content when the cream is skimmed off, but many skimmed milk makers now put these vitamins back. As well as protein this recipe has useful amounts of vitamin C and calcium and small amounts of vitamin A and the B vitamin riboflavine.

25g/1oz onion
75g/3oz potato
115ml/4floz water
¼ chicken stock cube
50g/2oz peeled prawns
150g/5oz canned sweetcorn
150ml/¼ pint skimmed milk
10ml/2 level teaspoons cornflour
Salt and pepper
Paprika

Bean Stuffed Potato (recipe page 22)

Peel and chop the onion and potato. Place in a saucepan with the water and stock cube. Cover and simmer for 10 minutes. Add the prawns, sweetcorn and skimmed milk. Simmer for 5 minutes. Blend the cornflour with a little cold water until smooth. Stir into the pan, then simmer for 2 minutes, stirring all the time. Season and pour into a bowl. Sprinkle with paprika and serve.

Serves 1/345 calories
0.5 fat units/10.4 grams fibre

Vitamin C

It is easy to get all the vitamin C you need — 210mg a week for the average woman. It is needed by the body to resist infection and there have been reports that large doses of vitamin C can cure the common cold. Later research, however, found no proof of this although there was some evidence that vitamin C could alleviate cold symptoms. The best sources of vitamin C are black-currants, oranges, grapefruit, strawberries and raspberries. Ounce for ounce, potatoes are not as rich in vitamin C, but because you eat them in larger quantities they can be a useful source. You do not need to eat vitamin C every day, but if you compile your dieting menus from the recipes in this book it is highly unlikely that you will go a day without eating at least some of your recommended requirement.

Strawberries in Raspberry Sauce

Frozen fruits can contain almost as much vitamin C as fresh. If you use fresh straw-berries for this recipe, 115g/4oz will contribute about 70mg vitamin C. Use frozen straw-berries and they will contribute about 55mg. The 50g/2oz raspberries provide about 15mg when fresh and 10mg when frozen. Use all fresh fruit and this simple dessert adds up to almost three days' vitamin C supply.

115g/4oz strawberries, fresh or frozen
50g/2oz raspberries, fresh or frozen
5ml/1 level teaspoon fruit sugar

Hull the strawberries and place in a serving dish. Mash the raspberries and sugar in a small bowl with a fork. Pour over the straw berries and serve.

Serves 1/60 calories
0 fat units/6.7 grams fibre

Chicken and Fruit Salad

Prepare this salad just before you are about to eat to make sure it retains the maximum amount of vitamin C. A small orange contributes 55mg vitamin C and the kiwi fruit 60mg. Watercress is also a good source of vitamin C, but just a few sprigs will not add much to your total. However, if you did eat 25g/1oz watercress it would supply the best part of your daily vitamin C requirement. The total vitamin C in this recipe is 120mg and it also supplies other vitamins.

1 small orange
1 kiwi fruit
75g/3oz cooked chicken
15ml/1 level tablespoon natural low-fat
  yoghurt
15ml/1 level tablespoon low-calorie salad
  cream
Few sprigs watercress

Peel and segment the orange, then cut each segment in half. Peel the kiwi fruit and cut in half lengthwise. Cut each half into slices. Discard all skin from the chicken and cut the flesh into small pieces. Mix the fruits with the chicken, yoghurt and low-calorie salad cream. Pile onto a plate and garnish with a few sprigs of watercress.

Serves 1/225 calories
2 fat units/.2.3 grams fibre

Jacket Potato with Cheese and Bacon (page 24)

Jacket Potato with Cheese and Onion (page 26)

Rice, Corn and Pepper Salad

Red and green peppers are a good source of vitamin C and the 115g/4oz in this recipe provides a whole 115mg — that is more than half a week's recommended dosage. Once cut, vegetables release an enzyme which starts to destroy the vitamin C, so do not prepare salads much before the time you intend to eat them. Peanuts are high in calories so they need to be added to salads with care, but they are also rich in protein and contribute a useful supply of minerals and vitamins. The vitamin C total for this recipe is 120mg. The recipe also contains 12g protein and some B vitamins.

15g/½oz long-grain brown rice
50g/2oz green pepper
50g/2oz red pepper
115g/4oz canned sweetcorn
25g/1oz dry roasted peanuts
30ml 2 tablespoons oil-free French dressing
Salt and pepper

Boil the rice in salted water until tender. Drain and rinse under the cold tap. Discard the seeds and white pith from the pepper and dice the flesh. Mix the rice, sweetcorn, pepper and peanuts with oil-free French dressing. Season lightly with salt and pepper.

Serves 1/335 calories
5 fat units/10.5 grams fibre

Jacket Potato with Cottage Cheese and Bacon
(see picture page 23)

This 200g/7oz potato provides about 25mg vitamin C when it is freshly picked but will lose some of the vitamins if it is stored for a long time and vitamin C is also affected by cooking. You retain more vitamin C if you bake a potato rather than boil it, and if you do boil it you should use the tiniest amount of water possible. This recipe contains 15mg vitamin C, 20mg protein and also some B vitamins.

200g/7oz potato
1 rasher streaky bacon
75g/3oz cottage cheese
Salt and pepper
Fresh chives, optional

Scrub and prick the potato, then bake in its jacket at 200°C/400°F/gas mark 6 for about 1 hour, or until soft when pinched. Grill the bacon until crisp, then cut into small pieces. Cut open the potato and scoop the flesh out into a basin leaving the skin intact. Mash the flesh with the cottage cheese and season. Stir in the bacon and pile back into the potato case. Reheat in the oven for 10 minutes. Sprinkle with a few chopped chives.

Serves 1/300 calories
2.5 fat units/5 grams fibre

Iron

A great deal of iron eaten in foods is not absorbed by the body. All meat contains iron in a form that is comparatively easy for the body to extract, and liver and kidneys are the best sources. There are also valuable cereal and vegetable sources, but more iron is absorbed if you eat a food high in vitamin C at the same meal. Many breakfast cereals contain iron and you will find that manufacturers often list the content on the box. But cereals also contain substances that can inhibit the absorption of iron. However, if you add fresh fruit to your cereal, this will aid iron absorption. The body does not store up more iron than it needs and it will lose any excess to requirements in the urine. When iron is lost during menstruation, your body takes in just enough from the food you eat to top up its store. If you go for a few days without eating any iron at all, your body will draw on its reserves until you swallow another helping. The recommended weekly intake of iron for the average woman is 84mg, but men need less as they do not have to compensate for a monthly drain on their iron reserves.

Liver and Orange Parcel
(see picture page 21)

This simple but very tasty liver recipe supplies 11mg iron, 24mg protein and 85mg vitamin C. You can increase the meal's iron content by choosing peas or spinach to serve with it. A 115g/4oz portion peas contains 2.6mg iron and the same amount of spinach contains 5mg. Canned carrots have slightly more iron than fresh ones and a 284g/10oz can contains 4mg. Carrots also contain carotene which is converted by the body into vitamin A. But a 115g/4oz portion liver once a week will give you all the vitamin A you need anyway.

115g/4oz lamb's liver
1 small orange
Sprig fresh thyme or pinch dried thyme
Salt and pepper

Slice the liver thinly (you can ask the butcher to do this when you buy it). Place on a large square of foil. Cut 2 slices from the middle of the orange, then cut away the rind. Place the slices on the liver. Add the sprig of fresh thyme or sprinkle on the dried. Squeeze the juice from the rest of the orange over the liver. Season lightly. Fold up the foil to make a parcel which is tightly sealed at the edges but loose enough to allow air to circulate around the liver. Place on a baking tray and cook at 190°C/375°F/gas mark 5 for 30 minutes.

Serves 1/240 calories
4 fat units/1.0 grams fibre

Simple Liver and Tomato Casserole

Liver is an excellent source of iron — the 115g/4oz in this recipe provides 10.6mg. Offal is the only food other than fruit and vegetables to supply a substantial quantity of vitamin C. Liver also supplies valuable amounts of nine other vitamins: B6 (pyridoxine), folic acid and B12 which aid blood cell formation, A, B1, B2, D, E and K. The can of tomatoes also adds 40mg of vitamin C to the total.

115g/4oz lamb's liver
1 small onion
227g/8oz can tomatoes
Pinch mixed dried herbs
Dash Worcestershire sauce
Salt and pepper

Slice the liver and finely chop the onion. Place in a casserole dish. Roughly chop the tomatoes and add to the dish with their juice, the herbs and Worcestershire sauce. Cover and cook at 170°C/325°F/gas mark 3 for 1¼ hours.

Serves 1/240 calories
4 fat units/2.4 grams fibre

Kidney Kebabs

Kidneys are not quite as rich in iron as liver, but this 150g/5oz portion contains 10mg. Like liver, kidneys contain protein in a low-fat form, and lots of vitamins. Although mushrooms are an excellent low-calorie vegetable they have little nutritional value except for some iron. Total iron for this recipe is 11mg; protein is 24mg; and vitamin C 45mg. It also supplies some vitamin A and a range of B vitamins.

150g/5oz lamb's kidneys
¼ green or red pepper
4 small button mushrooms
5ml/1 teaspoon oil
5ml/1 teaspoon tomato ketchup
1.25ml/¼ teaspoon Worcestershire sauce
1.25ml/¼ teaspoon French mustard

Cut the kidneys in half and discard the cores. If they are fairly large, cut each half into two pieces. Discard the pith and seeds from the pepper and cut the flesh into squares. Thread the kidneys, mushrooms and pepper onto 1 long or 2 short skewers. Mix together the oil, tomato ketchup, Worcestershire sauce and mustard. Brush onto the kebabs. Heat the grill, then cook the kebabs until the kidneys are just cooked. The cooking time will vary considerably, depending on the power of the grill but do not overcook

the kidneys or they will become tough. Brush frequently with the basting mixture and turn over while cooking.

Serves 1/180 calories
3.0 fat units/1.0 grams fibre

Chicken Liver Sauce with Spaghetti

Chicken livers have about the same nutritional value as lamb's, pig's and ox liver, and this recipe includes the same range of vitamins and minerals. The tomatoes add extra vitamin C. Totals come to 15mg iron; 32g protein; 50mg vitamin C; and the recipe also includes amounts of A and B vitamins.

1 small onion
Half 225g/8oz can tomatoes
Pinch mixed dried herbs
¼ chicken stock cube
115g/4oz chicken livers
50g/2oz button mushrooms
Salt and pepper
50g/2oz wholewheat spaghetti

Finely chop the onion and roughly chop the tomatoes. Place in a small saucepan with the juice from the tomatoes, herbs and stock cube. Bring to the boil, then cover and simmer for 10 minutes. Meanwhile, cut the chicken livers into small pieces, discarding any greenish bits. Chop the mushrooms. Add the mushrooms and livers to the saucepan, simmer for another 5 minutes. Stir occasionally and add a little water if the sauce starts to stick. While the sauce is cooking, boil the spaghetti in salted water for about 10 minutes, or until just tender. Drain and serve the sauce on top.

Serves 1/385 calories
2 fat units/8.2 grams fibre

Calcium

Milk is by far the best source of calcium, and cheese and yoghurt also contain generous quantities. The good news for slimmers is that when the fat is removed from milk to produce the lower-calorie, low-fat skimmed version its calcium is unaffected. If you drink 275ml/½ pint skimmed milk a day you will automatically be getting most of the calcium you need. The weekly recommended amount for an average woman is 3,500mg and 2 litres/3½ pints skimmed milk will supply 2,660mg. This means you probably only need to eat about another 120mg calcium a day to reach the recommended total. If you do not take milk in drinks, you should choose some recipes which include milk, yoghurt, eggs or cheese — pilchards, sardines and green vegetables are also good calcium sources. The adult requirement for calcium is lower than that for children and young people up to the age of 18. This is because calcium is needed

25

to ensure the healthy growth and development of bones and teeth. So if you are planning a balanced diet for an overweight youngster the easiest way to ensure they get all the calcium they need is to allow for a 568ml/1 pint skimmed milk a day in their eating plan (some of this could be used on a breakfast cereal).

Jacket Potato with Cheese and Onion
(see picture page 23)

Cheese is one of the best sources of calcium and this 40g/1½oz Edam provides 315mg. Edam is one of the best hard cheeses to choose because it is lower in fat and calories than cheeses such as Cheddar and Stilton. Cheese also supplies plenty of protein and lots of minerals and vitamins. The potatoes and spring onions/scallions in this recipe supply an extra helping of vitamin C. Calcium total for the recipe is 400mg. Protein is 16g; vitamin C, 20mg. There are also useful amounts of B vitamins.

200g/7oz potato
2 spring onions/scallions
40g/1½oz Edam cheese
30ml/2 tablespoons skimmed milk
Paprika

Scrub and prick the potato, then bake in its jacket at 200°C/400°F/gas mark 6 for about 1 hour or until soft when pinched. Cut open the potato and carefully scoop out the flesh. Discard the roots and tough leaves from the spring onions, then chop the bulbs. Grate the cheese. Mash the potato flesh with the milk and most of the cheese. Stir in the chopped onion and spoon into the potato case. Sprinkle the remaining cheese and a little paprika on top. Reheat in the oven for 10 minutes.

Serves 1/320 calories
3.5 fat units/5.2 grams fibre

Sardine and Potato Bake

Small fish like sardines, pilchards and whitebait are a good source of calcium, but do not push the bones to the side of your plate for this is where much of the calcium lies. The 50g/2oz sardines used in this recipe provide 310mg calcium and the egg provides another 30mg. Sardines also supply some B vitamins and vitamin D. Vitamin D regulates calcium in the body but you get most of what you need of this vitamin from the action of the sun shining on your skin. Apart from calcium, eggs also supply a whole alphabet of vitamins, protein and iron. This complete recipe supplies 400mg calcium; 27g protein; 5mg iron; 40mg vitamin C; and useful amounts of vitamin D and folate.

150g/5oz potatoes, weighed peeled
50g/2oz frozen peas
50g/2oz sardines canned in oil, drained
1 egg, size 3
1 tomato

Boil the potatoes until tender. Drain and mash. While the potatoes are cooking boil the peas as instructed on the packet, then drain and set aside. Preheat the oven to 200°C/400°F/gas mark 6. Drain the sardines well and pat off any excess oil with kitchen paper. Mash them. Lightly beat the egg. Add the sardines and egg to the potato and mix well. Chop the tomato and stir into the potato mixture with the peas. Turn into an ovenproof dish and bake for 30 minutes.

Serves 1/365 calories
5 fat units/8.2 grams fibre

Egg Florentine

Frozen spinach is just as high in calcium and vitamins as fresh spinach and this 175g/6oz portion contains a whole 1,020mg calcium. Added to that is 30mg calcium in the egg and 210mg in the cheese. So this is one of the highest calcium recipes you could cook and it will supply you with enough calcium for more than 2 days. The recipe is also high in vitamin C — total 45mg — and contains 8mg iron and 22g protein. It also contains useful amounts of vitamins A and folic acid.

175g/6oz frozen chopped spinach
1 egg, size 3
25g/1oz Edam cheese

Cook the spinach as instructed on the packet. While it is cooking poach the egg and grate the cheese. Drain the spinach and place in a heatproof dish. Place the egg on top and sprinkle on the cheese. Grill until the cheese melts.

Serves 1/220 calories
4.5 fat units/10.2 grams fibre

Planning your menus

The introduction to this book will tell you about a calorie-counted diet, the low-fat diet and the advantage of eating a healthy amount of fibre. Below we give four sample menus using the recipes in this book. Each day's menu will supply you with a variety of vitamins and minerals, but do not repeat the same menu every day of the week. The more varied your diet, the less likely it will be that you will go short of any essentials. So try these menus if you wish, and add some of your own choices to make up a weekly dieting plan.

We give a 1,000 calorie menu for super-fast weight loss; a 1,250 calorie menu which is suitable if you have between 6kg/1st and 19kg/3st to lose and a 1,500 calorie menu which you should begin with if you have over 19kg/3st to lose — men will also lose weight fast on this amount. We also show you how to keep in shape with a maintenance menu of 2,000 calories (men can add an extra 500 calories).

1,000 Calorie Menu

275ml/½ pint of skimmed milk for drinks throughout the day

Breakfast or Supper
Muesli with Yoghurt and Peach (page 72)

Light Meal
Prawn and Curd Cheese Sandwich made with wholemeal bread (page 47)

Main Meals
Kidney Kebabs (page 25)
25g/1oz brown rice, boiled
115g/4oz frozen peas, boiled
1 small orange or medium pear

Free Drinks
Water, black tea and coffee can be drunk in unlimited amounts

1,250 Calorie Menu

275ml/½ pint of skimmed milk for drinks throughout the day

Breakfast or Supper
Home-made Muesli (page 70)

Light Meal
Jacket Potato with Cheese and Onion (page 25)
1 medium orange

Main Meal
Hawaiian Chicken with Brown Rice (page 33)
115g/4oz French beans
Baked Apple with Sultanas (page 107)

Free Drinks
Water, black tea and coffee can be drunk in unlimited amounts

1,500 Calorie Menu

(see picture pages 20/21)

275ml/½ pint of skimmed milk for drinks throughout the day

Breakfast or Supper
Bran Cereal with Banana and Apricots (recipe page 71: picture page 20)

Light Meal
Speedy Pilchard Pizza (recipe page 40: picture page 21)
150g/5oz grapes

Main Meal
Liver and Orange Parcel (recipe page 24: see picture page 21)
225g/8oz potato, baked in its jacket
15ml/1 tablespoon low-fat natural yoghurt
Chopped chives or parsley
115g/4oz broccoli, boiled
115g/4oz carrots, boiled

Dessert
115g/5oz raspberries or strawberries, fresh or frozen
150g/5oz carton low-fat natural yoghurt (minus the tablespoon used to top potato)

Snack
Cottage Cheese, Ham and Gherkin Crispbreads (recipe and picture page 20)

Free Drinks
Water, black tea and coffee can be drunk in unlimited amounts

2,000 Calorie Menu

275ml/½ pint of skimmed milk for drinks throughout the day

Breakfast
Wheat and Mixed Dried Fruit (page 72)

Light Meal
Macaroni in Broccoli and Cheese Sauce (page 86)
1 medium apple

Main Meal
Liver and Bacon Casserole (page 171)
200g/7oz potato, baked in its jacket
115g/4oz frozen peas, boiled
Baked Banana with Sultanas and Nuts (page 109)

Snack
Chicken, Green Pepper and Pineapple Sandwich made with wholemeal bread (page 46)

Snack
Apricot and Curd Crispbread (page 98)

Free Drinks
Water, black tea and coffee can be drunk in unlimited amounts

Things with salad: how low can you go?

Quiche 535 calories
It is not just the topping that makes quiche a dieting baddy: the pastry alone costs 250 calories per average 150g/5oz slice! Recipes vary wildly; quiche from a delicatessen could be as much as 555 calories for this amount, and you are very unlikely to pay less than 350.

Chicken Joint 345 calories
Nearly half this calorie count is in the skin of the chicken. Remove it, and any fat beneath and you bring the calorie count down. This 225g/8oz wing and breast will lose 160 calories and come down to 185. Two cooked skinless drumsticks will be 130 calories.

Steak 290 calories
The more you cook a steak the more fat it loses. The 175g/6oz medium grilled steak here costs 290 calories. Grilled rare, it would soar to 310 calories; well-done, down to 260. Many restaurants serve bigger steaks. A 275g/10oz size done rare can cost 515 calories.

Tuna 200 calories
Drain off the oil tuna often comes in; this could add 80 more calories to the contents of a 100g/3½oz can shown. Tuna in brine is the best buy and a portion from a same-sized can will give the lowest count of 110 calories.

Roast Pork 160 calories
Pork is a fatty meat, sliced with a halo of fat. Cut every scrap of fat off and roast pork costs 52 calories for 25g/1oz. With fat it costs around 30 calories per 25g/1oz more. Cut the fat from the two slices shown to get 105 calories. Thicker slices with fat could cost 325.

Canned Salmon 155 calories
This salad treat is more likely to hurt your pocket than your diet. Fortunately it comes in little 100g/3½oz cans, just right for the generous portion shown here (all makes average 44 calories for 25g/1oz). Fresh salmon costs 56 calories per 25g/1oz steamed (off the bone).

If you gather a green salad, add a tomato perhaps and serve the lot without dressing, it is unlikely to cost more than 30 calories. What can make a big difference is what you serve with it.

Pilchards *145 calories*

At a lowly 36 calories for 25g/1oz, this fish in tomato sauce makes a good salad accompaniment. Most people will settle for two pilchards at around 145 calories. Buy a small can that contains just three, though, and you will probably eat the lot at 195 calories.

Salami *140 calories*

Salami certainly has a very high fat content but it also has such a strong flavour you are unlikely to eat more than the 25g/1oz shown here. If you did, each 15g/½oz slice would cost you an additional 70 calories! Choose smaller slices and you get five to each 25g/1oz.

Crab *110 calories*

Served plain, crab is 36 calories for 25g/1oz. Add mayonnaise, though, and those calories soar. A couple of tablespoons of ordinary mayonnaise zooms the cost of this 75g/3oz portion to over 300 calories. Beware of the fancy crab dishes some restaurants serve.

Ham *95 calories*

With all visible fat trimmed off, ham will not cost you more than 50 calories per 25g/1oz. Best buy is vacuum-packed lean ham — the slices are so thin that the 50g/2oz above looks right. Two thick-cut slices off the bone with fat could cost 360 calories.

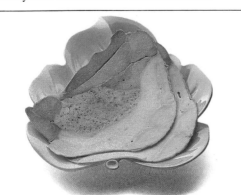

Roast Stuffed Turkey *100 calories*

At only 40 calories for 25g/1oz, turkey (without fatty skin) is a super slimmer's standby and you can safely choose from the variety of roasts and joints widely available. Even with the tasty herb stuffing shown, it is only 50 calories for 25g/1oz.

Roast Beef *90 calories*

Trim off all visible fat and roast beef is a good slimmer's buy at around 45 calories per 25g/1oz. With fat you will pay 20 calories more for each 25g/1oz topside — 25 for sirloin. Most restaurants dish up 115g/4oz and a portion of untrimmed sirloin could be 320 calories.

Easy meals

Meals for one should be simple, although they need not be any less delicious than a portion of a more elaborate creation. Our research shows that most people start a diet on their own, and in devising these recipes we have taken into account some other factors apart from calorie, fat unit and fibre counts.

To start with, your trip to the shops or supermarket should be as quick as possible so that you are not within hands' reach of lots of tempting items which are not on your slimming shopping list. None of these recipes requires you to buy a great many ingredients and a number of them can be made from items out of your store cupboard. By the way, never shop when you are hungry — plan to do it after breakfast or after lunch. The more hungry you are while you are shopping, the more tempting and less necessary foods you will buy, and the more you will eat when you get home.

As we know only too well from our own dieting experiences, recipes that call for half a banana or two-thirds of a can of tuna, or any other item that leaves a bit just asking to be finished off, are not the most successful dieting meals. Slimmers tend to have very tidy minds when it comes to left-overs and the chances are that any bits that cannot be turned into another meal, will get swallowed up anyway. Remember that it is often possible to buy some items in smaller quantities if you shop where the items are not prepackaged. For instance, although cheese packs are usually from 227g/8oz upwards, you could buy just 50g/2oz cut from a whole cheese. If you do have to buy more than you need for one recipe, plan to repeat the recipe or another to mark that food for a meal rather than a nibble.

The next important requirement for a just-for-one meal is that it should be easy to prepare and cook. Although many people will take a great deal of time and care over meals they cook to share, few of us like to put that amount of effort into meals for ourselves alone. There is also the added advantage that quick-to-prepare meals mean that you are not in that danger zone, the kitchen, for very long. Most people do their food preparation at a time when they are starting to feel hungry. Thus at a vulnerable time, they place themselves in close proximity to the prime appetite triggers — the sight and smell of food. Not surprisingly, they are tempted to help themselves to snacks. To decrease this temptation we have suggested that some of the following recipes can be prepared in advance — preferably after you have just eaten — ready to pop into the oven for your next meal.

You will find here recipes for both light meals and more substantial main meals. Where vegetables are not included, you can choose your own selection from the calorie chart at the back of the book. There are more meals for one in the breakfasts, packed lunches and vegetarian chapters and there are also puddings well worth trying in the desserts section.

Before you start your diet, sit down and devise your first week's menu. Write out your shopping list and make sure you have everything you need for the recipes you would like to try. If you plan to succeed, there is a good chance that you will.

All dishes shown on this spread make filling meals: 1 Seafood Soup (recipe page 58); 2 Pizza Omelet (recipe page 38); and 3 Citrus Chicken (recipe page 34)

Fish Meals

Canned, frozen or fresh, fish is usually a good low-calorie basis for a meal. Be wary, though, of fish canned in oil. Even when drained, your fish will have absorbed some fatty calories. Oily fish, such as mackerel, should also be carefully counted.

Tuna and Tomato Bake

It is well worthwhile keeping some tins of tuna in brine in your store cupboard. Do not be tempted to use tuna in oil instead. A small can of tuna in brine comes to about 110 calories, whereas the same amount of tuna in oil costs 195. Tuna goes well with tomatoes and this simple recipe can be made in less than half an hour. You could use Edam cheese instead of Lancashire, and bring the calories down to 310, fat units 3.

100g/3½oz can tuna in brine
2 tomatoes
1 spring onion/scallion
40g/1½oz fresh wholemeal breadcrumbs
1.25ml/¼ level teaspoon dried basil or
*   mixed herbs*
Salt and pepper
25g/1oz Lancashire cheese

Drain and flake the tuna. Slice the tomatoes. Discard the green leaves and roots from the spring onion/scallion and chop the bulb. Mix the chopped onion with the breadcrumbs and basil or mixed herbs. Season with salt and pepper. Spread half the crumb mixture over the base of a small ovenproof dish and cover with half the tomato and all the tuna. Arrange the remaining tomato on top. Grate the cheese and mix with the remaining crumb mixture. Sprinkle over the tomato and bake in a preheated oven at 190°C/375°F/gas mark 5 for 20 minutes.

Serves 1/330 calories
3.5 fat units/5.4 grams fibre

Curried Rice with Fish
(see picture page 41)

50g/2oz white long-grain rice
1.25ml/¼ level teaspoon curry powder
1.25ml/¼ level teaspoon turmeric
Pinch salt
225ml/8floz water
115g/4oz white fish fillet, e.g. cod, haddock
*   or coley, fresh or frozen*
¼ small red or green pepper
15ml/1 level tablespoon sultanas or raisins

Place the rice in a small saucepan with the curry powder, turmeric, salt and water. Add the fish if frozen but not if fresh. Cover the pan, bring to the boil and simmer gently for 10 minutes. Discard the white pith and seeds from the pepper and dice the flesh. Add to the pan with the sultanas and fresh fish if used. Cover the pan again and simmer for a further 10-15 minutes, or until the rice is tender. At the end of cooking, the water should have been absorbed. Carefully lift out the fish and discard the skin and bones. Flake the fish and mix with the rice.

Serves 1/325 calories
0.5 fat units/1.7 grams fibre

Cheesey Plaice on Vegetables
(see picture page 37)

1 medium leek
1 stick celery
50g/2oz carrot
50g/2oz mushrooms
2.5ml/½ level teaspoon dried oregano or
*   mixed herbs*
10ml/2 level teaspoons tomato purée
75ml/3floz water
Salt and pepper
150g/5oz plaice fillets, or similar flat
*   white fish, fresh or frozen*
40g/1½oz Edam cheese
1.25ml/¼ teaspoon oil
Lemon slices, optional
Parsley, optional

Thinly slice the leek; dice the celery and carrot and slice the mushrooms. Place all the vegetables in a saucepan with the oregano, tomato purée and water. Season with salt and pepper. Cover the pan, bring to the boil and simmer for 10-15 minutes. Meanwhile, slice the cheese very thinly and lay on the plaice fillets. Roll up and secure with wooden cocktail sticks. Brush with oil and grill under a low heat until cooked, turning frequently. Discard the cocktail sticks. Drain any excess water from the vegetables and place on a serving plate. Arrange the fish on top and garnish with lemon and parsley.

Serves 1/330 calories
5.5 fat units/7.5 grams fibre

Chicken Meals

Because it is so low in fat, chicken is an excellent meat for a slimmer to choose. However, always take care to remove the skin as an average grilled chicken breast with the skin comes to 200 calories, whereas with the skin removed it comes down to only 145 calories.

Drumsticks in Mushroom and Pepper Sauce

2 chicken drumsticks
½ small onion
Pinch dried thyme or mixed herbs
115ml/4floz water

¼ chicken stock cube
50g/2oz mushrooms
¼ small green or red pepper
Salt and pepper
7.5ml/1½ level teaspoons cornflour
15ml/1 level tablespoon skimmed milk
   powder

Skin the drumsticks and place in a small saucepan. Chop the onion and add to the pan with the herbs, water and stock cube. Season with salt and pepper. Cover the pan, bring to the boil and simmer for 20 minutes. Chop the mushrooms. Discard the pith and seeds from the pepper and dice the flesh. Add the mushrooms and pepper to the pan and simmer for another 10 minutes. Pour the stock off into a measuring jug and if necessary make it up to 75ml/3floz with water. Mix the cornflour and skimmed milk powder with 30ml/2 tablespoons cold water until smooth. Place the drumsticks on a plate and keep warm. Stir the cornflour mixture into the stock and return to the pan. Bring to the boil, stirring all the time, and then simmer for 1-2 minutes. Pour over the drumsticks and serve.

Serves 1/185 calories
2 fat units/2.0 grams fibre

Moira's Chicken with Baked Potato

1 chicken breast, 175g/6oz
30ml/2 level tablespoons natural yoghurt
15ml/1 level tablespoon tomato purée
1.25ml/¼ level teaspoon paprika
Salt and pepper
175g/6oz potato

Skin the chicken and place in a small ovenproof dish. Mix together the yoghurt, tomato purée and paprika. Season with salt and pepper, then spoon over the chicken, making sure that it is completely coated. Cover the dish and cook in a preheated oven at 180°C/350°F/gas mark 4 for 45 minutes. Prick the potato and push a skewer through the centre. Bake with the chicken.

Serves 1/325 calories
1.5 fat units/4.2 grams fibre

Peppery Chicken

(see picture page 37)

The garlic can be omitted from this recipe, but it will not taste as good nor save any calories. Spicy dishes can make a dieting meal more satisfying. Serve this with braised celery and grilled tomatoes as shown in the picture or other vegetables of your choice (calories not included).

1 chicken breast, 175g/6oz
1 small clove garlic
50g/2oz canned pimento, drained
15ml/1 tablespoon lemon juice
Salt and pepper
40g/1½oz Edam cheese

45ml/3 level tablespoons low-fat natural
   yoghurt
5ml/1 level teaspoon paprika
Chopped parsley, optional

Discard the skin from the chicken breast, then make narrow slits all over the flesh with the point of a sharp knife. Cut the garlic into slivers and insert into the slits. Place in an ovenproof dish. Cut the pimento into strips and arrange over the chicken. Pour over the lemon juice and season with salt and pepper. Cover the dish and cook at 180°C/350°F/gas mark 4 for 30 minutes. Drain and keep warm. Grate the Edam cheese and mix with the yoghurt and paprika. When the chicken is ready, spoon over the cheese mixture and grill for 2 minutes. Sprinkle with chopped parsley.

Serves 1/320 calories
5.5 fat units/0.6 grams fibre

Hawaiian Chicken

40g/1½oz long-grain rice, white or brown
¼ green or red pepper
75g/3oz cooked chicken
2 rings pineapple, canned in natural juice
30ml/2 tablespoons pineapple juice
2.5ml/½ teaspoon soya sauce
Salt and pepper
15ml/1 level tablespoon flaked almonds

Boil the rice until tender, then drain. While the rice is cooking, prepare the other ingredients. Discard the pith and seeds from the pepper and dice the flesh. Discard any skin from the chicken and cut the flesh into small pieces. Cut the pineapple into small pieces. Put the drained rice into a saucepan with the pepper, chicken, pineapple, juice and soya sauce. Season with salt and pepper and then heat through thoroughly. Sprinkle the almonds onto a piece of foil and grill until pale brown. Stir into the chicken mixture and serve.

		fat	grams
Serves 1	cals.	units	fibre
white rice	375	2.5	2.5
brown rice	370	3.0	3.9

Fruity Chicken Parcel

25g/1oz carrot
1 ring pineapple, canned in natural
   juice, drained
15ml/1 tablespoon pineapple juice from
   can
25g/1oz green pepper
15ml/1 level tablespoon peach chutney
   or mango chutney
Salt and pepper
115g/4oz chicken breast fillet

Thinly slice the carrot, then boil for 5 minutes. Drain and place in a basin. Cut the pineapple into small pieces and add to the carrot with the juice. Discard the white pith and seeds from the pepper and dice the flesh. Add to the basin with the chutney. Season with salt and pepper and place half the mixture in the centre of a piece of foil. Discard the skin from the chicken and place on top of the fruity mixture. Cover with the remaining mixture. Fold up the edges to make a loose parcel with tightly sealed joins. Place on a baking tray and cook in the oven at 190°C/375°F/gas mark 5 for 45 minutes.

Serves 1/210 calories
2 fat units/1.9 grams fibre

Citrus Chicken
(see picture page 31)

Fruit mixes particularly well with chicken. If you have an automatic oven, you can leave the prepared dish to cook later in the day or when you return from work. The French beans shown in our picture are a good accompaniment to this dish and a 75g/3oz portion will add 30 calories. It is suitable for freezing.

2 fresh apricots or 2 dried apricot halves
1 chicken breast, 175g/6oz weighed with bone
2.5ml/½ level teaspoon paprika
45ml/3 tablespoons frozen concentrated
*   orange juice, thawed*
30ml/2 tablespoons water
1.25ml/¼ teaspoon lemon juice
Salt and pepper

If dried apricots are used, soak them in cold water for at least 2 hours and then drain. Discard the water. If fresh apricots are used, plunge them into boiling water for 1 minute and then into cold water for 1 minute to loosen the skins. Skin them and cut each apricot in half, discarding the stones. Sprinkle the paprika onto the skin of the chicken breast and press it into the surface. Cook in a non-stick pan until it is lightly browned all over. Place in an ovenproof dish. Mix the undiluted orange juice, water and lemon juice in the pan, then pour over the chicken and season with salt and pepper. Arrange the apricots around the chicken. Cover the dish and cook at 190°C/375°F/gas mark 5 for 45 minutes.

Serves 1	cals.	fat units	grams fibre
fresh apricots	255	3	1.2
dried apricots	265	3	1.3

Chicken and Corn Parcel

150g/5oz chicken breast fillet or boned
*   chicken breast*
15g/½oz onion
75g/3oz canned sweetcorn with peppers,
*   drained*
15g/½oz fresh wholemeal breadcrumbs
15ml/1 tablespoon tomato ketchup
Salt and pepper

Discard any skin from the chicken and place it on a piece of foil large enough to

These colourful easy meals are: 1 Stuffed Piccalilli Tomato (recipe page 40); 2 Liver and Bacon Kebabs (recipe page 37); 3 Egg and Bacon Grill (recipe page 38); 4 Crumpet Pizza (recipe page 39); and 5 Devilled Pâté Toast (recipe page 39)

completely enclose it in a loose parcel. Finely chop the onion and mix with the sweetcorn, breadcrumbs and tomato ketchup. Season with salt and pepper, then pile on top of the chicken. Wrap the foil around to make a parcel. Bake at 190°C/375°F/gas mark 5 for 25-30 minutes.

Serves 1/295 calories
2.5 fat units/6.2 grams fibre

Beef and Pork Meals

The thing to remember with all meat is that the more fat it contains, the higher the calories. Lean meat may be more expensive than fattier cuts but your purse's loss will be your figure's gain. Also, you will end up with much more on your plate if you do not have to discard lots of fat.

Beef and Baked Bean Pie

115g/4oz very lean ground or minced beef
25g/1oz onion
1 tomato
225g/8oz canned baked beans in tomato
  sauce
Dash Worcestershire sauce
Salt and pepper
150g/5oz potatoes, weighed peeled
30ml/2 tablespoons skimmed milk

Brown the ground beef in a non-stick pan and then drain off all the fat. Finely chop the onion. Peel and roughly chop the tomato. Stir the onion, tomato, baked beans and Worcestershire sauce into the ground beef and season with salt and pepper. Turn into a small ovenproof dish, cover and cook at 180°C/350°F/gas mark 4 for 40 minutes. While the meat is cooking, boil the potatoes — then drain and mash with the skimmed milk. Season with salt and pepper and spread over the beef mixture. Increase the oven heat to 200°C/400°F/gas mark 6 and cook the pie for another 10-15 minutes.

Serves 1/470 calories
2.5 fat units/20.8 grams fibre

Pork and Pepper Pot with Rice

150g/5oz pork fillet or tenderloin
25g/1oz onion
¼ red or green pepper
115ml/4floz tomato juice
Few drops Tabasco or hot pepper sauce
2.5ml/½ teaspoon Worcestershire sauce
Salt and pepper
25g/1oz long-grain white rice
5ml/1 level teaspoon cornflour

Discard all visible fat from the pork and cut the lean into small bite-sized pieces. Finely chop the onion. Discard the white pith and seeds from the pepper and cut the flesh into strips. Place the pork, onion, pepper, tomato juice, Tabasco and Worcestershire sauce in a small saucepan and season with salt and pepper. Cover the pan, bring to the boil and simmer gently for 20 minutes. While the pork is cooking, boil the rice. Drain and keep warm. Blend the cornflour with a little cold water until smooth. Stir into the pork mixture and simmer for 1-2 minutes. Serve with the rice.

Serves 1/365 calories
3.5 fat units/1.1 grams fibre

Meatballs in Spicy Tomato Sauce

115g/4oz very lean ground or minced beef
25g/1oz onion
2 pinches chilli powder
15ml/1 level tablespoon tomato chutney
Salt and pepper
115ml/4floz tomato juice
5ml/1 teaspoon vinegar
5ml/1 teaspoon Worcestershire sauce
1.25ml/¼ level teaspoon mustard
2.5ml/½ teaspoon brown sugar
50g/2oz beansprouts

Finely chop the onion and mix with the beef, chilli powder and tomato chutney. Season with salt and pepper and divide into 6 equal portions. Roll between the palms of your hands (it is easier if you wet your hands first) to make small balls. Place the tomato juice, vinegar, Worcestershire sauce, mustard and brown sugar in a small saucepan. Season with salt and pepper and bring to the boil. Add the meatballs, one at a time, so that they are in a single layer in the sauce. Cover the pan and simmer gently for 30 minutes. Boil the beansprouts. Drain and serve the meatballs on top.

Serves 1/260 calories
2 fat units/1.3 grams fibre

Ham and Bacon Meals

Although well grilled bacon and ham is often fatty when raw, it loses lots of fat and calories when cooked. It also comes in convenient rashers, steaks or boiled portions which make calorie mistakes less likely.

Grilled Ham with Apple, Cheese and Mushrooms *(see picture page 41)*

1 ham or bacon steak, 135g/4½oz
115g/4oz mushrooms
1 small eating apple
1 processed cheese slice

Grill the ham or bacon steak until tender. Poach the mushrooms in a little salted water. Core and slice the apple and arrange on top of the steak. Grill for 2 minutes, or until the apple starts to soften. Top with the processed cheese slice and grill slowly until the cheese melts and the apple is hot. Drain the mushrooms and serve with the steak.

Serves 1/260 calories
4 fat units/4.3 grams fibre

Banana and Ham Mornay

If you buy vacuum-packed ham for this recipe, you may find that the very thin slices weigh under 25g/1oz. Ham also varies enormously in the amount of fat that surrounds it. Always cut off every visible scrap. Then reweigh your slices for you are allowed a whole 50g/2oz when the fat has been removed. This dish can be served on its own or with a salad.

50g/2oz Edam cheese
10ml/2 teaspoons cornflour
150ml/¼ pint skimmed milk
Salt and pepper
Tiny amount mustard, optional
1 medium banana
2 slices lean cooked ham, 25g/1oz each
15ml/1 level tablespoon fresh wholemeal
   breadcrumbs

Grate the cheese. Blend the cornflour with a little of the skimmed milk until smooth. Heat the remaining milk to boiling point and then pour onto the cornflour mixture, stirring continuously. Simmer for 2 minutes. Season with salt, pepper and a very small amount of mustard. Stir in three-quarters of the cheese. Peel the banana and cut in half lengthways. Discard all visible fat from the ham, then wrap a slice around each piece of banana. Place in a flameproof dish and pour the sauce on top. Sprinkle on the breadcrumbs and remaining cheese and brown under the grill.

Serves 1/430 calories
6 fat units/3.7 grams fibre

Bacon and Bean Nest

25g/1oz streaky bacon
40g/1½oz instant mashed potato powder
175ml/6floz boiling water
1 egg, size 3
150g/5.3oz can baked beans in tomato sauce
15g/½oz Edam cheese

Grill the bacon until crisp and then break into small pieces. Make up the instant potato using boiling water, as instructed on the packet. Stir in the bacon, then spread over the base and sides of a small ovenproof dish. Keep warm. Poach the egg and heat the baked beans. Pour the beans on top of the potato and place the egg on top. Grate the cheese and sprinkle on top. Grill until the cheese melts. Serve immediately.

Serves 1/435 calories
4.5 fat units/17.9 grams fibre

Liver and Kidney

You cannot go wrong with liver and kidney when you are dieting. Even if you fry them, they do not absorb many fatty calories. A 115g/4oz portion lamb's liver grilled without fat comes to 205 calories. The same size portion fried gains 30 calories. But there are many more interesting ways to serve offal than just plain grilled. Here are some ideal meals for one.

Bean and Kidney Casserole
(see picture page 41)

2 lamb's kidneys
½ small onion
¼ beef stock cube
1 tomato
1 small stick celery
150g/5.3oz can baked beans in tomato sauce
15ml/1 level tablespoon bottled brown sauce
Salt and pepper

Core and chop the kidneys. Finely chop the onion and place in a small saucepan with the crumbled stock cube and enough water to just cover. Bring to the boil, cover the pan and simmer gently for 10 minutes. Reserve 15ml/1 tablespoon stock and discard the rest. Place the kidneys, onion and reserved stock in a small casserole dish. Skin and chop the tomato and chop the celery. Add to the dish with the baked beans and brown sauce. Season with salt and pepper. Cover the dish and cook in a pre-heated oven at 190°C/375°F/gas mark 5 for 30 minutes.

Serves 1/250 calories
1.5 fat units/13 grams fibre

Kidney Stroganoff

115g/4oz lamb's kidneys
25g/1oz onion
25g/1oz mushrooms
5ml/1 teaspoon oil
5ml/1 level teaspoon butter
75ml/3floz water
¼ beef stock cube
5ml/1 level teaspoon tomatopurée
Salt and pepper
25g/1oz pasta shapes or noodles
5ml/1 level teaspoon cornflour
30ml/2 level tablespoons low-fat natural
   yoghurt

Halve and core the kidneys. Finely chop the onion and slice the mushrooms. Heat the oil and butter in a small pan until the butter melts and stops foaming. Add the kidneys and cook until they change colour. Remove and keep warm. Add the onion to the pan and cook until soft. Add the kidneys, mushrooms, water, stock cube and tomato purée. Season with salt and pepper. Cover the pan, bring to the boil and simmer for 8–10 minutes. You should have the same amount of liquid left after cooking. If not, add a little more water. Meanwhile, boil the pasta or noodles. Blend the cornflour with a little cold water until smooth and add to the kidneys. Bring to the boil, stirring all the

time, and simmer for 1 minute until the sauce has thickened and is smooth. Remove from the heat and stir in the yoghurt. Serve with pasta shapes or noodles.

Serves 1/330 calories
4.5 fat units/2 grams fibre

Liver and Bacon Kebabs
(see picture page 34)

Because it cooks so quickly, liver is an ideal kebab ingredient. Although liver is not very absorbent, and will not soak up much fat from the bacon, the tomatoes and mushrooms will take up every bit you brush on. So do measure the teaspoon of butter very carefully. We have pictured this recipe served on a bed of boiled cabbage — 115g/ 4oz weighed raw adds 25 calories, 0 fat units and 3 grams fibre.

The tasty dishes shown above are, reading clockwise: Speedy Pilchard Pizza (recipe page 40); Cheesey Plaice on Vegetables (recipe page 32); Peppery Chicken (recipe page 33); and Ploughman's Baked Potato (recipe page 38)

75g/3oz lamb's liver
50g/2oz streaky bacon
2 small tomatoes
¼ lemon
4 small mushrooms
Salt and pepper
5ml/1 level teaspoon butter
Pinch dried thyme

Cut the liver into 8 pieces. Discard the bacon rind and stretch the rashers with a knife. Divide into 8 pieces and wrap each one around a piece of liver. Quarter the tomatoes. Cut the lemon in 2 wedges. Thread the liver and bacon, tomatoes, lemon and mushrooms onto 2 skewers. Season with salt and pepper. Melt the butter by placing it in a cup and standing it in a pan of hot water. Add the thyme and brush onto the tomatoes and mushrooms. Grill the kebabs for about 10 minutes, turning occasionally.

Serves 1/360 calories
8 fat units/4 grams fibre

Eggs

Eggs contain invisible fat, which is what makes the fat units in these recipes higher, perhaps, than you might expect. However, if you are counting calories, egg meals are reasonable and filling. We use the medium size 3 eggs in these recipes. If you use the larger size 2, calories will increase by 10 per egg; if you use the smaller size 4, calories will decrease by 5 each egg.

Egg and Bacon Grill
(see picture page 34)

1 rasher back bacon
2 button mushrooms
1 tomato
1 egg, size 3
2 sprigs parsley, optional
1 small slice wholemeal bread, 25g/1oz

Grill the bacon until crisp, then cut the rasher in half. Keep warm in a low oven. Lightly brush the mushrooms with a little of the bacon fat, and place under the grill with the quartered tomatoes. Grill until just cooked. While they are grilling, poach the egg. Arrange the egg, mushrooms and tomato in a dish with the bacon and garnish with parsley. Toast the bread and serve with the supper snack.

Serves 1/255 calories
4 fat units/3.3 grams fibre

Ham and Corn Omelet

You can serve this omelet with a green vegetable such as broccoli (115g/4oz adds 30 calories/0 fat units/4.1 grams fibre, or a salad. If you can afford the extra calories and fat units, an additional 25g/1oz lean cooked ham will cost 47 and 0.5 fat units, 0 grams fibre respectively.

25g/1oz lean cooked ham
50g/2oz canned sweetcorn, drained
2 eggs, size 3
15ml/1 tablespoon water
Salt and pepper
5ml/1 level teaspoon buter

Discard all visible fat from the ham and dice the lean. Lightly beat the eggs and water together and season with salt and pepper. Melt the butter in a small non-stick omelet pan and brush all over the pan's surface. Add the egg mixture and cook until just set. Tilt the pan and lift the edges of the omelet while cooking so that the runny mixture goes underneath. Place the ham and sweetcorn in the centre and fold over.

Serves 1/290 calories
5.5 fat units/3.2 grams fibre

Pizza Omelet
(see picture page 30)

25g/1oz lean cooked ham
25g/1oz Edam cheese
2 eggs, size 3
10ml/2 teaspoons water
Salt and pepper
5ml/1 level teaspoon butter
10ml/2 level teaspoons tomato ketchup
1.25ml/¼ level teaspoon mixed dried herbs
Few sprigs watercress, optional

Discard all visible fat from the ham and chop the lean. Grate the cheese. Lightly beat the eggs and water together and season with salt and pepper. Melt the butter in a small non-stick omelet pan and brush all over the surface. Add the eggs and cook over a fairly high heat until the base is set, lifting the sides of the omelet as it cooks and tilting the pan so that the raw mixture runs underneath. Spread the tomato ketchup on top of the set omelet and sprinkle on the herbs. Scatter the ham on top and sprinkle over the cheese. Remove the pan from the heat and place under a hot grill until the cheese melts. Garnish with a few sprigs of watercress and serve immediately.

Serves 1/340 calories
8.0 fat units/0 grams fibre

Cheese Meals

Always weigh cheese very carefully and do not rely on guesswork chunks. It weighs heavier than many people imagine and an extra slither could add as much as 30 calories to your dish. Edam is lower in calories than most other hard cheeses, but if you wish to use the stronger flavoured Cheddar instead, count 32 more calories for each 25g/1oz.

Ploughman's Baked Potato
(see picture page 37)

1 potato, 200g/7oz
25g/1oz streaky bacon
40g/1½oz Edam cheese
1 pickled onion
30ml/2 tablespoons skimmed milk
Pinch grated nutmeg
Salt and pepper

Scrub the potato well, then prick all over with a fork. Bake in its jacket at 200°C/400°F/gas mark 6, for about 45 minutes, or until soft when pinched. Cut in half lengthwise and scoop the flesh out into a bowl, leaving the skin intact. While the potato is cooking, grill the bacon until crisp and then break into small pieces. Grate the Edam and chop the pickled onion. Mix about two-thirds of the cheese, the bacon, pickled onion, skimmed milk and nutmeg with the potato flesh. Season with salt and pepper and pile back into the potato cases. Sprinkle the remaining cheese on top. Return to the oven for 10-15 minutes, or until the cheese melts and the filling is heated through.

Serves 1/390 calories
5.0 fat units/5.2 grams fibre

Crumpet Pizza
(see picture page 34)

2 crumpets
1 tomato
Pinch mixed dried herbs
Salt and pepper
25g/1oz Edam cheese
4 anchovy fillets
4 black or green olives
Few sprigs watercress, optional

Toast the crumpets on both sides until golden. Slice the tomato and place on top. Sprinkle with herbs and season with salt and pepper. Grate the cheese and place on the tomato. Arrange the anchovies and olives on top. Grill until the cheese is melted and bubbling. Garnish with watercress.

Serves 1/285 calories
4.0 fat units/1.6 grams fibre

Cauliflower Cheese
(see picture page 41)

225g/8oz cauliflower
45ml/3 level tablespoons skimmed milk
 powder
15ml/1 level tablespoon cornflour
40g/1½oz mature Cheddar cheese
Salt and pepper
15ml/1 level tablespoon fresh breadcrumbs
15ml/1 level tablespoon grated Parmesan
 cheese
Little paprika, optional

Boil the cauliflower in salted water until just tender. Drain, reserving 115ml/4floz cooking water. Place the cauliflower in an ovenproof dish and keep warm. Let the liquid cool slightly, then whisk in the skimmed milk powder. Blend the cornflour with 30ml/2 tablespoons cold water, and then add to the milky liquid. Place in a saucepan and bring to the boil, stirring all the time. Grate the cheese and add to the sauce. Season with salt and pepper and pour over the cauliflower. Sprinkle the breadcrumbs, Parmesan and paprika on top. Grill until the topping starts to brown. Serve immediately.

Serves 1/335 calories
5.5 fat units/9.3 grams fibre

Bread and Crispbread Meals

Forget the old fashioned notion that bread is a dieting baddie. As long as you top it or fill it with something low in calories, bread can be the basis of a filling slimming meal. Here are some toast and pitta meals and topped crispbreads. You will find sandwiches and pitta parcels useful for packed lunches in the next chapter. The kind of bread you use only makes a small difference to your calories but using wholemeal can double your fibre. We have, therefore, given you a choice.

Devilled Pâté Toast
(see picture page 34)

50g/2oz chicken livers
¼ stock cube
Water
15ml/1 tablespoon tomato ketchup
5ml/1 teaspoon Worcestershire sauce
50g/2oz cottage cheese with chives and onion
 or with chives
Salt and pepper
1 large slice bread, 40g/1½oz
1 tomato
Mustard and cress

Cut the chicken livers into small pieces and place in a small saucepan with the crumbled stock cube, and enough water to just cover them. Bring to the boil, cover the pan and simmer gently for 5 minutes. Drain off any excess water. Add the tomato ketchup, Worcestershire sauce and cottage cheese to the livers and mash with a fork until well mixed. Toast the bread, then spread the pâté on top. Grill until heated. Quarter the tomato and arrange on the pâté with the mustard and cress.

Serves 1	cals.	fat units	grams fibre
white bread	265	2.0	2.1
brown bread	260	2.5	3.2
wholemeal bread	255	2.5	4.6

Herby Tomatoes on Anchovy Toast
(see picture page 41)

225g/8oz tomatoes
Salt and pepper
2 large slices bread, 40g/1½ oz each
35g/1.23oz pot anchovy fish paste
Large pinch fresh or dried basil or
 mixed herbs

Halve the tomatoes and season the cut sides with salt and pepper. Grill under a low heat until they begin to soften. Toast the bread and spread with anchovy paste. Place the tomatoes on top and sprinkle on the herbs.

Serves 1	cals.	fat units	grams fibre
white bread	285	1.5	5.5
brown bread	275	1.5	7.6
wholemeal bread	270	1.5	10.4

Sardine Pizza Toast
(see picture page 41)
1 large slice bread, 40g/1½oz
1 tomato
Pinch mixed dried herbs
Salt and pepper
2 sardines canned in tomato sauce
1 processed cheese slice

Toast the bread on one side only. Slice the tomato and place on the untoasted side. Grill until the tomato just starts to soften. Sprinkle with herbs and season with salt and pepper. Cut the sardines in half lengthwise and arrange on top. Cover with the cheese slice and grill until it melts.

Serves 1	cals.	fat unit	grams fibre
white bread	285	4	1.9
brown bread	285	4.5	3.0
wholemeal bread	280	4.5	4.4

Speedy Pilchard Pizza

1 large slice bread, 40g/1½oz
1 tomato
75g/3oz pilchards, canned in tomato sauce
Pinch dried basil or mixed herbs
Salt and pepper
40g/1½oz Edam cheese
1 stuffed olive, optional

Toast the bread. Slice the tomato and arrange on toast with the pilchards. Sprinkle with basil or mixed herbs and season with salt and pepper. Grill until hot. Thinly slice or grate the cheese and place on top. Grill until melted. Garnish with the sliced olive.

Serves 1	cals.	fat units	grams fibre
white bread	355	5.5	2.2
brown bread	350	5.5	3.3
wholemeal bread	345	5.5	4.7

Tasty Cheese Crispbreads
(see picture page 41)
25g/1oz red or green pepper
75g/3oz natural cottage cheese
15ml/1 level tablespoon canned sweetcorn
15ml/1 level tablespoon chopped dill cucumber
3 crispbreads
3 stuffed olives

Discard the white pith and seeds from the pepper and dice the flesh. Mix with the cottage cheese, sweetcorn and dill cucumber. Spread on the crispbreads. Slice the olives and use to garnish.

Serves 1/205 calories
2 fat units/3.5 grams fibre

Salad Meals

Forget about that limp lettuce leaf and dig into one of these delicious slimmers' salads. All are under 275 calories and make excellent light lunches.

Fish and French Bean Salad
(see picture page 41)
115g/4oz French beans or haricots vert, fresh or frozen
30ml/2 tablespoons oil-free French dressing
1 tomato
100g/3½oz canned tuna in brine
2 cans anchovy fillets
2 black or green olives
Salt and pepper

Cook the French beans or *haricots vert* in boiling, salted water until tender. Drain and, while still hot, toss in the oil-free French dressing. Leave to cool. Slice the tomato, then drain and flake the tuna. Drain the anchovy fillets and pat with kitchen paper to remove any excess oil. Stone and slice the olives. Arrange the beans, tomato and tuna in layers in a small bowl. Garnish with anchovies and olives and season with salt and pepper.

Serves 1/185 calories
0.5 fat units/4.8 grams fibre

Stuffed Piccalilli Tomato
(see picture page 34)
175g/6oz tomatoes
50g/2oz corned beef
15ml/1 level tablespoon piccalilli
15ml/1 level tablespoon natural yoghurt
Salt and pepper
1 small slice wholemeal bread, 25g/1oz
5ml/1 level teaspoon low-fat spread

Cut a slice off the top of the tomato and, using a small teaspoon, scoop out the seeds and core, taking care not to damage the tomato shell. Turn the shell upside-down to drain. Place the pulp in a basin, and discard the hard core. Dice the corned beef and add to the tomato pulp with the piccalilli and yoghurt. Season with salt and pepper. Pile back into the tomato shell. Spread the bread with low-fat spread and serve with the stuffed tomato.

Serves 1/245 calories
2.0 fat units/5.1 grams fibre

Coleslaw with Cottage Cheese and Prawns

Beware of bought coleslaw in mayonnaise for it can be as high as 400 calories for a 227g/8oz carton, and you would not normally serve it on its own.

50g/2oz white cabbage
1 carrot
1 stick celery
30ml/2 tablespoons low-calorie salad cream
30ml/2 tablespoons natural yoghurt
50g/2oz peeled prawns
50g/2oz cottage cheese with chives or with
  onion and chives
Salt and pepper

Shred the cabbage. Grate the carrot and thinly slice the celery. Mix all the ingredients and season with salt and pepper.

Serves 1/205 calories
3.0 fat units/4.2 grams fibre

Chicken, Celery and Apple Salad
(see picture page 41)

Celery and apple are very good salad partners. The combination of salad cream and yoghurt is a dressing mix that you could repeat with any plain salad. The amount we use here costs just 45 calories.

Some more ideas for easy meals for one: **1** *Fish and French Bean Salad (recipe page 40);* **2** *Herby Tomatoes on Anchovy Toast (recipe page 39);* **3** *Grilled Ham with Apple, Cheese and Mushrooms (recipe page 35);* **4** *Tasty Cheese Crispbreads (recipe page 40);* **5** *Cauliflower Cheese (recipe page 39);* **6** *Bean and Kidney Casserole (recipe page 36);* **7** *Curried Rice with Fish (recipe page 32);* **8** *Chicken, Celery and Apple Salad (recipe page 41);* and **9** *Sardine Pizza Toast (recipe page 40)*

50g/2oz cooked chicken
2 sticks celery
1 medium-sized apple
Little lemon juice
15ml/1 tablespoon low-calorie salad cream
30ml/2 tablespoons low-fat natural yoghurt
Salt and pepper

Discard all the skin from the chicken and cut the flesh into bite-sized pieces. Slice the celery. Core and dice the apple but leave the skin on. Toss in the lemon juice. Mix together the chicken, celery, apple, low-calorie salad cream and yoghurt. Season with salt and pepper.

Serves 1/190 calories
2.0 fat units/4.7 grams fibre

41

BUTTER

Of all slimming enemies, butter is the one that might most easily add to your weight without your noticing. It is not just that it costs 210 calories an ounce: butter is so palatable that we tend to use it to make other foods taste 'better' — on bread, in sauces, on vegetables, in the frying pan. A switch to a low-fat spread means half the calories; but all margarines cost the same as butter. Do not be fooled into thinking that margarines labelled 'high in polyunsaturates' or 'low-cholesterol' are any lower in calories than other margarines — they are not. For many women, cooking with butter (or margarine) is a habit, but one well worth breaking. If you use less butter than many recipes suggest, you will hardly notice the difference; indeed some do not need any butter at all. Next time you reach for your butter knife, reflect that 15g/½ oz contains as many calories as a small can of baked beans.

1 A chunk of garlic bread, like the one shown, has usually absorbed 25g/1oz butter bringing its total calories to 380. Plain French bread costs 170 calories for the same amount.
2 Spread the holey side of a crispbread and you will use about 55 calories' worth of butter. Flat side uses half as much.
3 Butter a tomato before grilling and you will raise the calorie count from 10 to 65.
4 Pour butter over your cooked sweetcorn (155 calories) and you will probably scoop up over 155 calories' worth and pay 310.
5 Machine-made toasted sandwiches are often recommended to be buttered both sides. Almost half this toasted sandwich's 345 total calories are in the butter.
6 Most restaurants' individual butter pots hold 25g/1oz. Many people use the lot with one bread roll (145 calories) bringing a pre-meal nibble total up to 355 calories.

7 Scrambled eggs are traditionally made with at least 25g/1oz butter which contributes 210 calories to the 480 calorie total.

8 Grilled white fish can absorb a lot of butter. The 175g/6oz piece above soaked up over 50 calories' worth, although the total cost of 185 calories still makes it a reasonable choice.

9 Nearly everyone will add at least 25g/1oz butter to a big jacket potato; the potato at 170 calories costs 40 calories less than the butter topping!

10 Grill a mushroom with butter and you convert a low-calorie food into a high-calorie menace. The mushroom shown here costs only 5 calories but has absorbed 55 calories' worth of butter.

11 Hard not to be generous and use more than 100 calories' worth of butter on hot toast. A poached egg would cost less and be much more filling.

Packed lunches

Even if you do not go out to work every day, there are probably going to be times during your diet campaign when you feel like a quick sandwich lunch or a light salad. During the summer there may also be days when you want to have a picnic meal down at the beach or even in the back garden. In this chapter you will find packed lunch and picnic meals that range from a saintly 165 calories up to a more substantial 400 calories.

If you know that nibbling is one of your main problems, do be careful where you store your packed lunch when you reach work. If you put it in an office drawer that you frequently open, the chances are that your sandwich will never see lunchtime. The

These are some of the sandwiches you would be best advised to avoid while you are dieting. All are made from two 50g/2oz slices bread and are spread with 25g/1oz butter: 410 calories before you add the filling:
Toasted Cheese Sandwich made with 75g/3oz Cheddar cheese: 835 cals/19 fat units/3 grams fibre
Sausage Butty made with 4 well-grilled pork chipolata sausages and a tablespoon tomato ketchup: 750 cals/1.5 fat units/3.4 grams fibre
Pâté and Tomato Sandwich made with 75g/3oz Brussels pâté and a sliced tomato: 830 cals/20 fat units/3.8 grams fibre
Luncheon Meat and Pickle Sandwich made with 75g/3oz luncheon meat and a rounded tablespoon sweet pickle: 775 cals/16 fat units/3.9 grams fibre
Salami Sandwich made with 50g/2oz salami: 735 cals/16.5 fat units/3 grams fibre
Cream Cheese, Nut and Raisin Sandwich made with 75g/3oz cream cheese mixed with a level tablespoon chopped nuts and a level tablespoon raisins: 905 cals/23 fat units/4.5 grams fibre
Chip Butty made with 125g/4oz average thickness chips and a tablespoon tomato ketchup: 770 cals/14.5 fat units/5.4 grams fibre

sight of food is a great appetite trigger and keeping a packed lunch within view is just as much a temptation to nibble as is the sight of left-overs in the refrigerator. And, be honest, if you eat all your packed meal before lunchtime are you really going to be able to miss a midday meal? It is more likely that you will go to the canteen or to the café and eat another lunch on top of your sandwiches or whatever else you have nibbled.

Missing meals is something that overweight people seem particularly reluctant to do. Recent research we have carried out shows that even women who have slimmed down to their target weight still tend to eat at precisely the same time each day. Effortlessly slim people are much less likely to be bullied into eating by the clock. If they are absorbed with a task they may decide to delay eating; and often delayed meals are missed altogether. Regular meals at the same time of day each day are a social habit rather than a health requirement for the normally fit adult, and people who refuse to be bullied by the clock have a natural head-start in calorie control. If you are sometimes able to delay or skip a meal you will be acquiring a habit that will not only help to get you slim but also to keep you in trim once you have reached your target weight.

Sandwiches are a favourite packed lunch and they can vary enormously in calorie value. All the sandwiches here on the right-hand side of the page are low in calories. Recipes are given in this chapter but here are the calories:
Toasted Steak Sandwich: 365 cals/3 fat units/3.1 grams fibre
Egg and Cress Sandwich: 305 cals/3.5 fat units/2.6 grams fibre
Fish Paste and Cottage Cheese Sandwich: 315 cals/2.5 fat units/2.3 grams fibre
Prawn, Curd Cheese and Cucumber Sandwich: 340 cals/2.5 fat units/2.4 grams fibre
Chicken, Green Pepper and Pineapple Sandwich: 355 cals/3.5 fat units/2.9 grams fibre
Cheese, Ham and Tomato Sandwich: 335 cals/3 fat units/3.1 grams fibre
Banana and Raisin Sandwich: 275 cals/0.5 fat units/5.2 grams fibre

Crusty Rolls

An average crusty roll costs 145 calories whether it is brown or white. Here is a way to make just one roll into a meal by scooping out some of the soft centre and adding a chunky filling. If you cannot bear to throw away those scooped-out breadcrumbs, they can be kept in a polythene bag in the refrigerator for up to six days and used in recipes requiring fresh breadcrumbs.

Prawn and Tomato Chutney Roll

1 crusty bread roll
25g/1oz cucumber
50g/2oz shelled prawns
15ml/1 level tablespoon tomato chutney
5ml/1 teaspoon oil-free French
    dressing
Salt and pepper

Cut the roll in half horizontally and remove about half of the crumbs. Dice the cucumber and mix with the prawns, chutney and oil-free French dressing. Season with salt and pepper. Pile onto the roll base and cover with the top half.

Serves 1/	cals.	fat units	grams fibre
white roll	215	1	1.6
brown roll	215	1	3.0

Cheese and Pickle Crusty Roll

1 crusty roll
25g/1oz Edam cheese
50g/2oz cottage cheese with chives
15ml/1 level tablespoon sweet pickle

Cut the roll in half horizontally and remove about half of the soft crumbs. Grate the Edam and mix with the cottage cheese and pickle. Pile onto the roll base and cover with the top half.

Serves 1/	cals.	fat units	grams fibre
white roll	285	3.5	1.5
brown roll	285	3.5	2.9

Chicken and Mango Chutney Roll

1 crusty bread roll
50g/2oz cooked chicken
15ml/1 level tablespoon low-calorie
    salad cream
15ml/1 level tablespoon mango chutney
1.25ml/¼ level teaspoon curry paste
    or powder

Cut the roll in half horizontally and scoop out about half of the soft crumbs. Discard the skin from the chicken and chop the flesh. Mix with the low-calorie salad cream, mango chutney and curry powder. Pile onto the roll base and cover with the top half.

Serves 1/	cals.	fat units	grams fibre
white roll	270	2.5	1.5
brown roll	270	2.5	2.9

Sandwiches

Sandwiches are one of the most common packed lunches and there is no need to give them up when you go on a diet. Learn to make them our low-calorie, low-fat way and you will never want to go back to high-calorie versions. Throughout this section, we give you a choice of white, brown or wholemeal bread. Calories and fat units are very similar but wholemeal bread is much higher in fibre.

Egg and Cress Sandwich
(see picture page 45)

1 egg, size 3
15ml/1 tablespoon low-calorie salad
    cream
2 large slices bread, 40g/1½oz each
Mustard and cress

Hard-boil the egg, then leave to cool in cold water. Shell, chop and mix with the salad cream. Make into a sandwich with the bread and a little mustard and cress.

Serves 1/	cals.	fat units	grams fibre
white bread	305	3.5	2.6
brown bread	295	3.5	4.7
wholemeal bread	285	3.5	7.5

Open Corned Beef and Cheese Sandwich
(see picture page 53)

You will need to pack this open sandwich in a rigid container. It goes very well with celery and tomato as shown in the picture and these should be packed separately.

1 small slice wholemeal bread, 25g/1oz
40g/1½oz corned beef
5ml/1 level teaspoon horseradish sauce
25g/1oz Edam cheese

Place the corned beef on the bread and spread with horseradish sauce. Grate the cheese and place on top.

Serves 1/245 calories
4 fat units/2.4 grams fibre

Chicken, Green Pepper and Pineapple Sandwich *(see picture page 45)*

50g/2oz cooked chicken
15g/½oz green or red pepper
1 pineapple ring canned in natural
    juice, drained
30ml/2 tablespoons low-calorie salad
    cream
Salt and pepper
2 large slices bread, 40g/1½oz each

Discard any skin from the chicken and then chop the flesh. Discard the white pith and seeds from the pepper and chop the flesh. Chop the pineapple. Mix all the ingredients together, except the bread, and season with salt and pepper. Make into a sandwich with the bread.

Serves 1/	cals.	fat units	grams fibre
white bread	355	3.5	2.9
brown bread	345	3.5	5.0
wholemeal bread	340	3.5	7.8

Cheese, Ham and Tomato Sandwich
(see picture page 45)

As well as making a packed lunch, this sandwich would be very tasty toasted.

2 large slices bread, 40g/1½oz each
25g/1oz cheese spread, plain or
  flavoured
25g/1oz lean ham
1 tomato

Spread the bread with cheese spread. Discard all visible fat from the ham. Slice the tomato and make into a sandwich with the bread and ham.

Serves 1/	cals.	fat units	grams fibre
white bread	335	3	3.1
brown bread	325	3	5.2
wholemeal bread	320	3	8.0

Prawn and Curd Cheese Sandwich
(see picture page 45)

25g/1oz cucumber
25g/1oz peeled prawns
50g/2oz curd cheese
2 large slices bread, 40g/1½oz each

Chop the cucumber and mix with the prawns and curd cheese. Make into a sandwich with the bread.

Serves 1/	cals.	fat units	grams fibre
white bread	340	2.5	2.4
brown bread	330	3.0	4.5
wholemeal bread	325	3.0	7.3

Banana and Raisin Sandwich
(see picture page 45)

Lemon juice prevents the banana from going brown but could be omitted if you eat the sandwich immediately. This filling is very moist and there is no need to use butter or low-fat spread on your bread.

1 small banana
Squeeze lemon juice
15ml/1 level tablespoon raisins or
  sultanas
2 large slices bread, 40g/1½oz each

Mash the banana with the lemon juice and then stir in the raisins or sultanas. Make into a sandwich with the bread.

Serves 1/	cals.	fat units	grams fibre
white bread	275	0.5	5.2
brown bread	265	1	7.3
wholemeal bread	260	1	10.1

Pinwheel Cheese Sandwich
(see picture page 53)

An attractive way to serve a sandwich, this is easy to prepare. By eating a small slice at a time you can slow down your eating and get maximum satisfaction from your calories. Serve, if you wish, with an apple and celery. A medium-sized apple will cost 50 calories. Celery is 5 calories a stick.

1 large slice bread, 40g/1½oz
25g/1oz Edam cheese
1.25ml/¼ level teaspoon French
  mustard
10ml/2 level teaspoons low-calorie
  salad cream
Salt and pepper

Discard the crusts from the bread. Using a rolling pin, roll the bread lightly to make it slightly thinner. Grate the cheese and mix with the mustard and low-calorie salad cream. Season with salt and pepper. Spread on the bread and roll up like a Swiss roll. Cut into slices.

Serves 1/	cals.	fat units	grams fibre
white bread	205	3	1.1
brown bread	200	3.5	2.2
wholemeal bread	195	3.5	3.6

Steak Sandwich
(see picture page 45)

Although this sandwich can be eaten cold, it is even better hot, and makes an ideal picnic barbecue meal. It is also delicious toasted.

1 thin slice rump steak, 75g/3oz
1 tomato
2 large slices bread, 40g/1½oz each
5ml/1 level teaspoon mustard or
15ml/1 level tablespoon tomato ketchup

Grill the steak until medium-well done. Discard all visible fat. Slice the tomato. Spread one slice of bread with mustard or tomato ketchup and make into a sandwich with the remaining slice, steak and tomato.

Serves 1/	cals.	fat units	grams fibre
white bread	365	3	3.1
brown bread	355	3.5	5.2
wholemeal bread	350	3.5	8.0

Fish Paste and Cottage Cheese Sandwich
(see picture page 45)

Fish paste is an ideal way to add flavour to your sandwiches without adding many calories or fat units. The ones that come in the tiny 35g/1¼oz jars are rarely above 60 calories/1.5 fat units per pot.

2 large slices bread, 40g/1½oz each
35g/1¼oz pot fish paste, any flavour
50g/2oz cottage cheese, natural or
  with chives

Spread the bread with fish paste and make into a sandwich with the cottage cheese.

Serves 1/	cals.	fat units	grams fibre
white bread	315	2.5	2.3
brown bread	305	3	4.4
wholemeal bread	300	3	7.2

French Bread Sandwiches

French bread has that lovely crunchy crust that makes a delicious sandwich. It is so light and airy that you get a nice big chunk for 65g/2½oz although you will probably find the wholemeal sort weighs a little heavier than the white. French bread is best eaten within a day of being made but will freeze for up to one week. After that time, the crust begins to separate.

French Bread with Fruity Chicken Filling
(see picture page 48)

50g/2oz cooked chicken or turkey
1 kiwi fruit or fresh peach
30ml/2 tablespoons low-calorie salad
  cream
Salt and pepper
65g/2½oz piece French bread
Few sprigs watercress

Discard any skin from the chicken and then chop the flesh. Peel and slice the kiwi fruit or peach. Mix the chicken and fruit with the low-calorie salad cream and season lightly with salt and pepper. Cut the French bread almost in half lengthways and fill with the chicken and fruit filling and watercress.

Serves 1/	cals.	fat units	grams fibre
white bread	380	3.5	3.8
wholemeal bread	365	3.5	8.7

French Bread with Beef Filling
(see picture page 48)

This is a very satisfying sandwich with plenty of bite and flavour. You can buy a portion of roast beef from a delicatessen or use left-overs from a joint. Be careful to cut off and discard all the fat you can see. It has been known for some absent minded dieters to cut off the fat and dispose of it straight into their mouths!

75g/3oz lean roast beef
2 gherkins
15ml/1 level tablespoon creamed
  horseradish sauce
15ml/1 tablespoon low-fat natural
  yoghurt
1.25ml/¼ level teaspoon English
  mustard
Salt and pepper
Lettuce
65g/2½oz piece French bread

Discard all visible fat from the beef and cut the lean into strips. Chop the gherkins and mix with the creamed horseradish, yoghurt and mustard. Season with salt and pepper. Shred the lettuce. Cut the French bread

French Bread with Beef Filling

French Bread with Fruity Chicken Filling

almost in half lengthways and fill with the beef mixture and lettuce.

Serves 1/	cals.	fat units	grams fibre
white bread	375	3	2.7
wholemeal bread	360	3	7.5

French Bread with Prawn Filling
(see picture page 49)

115g/4oz peeled prawns
15ml/1 tablespoon low-calorie salad cream
10ml/2 level teaspoons tomato ketchup
Squeeze lemon juice
Salt and pepper
Little lettuce
15g/½oz cucumber
65g/2½oz piece French bread

Mix the prawns with the low-calorie salad cream, tomato ketchup and lemon juice. Season with a little salt and pepper. Shred the lettuce and slice the cucumber. Cut the French bread almost in half lengthways and fill with the prawn mixture, lettuce and cucumber.

Serves 1/	cals.	fat units	grams fibre
white bread	370	2	2.4
wholemeal bread	355	2	7.3

French Bread with Lobster and Asparagus Filling
(see picture page 49)

At just 5 calories a spear, asparagus is one of life's little luxuries that every dieter can afford to include in a diet — as long as it is not served dripping with high-calorie butter or oily dressing. This low-calorie salad cream and ketchup mixture could also be used to top any left-over asparagus tips to turn them into a tiny snack. The amount of dressing shown here totals 65 calories.

65g/2½oz piece French bread
53g/1⅞oz pot lobster or crab paste or pâté
8 canned or cooked asparagus spears
30ml/2 tablespoons low-calorie salad cream
15ml/1 level tablespoon tomato ketchup
Squeeze lemon juice

Cut the French bread almost in half lengthways and then spread the cut surfaces with the lobster or crab paste or pâté. Drain the asparagus well and pile onto the French bread. Mix together the low-calorie salad cream, tomato ketchup and lemon juice and spoon over the asparagus.

Serves 1/	cals.	fat units	grams fibre
white bread	390	4	5.5
wholemeal bread	375	4	10.4

Pitta Bread Pockets

Pitta bread makes a pleasantly different packed lunch or picnic item. You can buy either white or wholemeal pitta breads from supermarkets or delicatessens. Calories vary little — 175 for a whole white pitta; 165 calories for wholemeal. However, the wholemeal pitta is higher in fibre, and you may find it a little more filling. Pitta bread can be frozen and you can take one out at a time to pack with filling. To make the pockets, cut the pitta bread in half, and then carefully slip a knife between the two layers, taking care not to split the side. Wrap the pitta bread in foil or put in a plastic bag and carry your chosen filling in a separate container. When you are ready to eat, spoon the filling into each pitta half.

French Bread with Prawn Filling

French Bread with Lobster and Asparagus Filling

Frankfurter Pitta Pocket

Although this recipe tastes best with a frankfurter, you could use a well-grilled chipolata sausage instead. Whereas a 25g/1oz frankfurter is 80 calories/2.5 fat units/0.3 grams fibre, a pork chipolata has 65 calories/2 fat units/0.1 grams fibre when cooked, so there would be a slight calorie and fat unit saving.

1 pitta bread
1 frankfurter, 25g/1oz
1 radish
15g/½oz green or red pepper
15ml/1 tablespoon low-calorie salad
  cream
2.5ml/½ level teaspoon mustard
Salt and pepper

Prepare the pitta bread as above. Slice the frankfurter and radish. Discard the white pith and seeds from the pepper and dice the flesh. Mix together the low-calorie salad cream and mustard, then season with salt and pepper. Stir in the frankfurter, radish and pepper. Pack in a plastic container. Spoon into the pitta when ready to eat.

Serves 1/	cals.	fat units	grams fibre
white pitta	290	4	2.6
wholemeal pitta	280	4	6.7

Chicken and Beansprout Pitta Pocket

Once only seen on Chinese restaurant menus, the beansprout has now infiltrated Western kitchens. Not only are beansprouts very low in calories — 3 per 25g/1oz canned; 5 raw — but they are beautifully crunchy and so light-weight that you get lots for your 25g/1oz.

1 pitta bread
50g/2oz cooked chicken
30ml/2 level tablespoons tomato or
  chilli chutney or relish
Pinch chilli powder, optional
25g/1oz beansprouts, fresh or canned

Prepare the pitta bread in the usual way. Discard any skin from the chicken and chop the flesh. Add the chilli powder to the chutney or relish, then stir in the chicken. Mix with beansprouts and pack into a container. Spoon into pitta pockets when ready to eat.

Serves 1/	cals.	fat units	grams fibre
white pitta	295	1.5	2.2
wholemeal pitta	285	1.5	6.3

Pork and Apple Pitta Pocket

The apple makes this filling lovely and moist and the nuts and raisins give it extra bite. Make sure you toss the apple well in lemon juice to prevent it turning brown.

1 pitta bread
25g/1oz lean roast pork
1 small apple
5ml/1 teaspoon lemon juice
15ml/1 level tablespoon low-fat
  natural yoghurt
15ml/1 level tablespoon raisins
15ml/1 level tablespoon roughly
  chopped walnuts

Prepare the pitta bread in the usual way. Discard all visible fat from the pork and chop the lean. Core and dice the apple and toss in lemon juice. Mix with the yoghurt, raisins, walnuts and pork. Pack in a plastic container. Spoon into the pitta pockets when ready to eat.

Serves 1/	cals.	fat units	grams fibre
white pitta	325	2	4.5
wholemeal pitta	315	2	8.6

Marinaded Drumsticks

Chicken drumsticks are ideal for picnics and packed lunches because they can be eaten easily with your fingers. They also come in conveniently controlled portions of 85 calories/1.5 fat units/0 grams fibre each when grilled. Remove the skin and you reduce this to 65 calories/1 fat unit/0 grams fibre. The following four recipes use a marinade to make each drumstick pair deliciously different. To start each recipe you need to remove the skin from the raw drumstick and make two deep cuts in the flesh on either side before proceeding with the marinade. The drumsticks are served with salads and in each case we give separate nutritional information so that you can mix and match if you wish.

Tandoori Drumsticks with Rice Salad

If you are eating out at an Indian restaurant, Tandoori chicken is usually the lowest-calorie dish you will find on the menu. These drumsticks have a really authentic taste and are so reasonable in calories that you will even be able to afford a rice salad accompaniment. If you do not have curry paste available, you could use curry powder instead.

Drumsticks:
2 chicken drumsticks
5ml/1 level teaspoon curry paste,
  hot or mild
30ml/2 level tablespoons natural
  yoghurt
1.25ml/¼ level teaspoon lemon juice
Pinch salt
Rice Salad:
40g/1½oz long-grain rice
15ml/1 tablespoon oil-free French dressing

Salt and pepper
50g/2oz cucumber
30ml/2 level tablespoons raisins or
 sultanas

Prepare the drumsticks as instructed above and place in a container. Mix together the curry paste, yoghurt, lemon juice and salt. Spread all over the drumsticks, cover and leave to marinade for 2-12 hours. Place in an ovenproof container, cover and cook at 180°C/350°F/gas mark 4 for 30-35 minutes. Cool, then pack. Boil the rice, then drain in a sieve. Rinse in cold water and drain again. Mix with oil-free French dressing. Dice the cucumber and add to the rice with the raisins or sultanas. Season with salt and pepper and pack in a container.

		fat	grams
Serves 1/	cals.	units	fibres
drumsticks	150	2	0
rice salad	215	0.5	2.1

Chinese-style Drumsticks with Beansprout Salad

You may have to go to a little extra trouble to find Five Spice Powder for this recipe, but it really is worth it to give the marinade that special Chinese flavour. You will find it in Chinese shops and supermarkets that stock a good range of spices. Alternatively, some of the big spice companies produce a Chinese flavouring which you could use instead.

Drumsticks:
2 chicken drumsticks
20ml/4 teaspoons soya sauce
10ml/2 level teaspoons liquid honey
2.5ml/½ level teaspoon Five Spice
 Powder
Pinch ground ginger
Beansprout salad:
1 stick celery
115g/4oz beansprouts, fresh or canned
115g/4oz canned sweetcorn with peppers
15ml/1 tablespoon oil-free French
 dressing
5ml/1 teaspoon soya sauce

Prepare the drumsticks as instructed above and place in a container. Mix together the soya sauce, honey, Five Spice Powder and ginger and spoon over the drumsticks. Cover and marinate for 2-12 hours. Place in an ovenproof dish, cover and cook at 180°C/350°F/gas mark 4 for 30-35 minutes. Cool, then pack.
 Slice the celery and mix with the beansprouts and sweetcorn with peppers. Toss the vegetables in oil-free French dressing and soya sauce and pack in a plastic container.

		fat	grams
Serves 1/	cals.	units	fibre
drumsticks	185	2.5	0
fresh beansprouts	130	0	8.6
canned beansprouts	125	0	10.8

Salads

Salads need not consist of a limp lettuce leaf and a few slices of cucumber and tomato! There are many lovely low-calorie mixtures that can be packed in plastic containers for a working lunch or for a picnic.

Stuffed Pepper with Apricots and Cheese
(see picture page 53)

Peppers are often stuffed and baked, but this recipe shows you how to use these crunchy low-calorie vegetables as the basis for an unusual salad mixture. If the stuffed pepper does not fit exactly into the container, wrap each half in cling film to prevent the filling spilling out.

1 small green or red pepper
50g/2oz button mushrooms
50g/2oz apricot halves, canned in
 natural juice, drained
25g/1oz Edam cheese
25g/1oz lettuce
15ml/1 tablespoon low-calorie salad cream
5ml/1 teaspoon lemon juice
Salt and pepper

Cut the pepper in half lengthways and discard the white pith and seeds. Plunge into boiling water for 2-3 minutes, then rinse in cold water. Chop the mushrooms, apricots and cheese. Shred the lettuce and mix with the chopped ingredients, low-calorie salad cream and lemon juice. Season and pile into the pepper shells.

Serves 1/165 calories
3.5 fat units/3.8 grams fibre.

Mediterranean Bean Salad

Mediterranean salads usually come drenched in oil dressing and each tablespoon of dressing will cost 75 calories/3 fat units. This recipe uses oil-free French dressing and the two tablespoons cost just 5 calories/ 0 fat units.

225g/8oz can butter beans
1 tomato
1 spring onion/scallion
¼ green or red pepper
½ clove garlic, optional
4 black olives
30ml/2 tablespoons oil-free French dressing
Salt and pepper

Drain the butter beans. Chop the tomato. Discard the roots and tough green leaves of the spring onion/scallion and chop the bulb. Discard the white pith and seeds from the pepper and dice the flesh. Crush the garlic and add to the oil-free French dressing. Stone the olives. Mix all the ingredients together and season with salt and pepper. Pack in a plastic container.

Serves 1/175 calories
0.5 fat units/9.6 grams fibre.

Cheesey Pasta Salad
(see picture page 53)

50g/2oz pasta shapes or noodles,
  white or wholewheat
25g/1oz Edam cheese
50g/2oz button mushrooms
25g/1oz red or green pepper
50g/2oz lettuce
15ml/1 level tablespoon low-calorie
  salad cream
Pinch of curry powder

Boil the pasta shapes or noodles until just tender. Drain and rinse under cold water, then drain again thoroughly. Dice the cheese and slice the mushrooms. Chop the celery. Discard the white pith and seeds from the pepper and dice the flesh. Shred the lettuce and arrange around the edge of a plate. Mix together the pasta, cheese, mushrooms, celery and pepper. Pile onto the plate and serve with low-calorie salad cream mixed with curry powder.

Serves 1/	cals.	fat units	grams fibre
white pasta	350	4	6.2
wholewheat pasta	330	4	10.1

Ham and Rice Salad

Rice salads are always filling and as long as you mix the rice with low-calorie ingredients and dressings, they make excellent slimmers' packed meals. This salad can be made in advance and kept in the refrigerator for about 12 hours. If you are intending to make up lots of rice salads during a week, cook the amount of rice you need all at once; it will store in the refrigerator unmixed and undressed for 7 days.

40g/1½oz long-grain rice, brown or
  white
30ml/2 tablespoons oil-free French
  dressing
50g/2oz lean cooked ham
2 rings pineapple, canned in natural
  juice, drained
50g/2oz cucumber
75g/3oz canned sweetcorn with
  peppers, drained
Salt and pepper

Boil the rice until tender and then drain in a sieve. Rinse in cold water and drain again. Turn into a bowl and stir in the oil-free French dressing. Leave until cold. Discard all visible fat from the ham and dice the lean. Cut the pineapple into small pieces and dice the cucumber. Mix all the ingredients and pack into a plastic container.

Serves 1/	cals.	fat units	grams fibre
white rice	370	1	6.6
brown rice	365	1.5	7.8

Melon, Prawn and Cheese Salad
(see picture page 53)

This fruity mixture is delicious on a hot day. But it is best served chilled so, if possible, pack it into a vacuum food jar or leave the salad in the refrigerator for half an hour before packing it in a container and carry it in an insulated bag.

275g/10oz melon
25g/1oz Edam cheese
50g/2oz grapes
50g/2oz peeled prawns

Discard the pips from the melon, then scoop out the flesh leaving the skin intact. Cut the flesh into bite-sized pieces. Cube the cheese, halve and pip the grapes. Mix all the ingredients together and pack into a container or serve in the melon shell.

Serves 1/220 calories
2.5 fat units/1.9 grams fibre

Smoked Haddock Coleslaw
(see picture page 53)

Bought coleslaw is usually made with mayonnaise which covers the low-calorie ingredients with masses of creamy calories. Mayonnaise is 120 calories/3.5 fat units a level tablespoon and it is wise to ban it from your store-cupboard while you are dieting. Low-calorie salad cream is an acceptable alternative which will save you about 95 calories/3 fat units per tablespoon, depending on the brand.

115g/4oz smoked haddock fillet
75g/3oz white cabbage
75g/3oz carrot
50g/2oz radishes
25g/1oz Edam cheese
15ml/1 tablespoon low-calorie salad cream
5ml/1 teaspoon lemon juice
Salt and pepper

Poach the smoked haddock in a small pan with just enough water to cover for 10-15 minutes, or until it flakes easily. Lift out and discard the skin and any bones. Flake the fish. Shred the cabbage. Grate the carrots and thinly slice the radishes. Cut the cheese into small cubes. Mix all the ingredients together and season with salt and pepper.

Serves 1/275 calories
4 fat units/5.7 grams fibre

Coleslaw with Blue Cheese

The strong flavour of blue cheese goes particularly well with grapes and coleslaw and makes this a favourite salad for cheese lovers. It will keep crisp in a container in the fridge overnight, so this is a salad you can make up in advance.

50g/2oz Danish Blue cheese
50g/2oz white cabbage
25g/1oz carrot
1 stick celery
25g/1oz grapes
30ml/2 level tablespoons low-calorie
  salad cream
Salt and pepper

Here's a colourful picnic spread for a hot summer's day: **1** Melon, Prawn and Cheese Salad (recipe page 52); **2** Open Corned Beef and Cheese Sandwich (recipe page 46); **3** Pinwheel Cheese Sandwich (recipe page 47); **4** Stuffed Pepper with Apricots and Cheese (recipe page 51); **5** Cheesey Pasta Salad (recipe page 52); and **6** Smoked Haddock Coleslaw (recipe page 52)

Cut the cheese into small cubes. Shred the cabbage; grate the carrot and thinly slice the celery. Halve and pip the grapes. Mix all the ingredients together and season with salt and pepper.

Serves 1/295 calories
8 fat units/3.5 grams fibre

Know your eggs

Though in terms of calories (42 per 25g/1oz), eggs are not particularly low, their great dieting advantage is that they come in portion-controlled packages. A large size 1 egg is 95 calories; size 2 is 90; a standard size 3 is 80 calories; size 4 is 75; size 5 is 70 and the smallest size 6 is 60. Raw, boiled or poached, an egg keeps a stable calorie count.

Like most foods, eggs gain in calories when fried. Add 20 calories to each egg. But there's no harm in having a fried egg with two crispy rashers of streaky bacon and a small slice of bread for a meal that costs around 265 calories. It's when you start adding sausages, fried bread and following up with buttered toast and marmalade that the traditional British breakfast can top 1,000 calories.

The egg contributes comparatively little to a Scotch egg's total — 290 to 350 calories depending on size. Most of the calories come in the fatty sausage meat that surrounds the egg. The Scotch egg absorbs even more calories when it's coated in breadcrumbs and fried. At an average 100 calories per 25g/1oz, veal, ham and egg pie is lower than a pork pie's 110, but this 115g/4oz slice would set you back 400 calories.

Beat up 3 eggs, fry in butter, fill with 75g/3oz cheese and an omelet could cost you 700 calories! But omelets can make excellent low-calorie meals if you use such low-calorie fillings as tomatoes or poached mushrooms. This omelet made from 2 eggs (size 3) filled with 2 sliced tomatoes, sprinkled with mixed herbs and cooked in a non-stick pan brushed with 1.25ml/¼ teaspoon oil, comes to only 185 calories.

One of the most fattening ways to eat eggs is scrambled. A couple of buttery-scrambled eggs on a slice of buttered toast can soon take you up to around 400 calories. No need to forgo scrambled eggs if you love them, though. Use 2 eggs (size 3), 30ml/2 tablespoons skimmed milk, cook in a non-stick pan and place on a large thin slice of unbuttered toast and the count comes down to 245.

Do not be fooled into thinking Egg Mayonnaise with salad is a safe slimming bet. It can be dangerously high in calories — because of the mayonnaise. The small salad here with 2 hard-boiled eggs coated with 60ml/2 rounded tablespoons mayonnaise comes to an astronomic 640 calories! Use low-calorie mayonnaise to reduce the calories to about 360; or low-calorie salad cream to cut the count down to around 260.

Eggs Benedict on Crab made with buttery Hollandaise Sauce could cost high. But here's a slimmer's version which makes a delicious 255 calorie mcal. Spread 40g/1½oz dressed crab on half a toasted bap. Top with poached egg; cover with sauce made with 15ml/1 tablespoon each tomato ketchup, low-calorie salad cream and natural yoghurt, stirred over a low heat.

Slenderest part of the egg is the white at 10 calories per 25g/1oz. You can make an Apple Snow pudding, mixing stewed apples, lemon rind, sugar and egg whites for just 165 calories. See the Desserts section for another Apple Snow recipe (page 110).

Soups and starters

Once you learn the low-fat, low-calorie way to make soups and starters, you will probably never want to return to making them by the traditional methods. You will find these recipes just as flavoursome as their high-calorie counterparts, and you will get just as much on your plate or in your bowl. All you will be missing is high-calorie fatty ingredients such as butter, oil, mayonnaise and cream. Soups make a warming beginning to a two or three-course meal, or can keep you going between meals if your will-power starts to weaken. We have given recipes for four portions but if you have a freezer it may be worth making a larger amount and freezing individual servings as emergency rations. Calories start at 50 calories — that is the same as a medium apple and about a third of the calories in a small packet of crisps.

Most soups are traditionally made by pre-frying vegetables — and that is the stage we omit in our recipes. Pre-frying adds lot of unnecessary calories to your soup. Just 25g/1oz butter costs 210 calories and 8 fat units, and it is an ingredient that you really will not miss once you get into the low-fat habit. Home-made soup is nothing like any product that you will get from a can or packet. Whereas some of the lower calorie manufactured soups are useful if you want to make a hot snack in minutes, few would compare for flavour and filling power with the ones we give recipes for here.

Most people usually only bother with a starter when they are serving a meal to family or friends. But although adding an extra course to the food you normally eat may not seem a good idea when you are dieting, eating a low-calorie starter does have some advantages, even for those people who normally stick to one main plateful. Many overweight people are fast eaters and often down more food than they really need because their first mouthfuls have not really 'registered' before they have crammed down a considerable amount. If you sit down to a starter or soup course, try delaying a little before serving up the second course. In this way, your stomach will have time to signal that it has received some food and the initial urge to satisfy hunger is considerably reduced.

All recipes in this section are for four people or more. We have indicated if the recipe can be frozen, and if you are cooking just for yourself or for two people it would be best to choose from these and freeze any remaining portions. If you are serving more than four people, the recipes can be increased accordingly. Do not be worried about giving low-calorie starters to special guests for they are unlikely to guess that the attractive dish set before them is to help you to control your weight. A starter can cost as little as 40 calories and many contain no fat units at all. Some of the starters can also be served as a light meal, either with additional salad or with bread or crispbreads.

Soups

Soups can be served as a starter in a main meal menu; can be eaten as a between-meal snack; or, with the addition of a slice of bread, will make a light meal on their own. All the following recipes serve four and most will freeze in individual portions if you do not want to share them with the rest of the family.

A selection of delicious soups and starters
1 *Herby Pea Soup (recipe page 59);*
2 *Cauliflower Soufflé (recipe page 64); and* **3**
Avocado and Lime Cocktail (recipe page 63)

Watercress soup
(see picture page 156)

Watercress is economical, low-calorie and excellent in a soup. Even if you are not normally a raw watercress fan, we would recommend that you try this recipe. The skimmed milk powder gives the soup a slightly creamy flavour. It freezes successfully.

150g/5oz watercress
1 medium onion
850ml/1½ pints water
2 chicken stock cubes
Salt and pepper
60ml/4 level tablespoons skimmed milk
  powder
30ml/2 level tablespoons cornflour

Wash the watercress and discard any yellow leaves and hard stalks. Chop the onion and place in a pan with the water and stock cubes. Season with salt and pepper. Bring to the boil, cover the pan and simmer for 10 minutes. Add the watercress and simmer for another 10 minutes. Purée in the blender or rub through a sieve. Blend the powdered skimmed milk with the cornflour and a little cold water to make a smooth paste. Add to the soup and return to the pan. Bring to the boil, stirring all the time, until the soup thickens slightly and simmer for 2-3 minutes.

Serves 4/60 calories
0 fat units/1.6 grams fibre per portion

Chilled Prawn and Mushroom Soup

115g/4oz shelled prawns
275ml/½ pint cultured buttermilk
283g/10oz can mushrooms in brine
5ml/1 teaspoon lemon juice
Salt and pepper
4 sprigs parsley, optional

Reserve 4 prawns for decoration and chop the remainder. Place the buttermilk, the mushrooms with their liquid and lemon juice in a liquidiser or processor and blend until smooth. If no liquidiser or processor is available, chop and pound the mushrooms into a purée and beat into the buttermilk mixture. Stir in the chopped prawns and season with salt and pepper. Chill for at least 1 hour. Stir and divide between 4 small serving bowls. Garnish with the reserved prawns and parsley.

Serves 4/60 calories
0 fat units/1.0 grams fibre per portion

Slimmer's Gazpacho
(see picture page 6l)

Gazpacho can be frozen without the cucumber garnish, in which case, add the diced cucumber just before serving.

575g/1¼ lb tomatoes
1 small green pepper
1 medium onion
1 clove garlic
15ml/1 tablespoon cider or wine vinegar
15ml/1 tablespoon olive oil or salad oil
Salt and pepper
¼ cucumber

Skin the tomatoes, then cut in half and squeeze out the seeds and juice. Rub the seeds and juice through a sieve, discarding the seeds. Discard the white pith and seeds from the pepper, then roughly chop the flesh. Slice the onion and crush the garlic. Place all the ingredients, except the cucumber, in a liquidiser or food processor and blend until smooth. Chill thoroughly.

4 Indian-Stuffed Tomatoes (recipe page 64); 5 Marinaded Mushrooms (recipe page 64); and 6 Florida Cocktail (recipe page 62) are interesting starters

57

Dice the cucumber and add to the soup just before serving.

Serves 4/60 calories
1 fat unit/2.6 grams fibre per portion

Chinese Sweetcorn and Crab Soup

The Chinese are famous for this subtle-tasting soup which is simple to make. It can be frozen with fresh or canned crab, but frozen crab should not be added until the rest of the soup has been thawed and re-heated. Instead of crab, you could add 75g/3oz shelled prawns. The calorie count would come down to 125 while fat and fibre counts would remain the same.

312g/11oz can sweetcorn kernels
2 spring onions/scallions
700ml/1¼ pints water
2 chicken stock cubes
10ml/2 teaspoons soya sauce
30ml/ 2 tablespoons dry sherry or
30ml/ 2 tablespoons extra water
30ml/ 2 level tablespoons cornflour
75g/3oz white crab meat, fresh, frozen or
  canned
Salt and pepper

Reserve 30ml/2 level tablespoons of the sweetcorn. Place the remainder in a liquidiser or food processor with the liquid from the can and blend until almost smooth. Place in a saucepan. Discard the roots and tough green leaves from the spring onions, and then chop the bulbs. Add to the pan with the water, stock cubes and soya sauce. Cover the pan, bring to the boil and simmer gently for 10 minutes. Mix the sherry or extra water with the cornflour until smooth. Stir into the soup and cook for 1-2 minutes, stirring all the time. Discard any pieces of shell from the crab and flake finely. Add to the soup with the reserved sweetcorn. Heat through and adjust the seasoning to taste. Serve hot.

Serves 4/130 calories
0.5 fat unit/4.6 grams fibre per portion

Onion Soup with Cheese
(see picture page 59)

Onion soup is so very low in calories if made this way that you can afford to add Cheddar cheese. The mature sort has lots of flavour so a little goes a long way. The soup will freeze and the cheese can be added before serving. Without cheese, the onion soup comes to 60 calories/0 fat units/1.7 grams fibre per portion.

450g/1lb onions
850ml/1½ pints water
2 beef stock cubes
30ml/2 level tablespoons cornflour
Salt and pepper
75g/3oz mature Cheddar cheese
Chopped parsley to garnish

Chop the onions and place in a saucepan with the water and stock cubes. Cover the pan, bring to the boil and simmer for 30 minutes. Blend the cornflour with a little cold water until smooth. Add to the soup, whisking all the time, and simmer, stirring continuously, for 2 minutes. Season with salt and pepper — you will not need much seasoning so taste it first. Grate the cheese and sprinkle on top. Garnish with chopped parsley.

Serves 4/150 calories
3 fat units/1.7 grams fibre per portion

Seafood Soup
(see picture page 30)

An impressive first course, this soup is not as expensive as it looks if you make it when tomatoes are plentiful and low-priced. Made with fresh prawns, the soup can be frozen; but frozen prawns should only be added if you are going to serve it immediately. If you make this or any of the other soups for supper guests, they can be prepared early in the day and reheated just before serving.

115g/4oz cod, coley, haddock or any similar
  white fish fillet
Small squeeze lemon juice
Water
Salt and pepper
1 small onion
575g/1¼lb tomatoes
1 cap canned pimento
1 chicken stock cube
15ml/1 level tablespoon tomato purée
15ml/1 level tablespoon cornflour
115g/4oz prawns

Place the fish in a small saucepan and add a small squeeze of lemon juice and enough water to just cover. Season with salt and pepper. Cover the pan, heat until simmering and cook very gently until the fish flakes easily — about 10 minutes. Drain the liquid into a measuring jug and make up to 700ml/ 1¼ pints with water. Discard the skin and bones from the fish and flake the white flesh finely. Set aside. Finely chop the onion. Cut the tomatoes in half and discard the seeds and juice. Chop the pimento.
  Place all the vegetables in a pan with the water, stock cube and tomato purée. Bring to the boil, cover the pan and simmer gently for 20 minutes. Purée in a liquidiser or food processor or rub through a sieve. Return to the pan. Blend the cornflour with a little cold water to make a smooth paste, then stir

into the soup. Bring to the boil, stirring all the time, and simmer for 2-3 minutes. Chop the prawns finely and add to the soup with the flaked fish. Taste and adjust the seasoning before serving.

Serves 4/100 calories
0 fat units/2.6 grams fibre per portion

Leek and Potato Soup

225g/8oz white part of leek (weighed
*   trimmed of roots and tough green leaves)*
1 stick celery
225g/8oz potato, weighed peeled
700ml/1½ pints water
2 chicken stock cubes
Salt and pepper
45ml/3 level tablespoons skimmed
*   milk powder*

Slice and wash the leeks and celery. Dice the potato. Place all the vegetables in a saucepan with the water and stock cubes. Season. Cover the pan, bring to the boil and simmer for 40 minutes or until all the vegetables are tender. Pour into a liquidiser or food processor and leave to cool slightly. Add the skimmed milk powder and run the machine until the mixture is smooth. Alter-natively, rub the soup through a sieve, then

Try one of the enticing soups and starters shown above: 1 Eggs Baked in Tomatoes (recipe page 65); 2 Cucumber Cups with Prawns (recipe page 60); 3 Pears with Cottage Cheese Dressing (recipe page 63); and 4 Onion Soup with Cheese (recipe page 58)

whisk in powdered milk. Return to the pan and reheat gently.

Serves 4/100 calories
0 fat units/3.2 grams fibre per portion

Herby Pea Soup
(see picture page 57)

It is a pity that pea soup has such a murky reputation, because made this way it could not be fresher nor more pleasant tasting. Peas are high in fibre, so this is a particularly filling sort of soup that could easily make a light meal if served with a crusty bread roll (adds 145 calories/½ fat unit and 1.5 grams fibre if white or 2.9 grams fibre if brown). This soup can be frozen also.

1 small onion
1 stick celery
450g/1lb frozen peas

1 chicken stock cube
5ml/1 level teaspoon mixed dried herbs
15ml/1 level tablespoon fresh mint or 5ml/
  1 level teaspoon dried mint
850ml/1½ pints water
5ml/1 level teaspoon sugar
Salt and pepper
15ml/1 level tablespoon cornflour
30ml/2 level tablespoons skimmed
  milk powder

Chop the onion and celery and place in a saucepan with the peas, stock cube, mixed herbs, mint, water and sugar. Season and then bring to the boil. Cover and simmer for about 30 minutes. Purée in a liquidiser or food processor or rub through a sieve. Pour most of the purée back into the saucepan and blend the remainder with the skimmed milk powder and cornflour in the liquidiser or food processor. Alternatively, mix them in a basin until smooth. Add to the saucepan and bring to the boil, stirring. Simmer for 2 minutes and serve hot.

Serves 4/95 calories
0 fat units/9.3 grams fibre per portion

Fish Starters

A fish starter is ideal when you are serving meat as a main course. Choose something in a tangy sauce if you are serving plain meat and vegetables. Or try a fruit and fish mixture with a spicy main course. All but one of the recipes given here are under 150 calories per portion.

Cucumber Cups with Salmon
(see picture page 61)

Low-calorie seafood sauce is 20 calories a tablespoon — the ordinary sort is about 75 calories. So when you switch to the low-calorie brands you will automatically be saving a considerable number of calories.

350g/12oz piece cucumber, washed
100g/3½oz can salmon
15ml/1 tablespoon low-calorie seafood
  sauce
3 small gherkins
Salt and pepper
4 tomatoes

Cut the cucumber into 8 equal pieces. Scoop the centre out of each with a small teaspoon to make cup shapes. Discard the centres. Flake the salmon and mix with seafood sauce. Chop the gherkins and add to the salmon. Season with salt and pepper, and pile into the cucumber cups. Chill thoroughly. Slice the tomatoes and arrange on four small serving plates with the cucumber cups.

Serves 4/60 calories
1 fat unit/1.1 grams fibre per portion

Cucumber Cups with Prawns
(see picture page 59)

At just 3 calories for 25g/1oz, cucumber is an ideal diet food. If you wish, you can prepare the prawn filling in advance and keep it in the refrigerator ready for piling into the cucumber cups when ready to serve.

450g/1lb cucumber, washed
2 mint leaves or pinch dried mint
50g/2oz canned pimento, drained
30ml/2 level tablespoons natural yoghurt
30ml/2 level tablespoons low-calorie seafood
  sauce
225g/8oz peeled prawns
Salt and pepper
½ lemon to garnish

Cut the cucumber into 8 evenly sized pieces. Scoop the centre out of each with a small teaspoon to make cup shapes. Discard the centres. Finely chop the fresh mint, if used, and the pimento. Mix into the yoghurt and seafood sauce. Stir in the prawns and season with salt and pepper. Pile into the cucumber cups and divide between 4 serving plates and chill. Cut the lemon into thin wedges and use to garnish.

Serves 4/90 calories
0.5 fat unit/0.5 grams fibre per portion

Prawn, Apple and Celery Cocktail
(see picture page 63)

Walnuts are 149 calories/5 fat units for 25g/1oz, so if you are a nut fan you had better get your family or friends to dispose of any left-overs from this recipe. If you buy nuts to add to any recipe, it is always best to buy the smallest packet you can find.

60ml/4 level tablespoons natural yoghurt
60ml/4 level tablespoons low-calorie salad
  cream
5ml/1 teaspoon lemon juice
1.25ml/¼ level teaspoon caster sugar
Salt and pepper
2 medium-sized eating apples
4 small sticks celery
225g/8oz peeled prawns
4 walnut halves
4 slices cucumber

Mix together the yoghurt, low-calorie salad cream, lemon juice and caster sugar. Season lightly with salt and pepper. Core and dice the apples. Chop the celery and add to the dressing with the apple and prawns. Divide between four serving dishes and garnish each cocktail with a walnut half and a slice of cucumber.

Serves 4/140 calories
2 fat units/2.2 grams fibre per portion

Smoked Mackerel with Cucumber Salad
(see picture page 63)

350g/12oz smoked mackerel fillet
115g/4oz cucumber
2.5ml/½ level teaspoon caster sugar
60ml/4 tablespoons white wine vinegar
10ml/2 level teaspoons chopped chives
Salt and pepper
8 lettuce leaves
1 lemon

Skin the smoked mackerel fillet and divide into 4 pieces. Peel and slice the cucumber and arrange on a plate. Sprinkle with caster sugar and vinegar. Leave to stand for 15 minutes. Arrange the mackerel and lettuce leaves on four serving plates. Place the cucumber at the side and sprinkle with chives, salt and pepper.

Serves 4/220 calories
7.5 fat units/0.5 grams fibre per portion

Salmon and Cottage Cheese Mousse
(see picture page 130)

Although this recipe is low in calories and fat units, it makes a fairly substantial starter. If you wish, you can serve non-dieting guests with accompanying toast or bread rolls, but the mousse is delicious just eaten on its own. Ungarnished mousses can be frozen.

200g/7oz can of salmon
1 small onion
150ml/¼ pint water
15ml/1 level tablespoon powdered gelatine

225g/8oz carton natural cottage cheese
2.5ml/½ teaspoon lemon juice
15ml/1 level tablespoon chopped parsley
Salt and pepper
Watercress sprigs
½ lemon
4 slices cucumber

Drain the juice from the salmon into a small saucepan. Finely chop the onion and add to the pan with half the water. Cover the pan and simmer gently for 5 minutes. Meanwhile, place the remaining water in a small basin or a cup and sprinkle on the gelatine. Leave to soak for 5 minutes. Stand the basin or cup in a pan containing a little simmering water and leave until the gelatine has dissolved. Roughly flake the salmon and place in a liquidiser or food processor with the onion and cooking juices, dissolved gelatine, cottage cheese and lemon juice. Season with salt and pepper. Blend until smooth. Stir in the chopped parsley. Pour into four small moulds or empty yoghurt or cottage cheese cartons. Chill until set. Turn out and garnish with watercress, lemon wedges and cucumber.

Serves 4/145 calories
2.5 fat units/0 grams fibre per portion

Any one of the exciting ideas for appetisers shown below would be suitable for entertaining: **1** *Slimmer's Gazpacho (recipe page 57);* **2** *Pears with Blue Cheese (recipe page 62);* **3** *Cucumber Cups with Salmon (recipe page 60);* **4** *Melon with Mint Liqueur (recipe page 62); and* **5** *Grilled Spiced Grapefruit (recipe page 62)*

Fruit Starters

Refreshing fruit starters are ideal to serve before a slightly heavier main course. When you are planning your menu, though, take into account the dessert. A fresh fruit starter is best followed by a mousse, ice-cream or custard pudding.

Grilled Spiced Grapefruit
(see picture page 61)

This is one of the lowest calorie ways to start a meal and is ideal when you want to spend a little extra on the main course. You can mix the sugar and cinnamon in advance but do not put it on top of the grapefruit until you are ready to grill it. The sugar will gradually melt into the grapefruit if left for any length of time. Brown sugar gives a better colour, but white could be used instead if you wish — calories are exactly the same.

2 medium grapefruit
20ml/4 level teaspoons soft brown sugar
5ml/1 level teaspoon ground cinnamon
2 glacé cherries

Cut the grapefruit in half and loosen the segments using a small knife. Mix together the brown sugar and cinnamon and sprinkle this over the cut surface of the grapefruit. Cook under a medium grill until the sugar melts and the grapefruit is heated through. Cut the cherries in half and place in the centre of the grapefruit. Serve immediately.

Serves 4/40 calories
0 fat units/0.5 grams fibre per portion

Florida Cocktail
(see picture page 57)

This popular starter is a safe choice if you are uncertain of your guests' tastes. If you use sweet oranges and the less tart varieties of grapefruit, this amount of sugar will be ample. However, if guests have a particularly sweet tooth, you can offer them extra sugar separately.

2 grapefruit
2 large oranges
10ml/2 level teaspoons caster sugar

Cut each grapefruit in half. Using a grapefruit knife or a small sharp knife, cut out the segments and place in a basin with any juice. Cut away the membranes and core from the grapefruit and discard. Cut the edges of the shells into a zig-zag pattern. Using a sharp knife, cut away the skin and pith from the oranges, then cut out the segments by slipping the knife between the fruit and the membrane. Mix the fruits together and divide between the grapefruit shells with any juice. Sprinkle on the caster sugar and serve chilled.

Serves 4/65 calories
0 fat units/2.6 grams fibre per portion

Melon with Mint Liqueur
(see picture page 6l)

There is no need to buy a large bottle of Crème de Menthe if you are not certain you will be repeating the recipe — liqueurs are usually available in miniature-sized bottles and one of these will be ample. You could also use orange liqueur for this recipe.

675g/1lb 8oz Honeydew or yellow melon
* weighed with skin*
45ml/3 tablespoons Crème de Menthe
4 sprigs of mint, optional

Cut the melon in half and discard the pips. Using a small ball scoop, cut out as many balls as possible. Cut the remaining flesh away from the skin and cut into bite-sized pieces. Place the melon in a bowl and sprinkle on the Crème de Menthe. Cover with cling film and chill for at least 1 hour. Divide between 4 glasses, reserving the best shaped balls to place on top. Decorate with mint sprigs.

Serves 4/60 calories
0.5 fat units/1.0 grams fibre per portion

Melon and Ham Gondola
(see picture page 63)

675g/1lb 8oz slice Honeydew or
* yellow melon, weighed with skin*
115g/4oz lean smoked ham
10ml/2 teaspoons lemon juice
Black pepper
4 slices lemon to garnish

Chill the melon thoroughly. Cut into four even wedges and discard the pips and skin. Remove all visible fat from the ham and divide the lean into four portions. Wrap a slice around each melon wedge. Sprinkle with lemon juice and black pepper. Garnish with lemon slices.

Serves 4/75 calories
0.5 fat units/0.9 grams fibre per portion

Pears with Blue Cheese
(see picture page 61)

You will usually need to go a little easy on Danish Blue cheese at 103 calories/3 fat units/0 grams fibre per 25g/1oz. But mix it with cottage cheese and you will still get that pleasantly strong flavour, although the total calories and fat units have been

'diluted'. Roquefort is expensive but has the best flavour — it would also save you 5 calories per portion. Fat comes down to 1.5, fibre stays the same.

2 large ripe dessert pears, 225g/8oz each
Lemon juice
50g/2oz Danish Blue or Roquefort cheese
113g/4oz carton natural cottage cheese
Paprika
Few lettuce leaves

Cut the pears in half lengthwise and remove the cores. Brush the cut surfaces with lemon juice. Crumble the Danish Blue (or the Roquefort) cheese and mix with the cottage cheese. Pile into the pear cavities and dust with paprika. Arrange some lettuce on four individual plates and serve the pears on top.

Serves 4/110 calories
2 fat units/4.2 grams fibre per portion

Pears with Cottage Cheese Dressing
(see picture page 59)

450g/1lb ripe dessert pears
Little lemon juice
227g/8oz carton natural cottage cheese
30ml/2 tablespoons tarragon vinegar or
*   white wine vinegar*

*Here are four colourful cold starters for you to choose from: **1** Eggs with Herb Dressing (recipe page 65); **2** Smoked Mackerel with Cucumber Salad (recipe page 61); **3** Melon and Ham Gondola (recipe page 62); and **4** Prawn, Apple and Celery Cocktail (recipe page 60)*

2.5ml/½ level teaspoon finely grated
*   lemon rind*
Paprika
Watercress sprigs to garnish

Cut each unpeeled pear into eight slices lengthwise, and brush the cut surfaces with a little lemon juice. Sieve the cottage cheese and then mix with the vinegar and lemon rind. Beat together well, and then gently stir in the pear slices. Divide between four serving plates and chill thoroughly. Sprinkle with paprika and garnish with watercress sprigs before serving.

Serves 4/85 calories
0.5 fat units/4.2 grams fibre per portion

Avocado and Lime Cocktail
(see picture page 56)

Avocados are the exception to the rule that fruit is fat-free. A medium avocado will cost 470 calories and 17 fat units!

30ml/2 tablespoons lime cordial
5ml/1 teaspoon white wine vinegar or cider
 vinegar
2.5ml/½ level teaspoon French mustard
Salt and pepper
1 medium avocado
Little lemon juice
115g/4oz white grapes
1 medium-sized green eating apple
1 stick celery

Place the lime cordial, vinegar, French mustard and salt and pepper in a small jar with a lid. Shake until well blended. Cut the avocado in half lengthwise and carefully ease out the stone. Discard the skin and cut the flesh into bite-sized pieces. Brush with lemon juice. Halve and pip the grapes. Core the apple but do not peel, then cube the flesh. Brush with lemon juice. Slice the celery. Arrange the fruit and celery in four glasses or dishes and spoon over the dressing.

Serves 4/155 calories
4 fat units/2.2 grams fibre per portion

Vegetable Starters

These will suit almost any main course, but for variety's sake it is best not to serve cauliflower with your main dish when you are starting with a cauliflower soufflé, or mushrooms as a main course accompaniment when you are serving a mushroom starter.

Marinaded Mushrooms
(see picture page 57)

4 tomatoes
1 clove garlic
1 large sprig parsley
150ml/¼ pint dry white wine
2.5ml/½ level teaspoon ground coriander
1 bay leaf
Pinch dried thyme
2.5ml/½ level teaspoon salt
Black pepper
450g/1lb button mushrooms

Skin the tomatoes, then cut each in half and squeeze out the seeds and juice (either discard this or save it to add to a casserole or soup). Chop the tomato flesh. Crush the garlic. Place all the ingredients except the mushrooms in a saucepan. Cover the pan, bring to the boil and simmer gently for 5 minutes. Discard the tough ends of the stems of the mushrooms. Add the mushrooms to the pan, return to the boil and simmer for 8 minutes. Turn into a bowl and chill. Remove the bay leaf; divide the mixture between four serving dishes.

Serves 4/50 calories
0 fat units/3.6 grams fibre per portion

Indian-Style Stuffed Tomatoes
(see picture page 57)

25g/1oz white long-grain rice
15ml/1 tablespoon oil-free French dressing
10ml/2 level teaspoons mango chutney
Good pinch curry powder
50g/2oz cooked chicken
¼ small green pepper
8 medium tomatoes
Lettuce leaves

Cook the rice in boiling water until tender. Drain in a sieve, rinse in cold water and drain again. Mix with the oil-free French dressing, mango chutney and curry powder. Discard any skin from the chicken and chop the flesh. Discard the white pith and seeds from the pepper and dice the flesh. Add the chicken and pepper to the rice and season with salt and pepper. Cut a slice off the stem end of the tomatoes and carefully scoop out the core and seeds, using a small teaspoon or a grapefruit spoon. Leave the tomatoes upside-down to drain for 5 minutes — the core and seeds can be saved to use in stew or soup. Fill the tomatoes with the rice mixture and replace the lids at an angle. Serve 2 tomatoes per portion on a bed of lettuce.

Serves 4/75 calories
0 fat units/1.8 grams fibre per portion

Cauliflower Soufflé
(see picture page 56)

This starter will impress your guests, but do make sure they are ready to eat as soon as the soufflé comes out of the oven — any delay and your lovely soufflé will collapse.

175g/6oz cauliflower, weighed without
 leaves or hard stalks
30ml/2 level tablespoons powdered
 skimmed milk
25g/1oz low-fat spread
15ml/1 level tablespoon plain flour
2 eggs, size 3
25g/1oz mature Cheddar cheese
Salt and pepper

Preheat the oven to 190°C/375°F/ gas mark 5. Cook the cauliflower in boiling salted water until tender — about 15 minutes. Drain and reserve 115ml/4floz of the cooking liquid. Leave this to cool slightly, then stir in the powdered skimmed milk. Purée the cauliflower in a food processor or liquidiser. Grease four individual soufflé dishes with a little of the low-fat spread. Place the remainder in a small saucepan with the milky cooking liquid and the flour. Bring to the boil, whisking all the time until smooth, then simmer for 1-2 minutes. Add the cauliflower. Separate the eggs and grate the cheese. Beat the yolks and cheese into the sauce and season with salt and pepper. Whisk the egg whites until stiff and fold in gently. Turn into the prepared soufflé dishes and cook in the preheated oven for about 25 minutes, or until well-risen. Serve immediately.

Serves 4/120 calories
3 fat units/0.9 grams fibre per portion

Egg Starters

Eggs are filling so always serve an egg-based starter with a light main course. All these recipes use standard size 3 eggs but you can use a larger or smaller size if you wish. A larger size 2 egg will cost you 10 calories, 0.5 fat units more, and a smaller size 4 egg will cost 5 calories less, the fat units remaining the same. For other egg calories see the chart at the back of the book. Eggs do not contain any fibre.

Eggs with Herb Dressing
(see picture page 63)

4 eggs, size 3
60ml/4 level tablespoons low-calorie salad
*   cream*
60ml/4 level tablespoons natural yoghurt
15ml/1 level tablespoon finely chopped fresh
*   herbs of your choice*
10ml/2 level teaspoons finely chopped chives
4 lettuce leaves
1 tomato
Watercress sprigs

Hard-boil the eggs, and then cool in cold water. Shell and cut each in half lengthwise. Mix together the low-calorie salad cream, yoghurt, herbs and chives. Shred the lettuce and arrange on four serving plates. Place the eggs on top and coat with herb dressing. Cut the tomato into wedges and use to garnish with the watercress.

Serves 4/120 calories
3 fat units/0.3 grams fibre per portion

Eggs Baked in Tomatoes
(see picture page 59)

4 large firm tomatoes, 115g/4oz each
Garlic salt or salt
Black pepper
4 eggs, size 3
10ml/2 level teaspoons tomato ketchup
20ml/4 level teaspoons natural yoghurt
20ml/4 level teaspoons grated Parmesan
*   cheese*
1 large slice of bread, 40g/1½oz
Lettuce leaves

Cut a slice off the stem end of the tomatoes and carefully scoop out the pulp, leaving the shells intact. Turn upside-down and leave to drain for 30 minutes. Sprinkle the inside with garlic salt or salt and pepper. Place on a baking sheet and break an egg into each

shell. Blend the tomato ketchup and yoghurt and carefully spoon over the egg. Sprinkle on the Parmesan cheese. Bake at 180°C/ 350°F/ gas mark 4, for 15 minutes, or until the eggs have just set. Cut the bread into four small squares and toast. Shred the lettuce. Place a tomato on a piece of toast on each of 4 serving plates and garnish with shredded lettuce.

Serves 4 Per portion	cals.	fat units	grams fibre
white bread	140	2	2.0
brown bread	135	2	2.2
wholemeal bread	135	2	2.6

Spreads and Pâtés

All spreads and pâtés can be made in advance and many gain from being left in the refrigerator for several hours before serving.

Blue Cheese Spread

75g/3oz streaky bacon
25g/1oz mushrooms
75g/3oz Danish Blue cheese
113g/4oz carton cottage cheese with chives
Salt and pepper

Grill the bacon until crisp. Pat with kitchen paper to remove any excess grease. Finely chop the bacon and mushrooms. Grate Danish Blue cheese and mix with the cottage cheese, bacon and mushrooms. Season with salt and pepper but taste first as you may not need salt if the bacon is salty. For a smoother spread, place all the ingredients in a liquidiser or food processor and blend until smooth.

Serves 4/155 calories
3.5 fat units/0.2 grams fibre per portion

Smoked Trout Pâté

2 smoked trout, 160g/5½oz each
113g/4oz carton natural cottage cheese
150g/5oz carton natural low-fat yoghurt
15ml/1 tablespoon lemon juice
Pinch cayenne pepper
Black pepper and salt
4 slices cucumber
4 small wedges lemon

Skin and bone the smoked trout. Flake the flesh and place in a liquidiser or food processor with the cottage cheese, yoghurt, lemon juice, cayenne pepper and a little black pepper. Blend until smooth. Taste and add salt if necessary. Divide between individual containers and chill. Garnish with slices of cucumber and lemon wedges before serving.

Serves 4/130 calories
1.5 fat units/0 grams fibre per portion

65

Chinese Spare Ribs *500 calories*
Cooked to a real Chinese recipe, the spicy sauce that makes spare ribs so succulently special contains sugar, oil and sherry. Take-away and restaurant counts vary wildy. Do not count less than 335 calories for ribs with little meat and you could pay as high as 670 calories.

Fried Scampi *445 calories*
Scampi's breadcrumb coating soaks up the fat it is cooked in — 90 calories for 25g/1oz. Most restaurants serve 115g/4oz and bring a bowl of tartare sauce. If you are lavish with sauce (at 40 calories each level tablespoon), you could pay as much as 500 calories.

Bhajias *435 calories*
Each puff-ball is made from a thick spiced batter enclosing vegetables or prawns, then deep-fried. Indian restaurants give two big bhajias in each portion. Eat both of these and you will not pay less than 435 calories. Even small ones will be around 200 calories each.

Avocado Vinaigrette *385 calories*
The avocado is a fatty fruit — no less than 63 calories per 25g/1oz. Vinaigrette or prawn cocktail fillings cost a calorie fortune, too. Most people use 2 tablespoons vinaigrette at 75 calories each. Cocktail sauce is about 55 calories per level tablespoon, plus 30 for prawns.

Spaghetti Bolognese *360 calories*
The average 115g/4oz spaghetti portion costs 130 calories. But it's the sauce that can pile on the calories. Most places dole out 200 calories' worth of bolognese sauce at least. Napolitana could be a little lower if the chef does not add oil. Highest is *alburro* at about 300 calories.

Pâté *360 calories*
Restaurant pâtés are sure to be high in calories. Reckon on 120 calories for 25g/1oz. Many places serve 75g/3oz. Add another 65 calories for one slice of unbuttered toast (25 per Melba toast triangle). No pâté is likely to be less than 60 calories per 25g/1oz.

How much does that first course really cost you? As you will see here, some starters could almost finish off a diet!

Ravioli *325 calories*
The stuffing of these pasta envelopes in savoury sauce may be minced meat and vegetables or cheese. The savoury sauce may or may not be rich in wine and cream; but if eating out it is best to reckon your calorie cost at anything from 250 to 400 calories.

Humus *310 calories*
This savoury paste is made from chick peas, garlic and sesame seed Tahina paste usually served with a topping of olive oil and paprika. Most people eat 65g/2½oz humus (at 50 calories for 25g/1oz) plus a dessertspoon of oil (80 calories) and half a pitta (105 calories).

Whitebait *300 calories*
These baby fish (the young of the herring) arrive at the table dipped in flour and deep-fried. They absorb a lot of fat and cost 150 calories for 25g/1oz. The average restaurant serving is 50g/2oz but a generous restaurant might well serve 75g/3oz at 450 calories.

Corn on the Cob *315 calories*
A corn on the cob scores 155 calories — the rest comes from the butter. Most people eat 20g/¾oz butter with their sweetcorn — 160 calories' worth. Using just 7g/¼oz butter would reduce the cost to 210 calories. Use low-fat spread and score around 180 calories.

Samosas *280 calories*
This Indian speciality is made of butter-and-milk pastry filled with spicy fried meat or vegetables and deep-fried in hot fat. You will get two big samosas in most restaurants, so your cost could be as high as 320 calories. Even one tiny samosa is 90 calories.

Spring Roll *240 calories*
This Chinese stuffed pancake is made of flour and egg dough, rolled around stir-fried mixes of bean-shoots, vegetables, chicken, prawns, pork, etc, and deep-fried. You are not going to pay less than 240 per roll from a Chinese restaurant and you could pay up to 300 calories.

Cream of Tomato Soup *220 calories*
Cream of tomato is a high calorie soup. The reason is the sugar, cream, vegetable oil and starch thickeners that find their way into the can along with the tomatoes. If you have a dash of cream (as some restaurants serve it) there could be as many as 340 calories.

Artichoke *220 calories*
The luxurious artichoke has an amazingly low calorie count, just 4 calories for 25g/1oz. Trouble is, this tiny count is usually swamped in high-calorie butter or vinaigrette dressing. Substitute oil-free French dressing and your score plummets down to below 20 mark!

French Onion Soup *175 calories*
This soup is usually 45 to 75 calories for the 275ml/½pint shown here. Home-made recipes using butter to pre-fry onions and a stock cube, come higher; about 145 calories a bowlful. The traditional toasted cheese topping can add an extra 125 calories.

Prawn Cocktail *175 calories*
At a mere 30 calories an ounce, prawns are a slimmer's friend — but they are often swamped in high-calorie seafood sauce (105 calories per 25g/1oz). A few prawns in oceans of sauce give a top figure of 220. At home, use low-calorie sauce at 20 calories per level tablespoon.

Smoked Trout *170 calories*
Naturally oily fish are the ones most commonly smoked, so they tend to be high-calorie. Trout gives the lowest count at 38 calories for 25g/1oz; smoked eel is 55 and smoked mackerel 70 calories. On the bone, you seldom get less than 115g/4oz.

Crudités with Dip *150 calories*
Vegetables and salads are so low in calories you can be greedy as you like and still eat less than 20 calories' worth. The dip is the 'danger'. The cost is from 130 to 160 calories per 25g/1oz and you would scoop up that amount without trying!

Potted Shrimps *125 calories*
The frozen potted shrimps pictured here come in a tiny 50g/2oz pot and are less generous with butter than some of the recipes used in restaurants. The recipe calls for the shrimps (33 calories per 25g/1oz) to be covered with butter and allowed to set.

Smoked Salmon *80 calories*
Smoked salmon costs 40 calories an ounce, but it's a rare restaurant that will give more than 50g/2oz on your pricey plate. Go easy though on the brown bread and butter accompaniment (30 calories per delicate triangle).

Orange juice *60 calories*
Most restaurants buy in sweetened juices so your average 115ml/4floz can cost as high as 60 calories for orange and 70 for grapefruit. Unsweetened juices — including fresh-pressed fruits — bring calories down to 45 calories for orange and 35 for grapefruit.

Consommé *50 calories*
Consommé is always low-calorie. The average restaurant serving is the 275ml/½ pint shown and calories will always be about the same per bowlful. Careful, though. If you munch a roll (145 calories) and butter (210 calories per 25g/1oz) you will undo all the good work.

Melon *30 calories*
At a mere 4 calories per 25g/1oz (5 for Ogen), melon served plain and simple is a foolproof safe starter. Ginger works out at about 8 calories per teaspoon and even a level teaspoon of sugar (17 calories) will only bring your total cost to around 50 calories.

Grapefruit Half *25 calories*
A plain grapefruit half is the perfect starter at about 20 calories (the half glacé cherry costs 5). The sugar needed to turn sour into sweet does not make the calories climb too much. Most people sprinkle on a rounded teaspoon — 35 extra calories' worth.

Breakfasts and brunches

Ignore any so-called slimming experts who trot out the old 'you must eat breakfast' advice. 'Eat breakfast only if you want it' is sound slimming sense. That is why we have made this chapter a combination of breakfast and brunch recipes. A bowl of cereal need not be eaten first thing in the morning just because that is the time advertisements entice you to indulge. If you really cannot face a morsel before 11.30am save your breakfast-type meal until then or keep it for a late night snack. A housewife could choose a brunch mid-morning, have a light meal when the children come home from school and still have enough calories left to enjoy a substantial evening meal

There is now some evidence to indicate that people's biological time clocks vary quite a bit, and that left to follow the dictates of our own biology rather than the many other factors that influence our eating, we would naturally tend to eat at different times from each other. If we become very clock-bound into eating a meal at set times of each and every day the body tends to expect that meal at that time. For a while we may experience what might almost be termed as 'withdrawal symptoms' if we miss that meal. There are some scientific indications that, in a physical sense, the body does show a rumbling resentment for a while should a meal — one that it has been taught to expect at a precise time — be withdrawn. So there is no reason, and a positive disadvantage, in forcing breakfast down yourself if you do not already eat it. In fact, about 27 per cent of adult Britons do not eat breakfast, and reports suggest that a similar pattern is evident in other countries.

But does breakfast give you the 'energy' to get through the morning? Well, just

Here are two high-fibre breakfast cereal dishes: 1 Home-made Muesli (recipe page 72); and 2 Bran Flakes and Fruit (recipe page 71)

3 Bran Cereal with Banana and Apricots (recipe page 71) and 4 Wheat and Mixed Dried Fruit (recipe page 72) are tasty ideas for a fibre-rich breakfast cereal bowl

4

3

remember that 'energy' equals calories and if you are overweight you are already carrying around your own energy store. Although there have been reports that suggest that missing breakfast could lead to dizziness and mid-morning dopiness, nutritionist Dr Nigel Dickie, in an extensive investigation of the research evidence and in a study of the performance of nearly 500 school-children, found that there was little to support this theory. If you have been accustomed to eating breakfast and decide to miss it, you will not come to any harm if you are in normal health and carrying some surplus pounds.

Cereal Breakfasts

Mix a little fresh or dried fruit with your breakfast cereal and you will add flavour and fibre. All these recipes can be tossed together in minutes.

Bran Flakes and Fruit
(see picture page 70)

Raisins not only add sweetness to your cereal but they are also a good source of fibre. Do not toss them into your breakfast bowl by the handful as they cost 70 calories for 25g/1oz, or 25 calories for a level 15ml tablespoon.

1 small apple
25g/1oz bran flakes
15ml/1 level tablespoon raisins
115ml/4floz skimmed milk

Core and dice the apple but do not peel it. Mix with bran flakes and raisins. Serve with skimmed milk.

Serves 1/180 calories
0.5 fat units/6.4 grams fibre

Bran Cereal with Banana and Apricots
(see picture page 71)

Dried apricots are not as sweet as raisins or

71

sultanas and are lower in calories — 52 for 25g/1oz, or 10 calories for each apricot half. However they are higher in fibre and make a very filling breakfast ingredient.

2 dried apricot halves
1 small banana
25g/1oz bran breakfast cereal,
  eg. farmhouse bran
115ml/4floz skimmed milk

Chop the dried apricots. Slice the banana and mix with the cereal and apricots. Serve with skimmed milk.

Serves 1/195 calories
0.5 fat units/11.2 grams fibre

Home-made Muesli
(see picture page 70)

It is very simple to make your own muesli; and if you are going to breakfast on muesli regularly, you could mix up a week's supply in a jar or plastic bag. Each day's mix will weigh approximately 50g/2oz. This recipe is higher in fibre than most brands.

15g/½oz porridge oats
15g/½oz All-Bran
3 dried apricot halves
7g/¼oz hazelnuts
15ml/1 level tablespoon sultanas
115ml/4floz skimmed milk

Place the porridge oats and All-Bran in a serving bowl. Chop the dried apricots and halve the hazelnuts. Add to the cereals with the sultanas and serve with milk.

Serves 1/215 calories
2 fat units/10.2 grams fibre

Wheat and Mixed Dried Fruit
(see picture page 71)

15g/½oz dried dates, weighed without stones
1 dried peach half
1 dried fig
2 wheat breakfast biscuits, eg Weetabix
115ml/4floz skimmed milk

Chop the dates, peach and fig. Crumble the wheat biscuits and mix with the fruit. Serve with skimmed milk.

Serves 1/250 calories
1 fat unit/9.6 grams fibre

Yoghurt Mixtures

Natural yoghurt is a lovely basis for fruit and cereal mixtures. Make sure that you buy the sort marked low-fat, as whole milk natural yoghurts cost more calories and fat units. All these yoghurt mixtures could be taken to work in a plastic container if you like to eat your breakfast as a mid-morning

snack. The ones with cereal will not, however, be quite as crunchy as they are when freshly made.

Orange and Raisin Yoghurt

1 medium orange
15ml/1 level tablespoon raisins
1 small carton natural low-fat yoghurt,
  150g/5oz
15ml/1 level tablespoon wheat germ

Peel and segment the orange, then mix with raisins and yoghurt. Turn into a serving dish and sprinkle the wheat germ on top.

Serves 1/200 calories
1 fat unit/4.2 grams fibre

Grapefruit, Apple and Yoghurt
(see picture page 156)

This breakfast can be shared or you could save half for an evening snack. Do not sprinkle with muesli until you are about to eat. Make sure the apple is well coated with the yoghurt and it will not go brown.

1 grapefruit
1 small eating apple
60ml/4 level tablespoons natural low-fat
  yoghurt
10ml/2 level teaspoons honey
30ml/2 level tablespoons muesli

Halve the grapefruit and remove the segments. Cut out the membranes and discard them. Save the empty shells. Core and dice the apple and mix with the yoghurt, grapefruit and honey. Spoon into the grapefruit shells and sprinkle the muesli on top.

Serves 2/105 calories
0.5 fat unit/1.9 grams fibre per portion

Muesli with Yoghurt and Peach

If fresh peaches are not available, you can substitute four slices from a can of peaches in natural juice, water or low-calorie syrup.

30ml/2 level tablespoons muesli
1 small carton natural low-fat yoghurt,
  150g/5oz
1 fresh peach

Mix the muesli with the yoghurt and place in a bowl. Stone and slice the peach and arrange on top.

Serves 1/195 calories
0.5 fat unit/2.4 grams fibre

Yoghurt with Muesli and Grapes

Black grapes are slightly lower in calories than white grapes, but if you wish to use white grapes for this recipe they will add only 5 calories. White grapes are slightly higher in fibre, too, so the fibre figure would come up to 4.3 grams.

50g/2oz black grapes
1 small carton hazelnut yoghurt, 150g/5oz
30ml/2 level tablespoons muesli

Halve the grapes and stir into the yoghurt. Place in a bowl and sprinkle with muesli.

Serves 1/230 calories
1.5 fat units/3.6 grams fibre

Toast and Crusty Roll Brunches

Some of these recipes are quick and easy enough to prepare for an early breakfast, but most require a little more time to put together and are ideal when you are planning a late brunch.

Creamed Mushrooms on Toast

¼ chicken stock cube
115ml/4floz water
115g/4oz button mushrooms
45ml/3 level tablespoons skimmed milk
*   powder*
10ml/2 level teaspoons cornflour
Salt and pepper
1 small slice bread, 25g/1oz

Crumble the stock cube into 75ml/3floz water in a small pan. Add the mushrooms, cover the pan and simmer for 5 minutes. Blend the skimmed milk powder and cornflour with the remaining water to make a smooth paste. Add to the pan, stirring all the time, and bring back to boiling point. Simmer,

stirring, for 1 minute and season with salt and pepper. Toast the bread and serve the mushroom mixture on top.

Serves 1/	cals.	fat units	grams fibre
white bread	165	0	3.6
brown bread	160	0	4.3
wholemeal bread	160	0	5.2

Tangy Mushrooms on Toast
(see picture page 73)

Not only are mushrooms low in calories — only 4 for 25g/1oz — but they are also very light in weight and the amount we use here makes a generous-looking portion.

115g/4oz button mushrooms
15ml/1 level tablespoon low-fat spread
30ml/2 tablespoons water
Salt and pepper
15ml/1 level tablespoon tomato chutney
Dash Tabasco or hot pepper sauce
1 large slice bread, 40g/1½oz

Place the mushrooms in a small saucepan with low-fat spread and water. Season with salt and pepper. Cover the pan and heat to boiling point. Cook over a low heat for 5 minutes. Discard any excess liquid and stir

Things on toast make tasty and filling ideas for breakfasts and brunches: 1 Honey and Banana Toast (recipe page 74); 2 Crab and Asparagus Toast (recipe page 75); 3 Tangy Mushrooms on Toast (recipe page 73); 4 Salmon and Gherkin Toast (recipe page 74); 5 Kipper Pâté on Toast (recipe page 75); and 6 Chicken, Pineapple and Pepper Toast (recipe page 75)

in the tomato chutney and Tabasco or pepper sauce. While the mushrooms are cooking, toast the bread. Pile the mushrooms on top and serve.

Serves 1/	cals.	fat units	grams fibre
white bread	190	2	4.3
brown bread	185	2.5	5.2
wholemeal bread	185	2.5	6.7

Chicken and Sweetcorn Toast

You could use turkey or ham instead of chicken for this recipe if you have some left-overs of either which you would like to use up. Fat and fibre figures remain the same but the calories will be 5 higher if you use ham.

25g/1oz cooked chicken
15g/½oz Edam cheese
25g/1oz sweetcorn, canned
15ml/1 level tablespoon low-calorie
    salad cream
Salt and pepper
1 small slice bread, 25g/1oz

Discard the skin from the chicken and chop the flesh. Grate the Edam cheese. Mix together the chicken, cheese, sweetcorn and low-calorie salad cream. Season with salt and pepper. Toast the bread on one side only. Spread the chicken mixture on the other side and grill until hot.

Serves 1/	cals.	fat units	grams fibre
white bread	200	3	2.4
brown bread	200	3	3.0
wholemeal bread	195	3	4.0

Honey and Banana Toast
(see picture page 73)

1 large slice bread, 40g/1½oz
1 small banana
10ml/2 level teaspoons honey
2 walnut halves

Toast the bread. Slice the banana and mix gently with the honey. Place on the toast. Chop the walnuts and sprinkle on top.

Serves 1/	cals.	fat units	grams fibre
white bread	220	1.5	3.4
brown bread	215	1.5	4.5
wholemeal bread	210	1.5	5.9

Salmon and Gherkin Toast
(see picture page 73)

The flavour of canned salmon goes well with spicy gherkins. Remember that when you buy a can of salmon, the weight given on the can includes the weight of the water or brine. You will get just over 50g/2oz of drained salmon from a small 100g/3½oz can.

50g/2oz canned salmon, drained
10ml/2 teaspoons low-calorie salad cream
Dash of vinegar
3 small gherkins
1 large slice bread, 40g/1½oz

Flake the salmon and mix it with the low-calorie salad cream and vinegar. Chop one gherkin and add to the salmon mixture. Toast the bread, top with salmon and grill untill hot. Place the remaining two gherkins on top and serve.

Serves 1/	cals.	fat units	grams fibre
white bread	205	3	1.2
brown bread	200	3	2.1
wholemeal bread	195	3	3.6

Bacon and Tomatoes on Toast
The more you grill bacon, the more fatty calories it loses. So it is important to crisply grill your rasher until it is brittle enough to crumble.

1 rasher streaky bacon
2 tomatoes
1 large slice bread, 40g/1½oz
Half a 35g/1¼oz pot liver and bacon or
    smokey bacon paste

Grill the bacon until crisp. Halve the tomatoes and grill until they just begin to soften. Toast the bread alongside the tomatoes. Spread with meat paste and top with tomatoes and bacon.

Serves 1/	cals.	fat units	grams fibre
white bread	205	2	2.8
brown bread	200	2	3.7
wholemeal bread	195	2	5.2

Hawaiian Toasts

Pineapple goes extremely well with bacon or ham. If fresh pineapples are available you could substitute a fresh slice for the canned ring.

1 bacon or ham picnic steak, 100g/3½oz
1 small slice bread, 25g/1oz
2.5ml/½ level teaspoon mustard
1 tomato
1 ring pineapple, canned in natural juice,
    drained

Grill the bacon or ham steak and discard all visible fat. Toast the bread and spread with mustard. Top with the sliced tomato, bacon steak and pineapple. Grill until hot.

Serves 1/	cals.	fat units	grams fibre
white bread	205	1.5	2.1
brown bread	205	1.5	2.7
wholemeal bread	200	1.5	3.7

Bacon Pizza Toast
(see picture page 77)

1 small slice bread, 25g/1oz
25g/1oz streaky bacon
5ml/1 level teaspoon yeast extract
1 tomato
1 processed cheese slice
1 olive
Parsley to garnish, optional

Toast the bread on one side only. Cut the bacon rashers in half lengthwise, and then grill well. Spread the untoasted side of the bread with yeast extract. Slice the tomato and place on top. Cover with the cheese slice and grill until melted. Halve and stone the olive and arrange on top with the bacon and parsley, if used.

Serves 1/	cals.	fat units	grams fibre
white bread	220	3.5	1.8
brown bread	215	3.5	2.4
wholemeal bread	215	3.5	3.4

Ham and Corn Scramble on Toast

25g/1oz lean cooked ham
1 egg, size 3
15ml/1 tablespoon skimmed milk
25g/1oz canned sweetcorn, drained
Salt and pepper
1 small slice bread, 25g/1oz

Discard all visible fat from the ham and chop the lean. Lightly beat together the egg and milk. Stir in the sweetcorn and ham and salt and pepper. Turn into a non-stick pan and cook over a low heat, stirring all the time until lightly set. While the eggs are cooking, toast the bread. Pile the eggs onto the toast and serve immediately.

Serves 1/	cals.	fat units	grams fibre
white bread	225	2.5	2.4
brown bread	225	2.5	3.0
wholemeal bread	225	2.5	4.0

Crab and Asparagus Toast
(see picture page 73)

1 large slice bread, 40g/1½oz
Half a 35g/1¼oz pot crab paste or spread
4 canned or cooked asparagus spears,
*   drained*
25g/1oz Edam cheese

Toast the bread and spread with the crab paste. Arrange the asparagus on top. Grate the cheese and sprinkle over the asparagus. Grill until the cheese melts and the asparagus is hot.

Serves 1/	cals.	fat units	grams fibre
white bread	230	3.5	2.8
brown bread	230	4	3.7
wholemeal bread	225	4	5.2

Chicken, Pineapple and Pepper Toast
(see picture page 73)

50g/2oz cooked chicken or turkey
1 ring pineapple canned in natural
*   juice, drained*
30ml/2 tablespoons low-calorie salad
*   cream*
1 large slice bread, 40g/1½oz
1 ring green pepper

Discard the skin from the chicken and chop the flesh. Chop the pineapple ring and mix with the chicken and low-calorie salad cream. Toast the bread and top with the chicken mixture. Garnish with the pepper ring.

Serves 1/	cals.	fat units	grams fibre
white bread	260	3.5	1.8
brown bread	255	4.0	2.7
wholemeal bread	250	4.0	4.2

Bean and Cheese Medley on Toast
(see picture page 77)

½ stick celery
15g/½oz green pepper
25g/1oz cauliflower
150g/5.3oz canned baked beans in tomato
*   sauce*
25g/1oz Edam cheese
1 small slice bread, 25g/1oz

Chop the celery and green pepper. Cut the cauliflower into small florets. Place all the vegetables in a small saucepan with the baked beans and heat through gently. Cut the Edam into small cubes and stir into the mixture. Toast the bread and serve the bean mixture piled on top.

Serves 1/	cals.	fat units	grams fibre
white bread	270	3	13.0
brown bread	270	3	13.6
wholemeal bread	265	3	14.6

Kipper Pâté on Toast
(see picture page 73)

A strong-flavoured pâté, this could be made up in a larger quantity and frozen in individual portions. The pâté on its own comes to 225 calories/4 fat units/0 grams fibre.

50g/2oz cooked kipper fillet
50g/2oz curd cheese
Dash lemon juice
Salt and pepper
1 large slice bread, 40g/1½oz
Sprig of watercress, optional

Flake the kipper fillet finely and mix with the curd cheese and lemon juice. Season with salt and pepper. Toast the bread and spread with kipper pâté. Garnish with watercress if liked.

Serves 1/	cals.	fat units	grams fibre
white bread	325	4.0	1.2
brown bread	320	4.5	2.1
wholemeal bread	315	4.5	3.6

Egg, Bacon and Rice Brunches

These are all suggestions for late-start meals which take a little time to prepare and cook. All are substantial enough to keep you going through the day to an evening meal.

Scrambled Eggs with Tomato and Pepper
(see picture page 77)

¼ small green or red pepper
1 tomato
2 eggs, size 3
30ml/2 tablespoons skimmed milk
5ml/1 level teaspoon low-fat spread
1 large slice bread, 40g/1½oz
Watercress, optional

Discard the pith and seeds from the pepper and slice the flesh. Skin the tomato by plunging into boiling water for one minute, or hold it on a fork in the gas flame until it 'pops'. The skin will now peel off easily. Quarter the tomato and discard the seeds. Beat the eggs and the skimmed milk together. Season with salt and pepper. Pour into a non-stick pan, add the low-fat spread, and cook over a low heat, stirring all the time until just beginning to set. Add the pepper and tomato and continue cooking until the eggs are scrambled. While the eggs are cooking, toast the bread and serve the mixture on top. Garnish with watercress.

Serves 1/	cals.	fat units	grams fibre
white bread	300	4.5	2.3
brown bread	295	5	3.2
wholemeal bread	290	5	4.7

Fluffy Cottage Egg

This light ham and egg mixture is good served with crispbreads, unbuttered toast or a savoury cracker.

5ml/1 level teaspoon low-fat spread
1 egg, size 3
25g/1oz ham
50g/2oz natural cottage cheese or with chives
Salt and pepper

Preheat the oven to 190°C/375°F/gas mark 5. Grease a ramekin or a small ovenproof dish with the low-fat spread. Separate the egg. Discard all visible fat from the ham and chop the lean. Add to the egg yolk with the cottage cheese and season with salt and pepper. Whisk the egg white until stiff and

fold in gently. Turn into the dish and cook for 15 minutes. Serve immediately.

Serves 1/180 calories
3.5 fat units/0 grams fibre

Egg and Bacon Bake

50g/2oz streaky bacon
5ml/1 level teaspoon fresh chopped chives or 2.5ml/½ level teaspoon dried chives
1 egg, size 3
115ml/4floz skimmed milk
Salt and pepper
25g/1oz mature Cheddar cheese, grated

Grill the bacon until crisp, then break into small pieces. Place in a small ovenproof dish and sprinkle on the chives. Lightly beat together the egg and milk and season with salt and pepper. Pour over the bacon and chives. Sprinkle the cheese on top. Stand the dish in a roasting tin containing a little hot water and cook at 180°C/350°F/gas mark 4 for about 30 minutes, or until set in the middle. Serve warm or cold.

Serves 2/185 calories
4 fat units/0 grams fibre per portion

Sausage and Rice Brunch
(see picture page 77)

25g/1oz long-grain brown or white rice
75g/3oz mixed vegetables, frozen
2 pork chipolata sausages
5ml/1 level teaspoon French mustard
5ml/1 level teaspoon vinegar
2 spring onions/scallions
Salt and pepper

Cook the rice and the frozen vegetables separately in boiling, salted water. While they are cooking, grill the sausages well and then cut into slices. Drain the vegetables and rinse with cold water. Drain again. Repeat with the rice. Mix together the mustard and vinegar. Chop the bulbs of the spring onions/scallions and discard the rest. Mix all the ingredients together and season with salt and pepper.

Serves 1/	cals.	fat units	grams fibre
white rice	295	4.0	5.5
brown rice	290	4.0	6.4

Kedgeree

175g/6oz smoked haddock fillet
150ml/¼ pint skimmed milk
1 bay leaf
1 sliced onion
75g/3oz long-grain white rice
1 egg, size 3

75g/3oz peas, frozen
Salt and pepper

Place the smoked haddock in a casserole dish with the milk, bay leaf and onion. Cover and cook at 180°C/350°F/gas mark 4 for 20 minutes, or until the fish flakes easily. Discard the onion and bay leaf. Lift the fish onto a plate and discard the skin and bones. Flake the fish and set aside. Strain the milk into a measuring jug, and make it up to 250ml/ 9floz with water. Heat to boiling point. Rinse out the dish and pour back the liquid. Add the rice, cover and cook for 25 minutes at 180°C/350°F/gas mark 4. While the rice is cooking, hard-boil the egg and then leave to cool in cold water. Shell and chop. Add the peas to the rice after 25 minutes. Cook for another 10 minutes and then stir in the fish and egg and return to the oven to heat through — about 5 minutes. Taste and season with salt and pepper if necessary.

Serves 2/330 calories
1 fat unit/3.8 grams fibre per portion

Bubble and Squeak

1 rasher streaky bacon
150g/5oz boiled potatoes, weighed
  cooked

These are more substantial breakfast and brunch dishes: **1** *Bean and Cheese Medley on Toast (recipe page 75);* **2** *Bacon Pizza Toast (recipe page 75);* **3** *Sausage and Rice Brunch (recipe page 76); and* **4** *Scrambled Eggs with Tomato and Pepper (recipe page 76)*

150g/5oz boiled cabbage, weighed cooked
1 pickled onion
5ml/1 teaspoon soya sauce
Salt and pepper
2.5ml/½ teaspoon oil
2.5ml/½ level teaspoon butter.

Grill the bacon until crisp, then break it into small pieces. Mash the potato and chop the cabbage or place both in a food processor and chop finely. Chop the pickled onion and add to the bacon, potato and cabbage with the soya sauce. Season with salt and pepper. Heat the oil in a small, non-stick frying pan. Add the butter and when it has melted, brush both fats over the pan's surface. Add the vegetables and smooth the top down. Cook over a moderate heat until the base is golden-brown. Turn over carefully and cook until the other side is brown and the vegetables are heated through.

Serves 1/ 240 calories
2.5 fat units/5.4 grams fibre

Breakfasts: how low can you go?

Croissant with Butter and Jam
380 calories
Croissants are made from buttery yeast pastry and just one 65g/2½oz delicacy is a wicked 280 calories. Eaten with no butter or jam, a small 40g/1½oz croissant gives the lowest cost: 165 calories. With extra butter and jam, it could be over 400 calories.

Kipper with Bread and Butter
430 calories
The herring is a very oily fish, even when it is smoked and transformed into a kipper. This grilled 175g/6oz kipper costs 280 calories, and that's before you add bread and butter.

Kedgeree *360 calories*
This mix of smoked haddock, hard-boiled eggs and rice depends for its appeal on the butter it is cooked with; and some recipes call for cream as well. A really mean version might come as low as 270 calories but play safe and reckon on high rather than lower.

Mushrooms on Toast *315 calories*
Mushrooms (only 4 calories per 25g/1oz raw) soak up fatty calories. The 115g/4oz buttons here cost 160 calories fried — flat mushrooms would cost 240. Sliced and fried mushrooms soak up another 40 calories per portion. Cut costs with poached mushrooms and low-fat spread on toast: 140 calories.

Egg in Milk *270 calories*
Raw egg beaten into milk or fruit juice can cost high. Beat a size 3 standard egg into 275ml/½pint whole milk and you toss back no fewer than 270 calories. Use skimmed milk and this total comes down to 180. Beat the egg into sweetened orange juice and you pay 230 calories: 190 for unsweetened juice.

Muesli *285 calories*
Muesli is considered a nutritional goody, but it does weigh heavy. Standard muesli costs from 105 to 110 calories per 25g/1oz; and crunchy kinds cost from 115 to 130. Most people tip into their bowl at least 50g/2oz muesli and an average of 115ml/4floz milk.

You can decide on a low calorie breakfast — or all too easily find you have let a whole day's dieting allowance slip down. Here are some favourite breakfast choices.

Porridge *225 calories*
The true Scot who cooks his oatmeal in water pays around 115 calories a plateful. Porridge made with half milk, half water, costs 225 calories for about 275ml/½ pint served with a teaspoon of sugar. Cut costs by making with water, skimmed milk and low-calorie sweetener.

Cornflakes *195 calories*
Most flaked and puffed cereals cost 100 calories per 25g/1oz. Few people ever want more than the 25g/1oz shown and many find 15g/½oz sufficient. Nearly everybody pours on at least 150ml/¼ pint milk. Skimmed milk cuts above costs by 45 calories.

Toast, Butter and Marmalade
185 calories
If you go carefully with the butter (7g/¼oz) and marmalade (10ml/2 level teaspoons) your toasty slice won't cost more than this. It is easy to be lavish and use twice as much butter and preserve, increasing the cost to 265 calories. Low-fat spread and a scrape of marmalade or jam would be lowest; 130 calories.

Fried Sausage and Tomato *140 calories*
Well-grilled — or even well-fried — the sausage loses most of its fat into the pan; and even the biggest beef or pork one is unlikely to cost more than 130 calories. Chipolatas cost from 50 for beef to 65 for pork. Grill a tomato and you get breakfast for 140 calories.

Stewed Prunes *85 calories*
Prunes are dried plums and are naturally sweet. Stewed prunes are nicely low in calories and they truly do not need any extra sugar. This 115g/4oz bowl is the amount most people would serve. Canned prunes come in syrup and a 215g/7½oz can could be 235 calories.

Boiled Egg *80 calories*
Each egg comes with its own built-in calorie limit; even the biggest costs only 95 calories. Boiling (or poaching in water) adds nothing. Each 25g/1oz slice of buttered bread or toast costs another 120 calories. Low-calorie crispbreads and low-fat spread cut the cost.

Vegetarian meals

You do not have to be a vegetarian to choose recipes from this section, although if you are you will find plenty of tasty dieting meals to suit you — ranging from light meals for one to main meals to share with the family. Modern nutrition puts a lot less emphasis on animal protein intake, so you can safely stop making meat or fish the conscious basis of every 'proper' meal. We all need protein, of course, as part of a balanced diet, but it does not only come from meat, fish, cheese and eggs. Vegetables also contain protein and it is the sort that comes un-partnered by high-calorie fat. It's not news that vegetables tend to be big slimming aids, simply because most of them are low in calories. What is news is the type of vegetables emerging as the fit-

and-slim superstars. In fact, most turn out to be the ones that were not considered in the past as being very good for dieters because they were higher in calories than their leafier relations. Avoid them no more. The new superveg are beans of all kinds, peas of all kinds, and that lovely vegetable sweetcorn. What they all have in common is a generous content of dietary fibre.

What about vegetables that you serve as an accompaniment to meals? Are there good and bad ways of serving them? From a slimmer's point of view, and for healthy eating, too, all vegetables should be eaten without a fatty or creamy topping. Also, they are best plain boiled or steamed and not cooked in fat — or, if suitable, enjoyed raw. But how about their nutritional value? Vegetables tend to lose nutrients mainly by 'leakage' into their cooking water: so it is good sense to cook them in as little water as possible, and then retain the drained-off liquid for making soup and gravy. But hanging on to vitamin C, by far the most easily lost vitamin, calls for extra consideration. However 'economically' you cook vegetables, they will carry on losing vitamin C at quite a rate unless you eat them immediately. Hotplates and stay-warm trolleys may keep a meal eatable but they murder vitamin C. Salads can also 'leak' vitamin C. Most vegetables contain an enzyme which speeds up vitamin C's dissipation once bruising or cutting exposes inner surfaces to air, so do not slice or grate a moment earlier than you must.

Do cooking methods much affect food values? Experiments show no marked difference between vegetables cooked in a steamer or pressure cooker, or in a saucepan with minimum water. But leafy vegetables, such as broccoli, cooked completely covered with water can lose up to 80 per cent of their vitamin C. To a minor degree, copper pots and a pinch of cooking soda to preserve colour will also accelerate vitamin C's destruction. So the rules for vegetables are: buy fresh vegetables; cut, grate or chop just before eating or cooking; cook in a little water, and then serve immediately.

Meals for One

Here are some vegetarian meals that can be served as a light lunch or as your main meal of the day. If you are cooking for two or more, just increase quantities accordingly.

Piperade

This recipe tastes good served hot or cold. It is best served with crusty bread or with toast — you should not need to butter either as the Piperade is nice and moist.

¼ small red pepper
¼ small green pepper
1 tomato
1 spring onion/scallion
2 eggs, size 3
15ml/1 tablespoon skimmed milk
Salt and pepper
10ml/2 level teaspoons butter

Discard the white pith and seeds from the peppers, then cut the flesh into strips. Cook in boiling salted water for 5 minutes, then drain and set aside. Halve the tomato, discard the seeds and chop the flesh. Discard the roots and tough green leaves from the spring onion and chop the bulb. Lightly beat the eggs and milk together and season with salt and pepper. Melt the butter in a small non-stick pan and add the tomato and onion. Cook over a moderate heat, stirring frequently, for 2 minutes. Add the peppers and egg mixture. Reduce the heat and cook, stirring all the time, until creamy. Serve immediately or turn into a bowl and leave until cold.

Serves 1/255 calories
6.5 fat units/1.6 grams fibre

Carrot, Peanut and Raisin Salad

Weigh your peanuts very carefully — at 168 calories for 28g/1oz of the roasted and salted kind, a slip of the hand could add considerably to your total for this recipe. Dry roasted peanuts cost only a few calories less.

75g/3oz carrot
30ml/2 level tablespoons raisins
25g/1oz dry roasted or roasted, salted
    peanuts
15ml/1 tablespoon unsweetened
    orange juice
15ml/1 level tablespoon low-fat
    natural yoghurt
Salt and pepper

Scrub the carrots if new; peel if old, then grate them. Mix with the raisins and peanuts. Mix together the orange juice and yoghurt and season lightly with salt and pepper. Stir into the salad.

Serves 1/245 calories
5.5 fat units/6.1 grams fibre

Brown Rice Risotto

This is a very easy one-pan dish that makes a satisfying midday meal. If you wish to substitute another cheese for Edam, check the chart at the end of the book for calorie and fat unit differences.

25g/1oz onion
2 tomatoes
25g/1oz long grain brown rice
200ml/7floz water
1.25ml/¼ level teaspoon dried mixed
    herbs
Salt and pepper
50g/2oz mushrooms
50g/2oz frozen peas
25g/1oz Edam cheese

Finely chop the onion and roughly chop the tomatoes. Place in a small saucepan with the rice, water and herbs. Season with salt and pepper. Cover the pan, bring to the boil and simmer gently for 30 minutes. Chop the mushrooms and add to the pan with the peas. Simmer for a further 15 minutes. Stir occasionally during the last 15 minutes and add a little extra water if the mixture becomes too dry. Grate the cheese and sprinkle on top before serving.

Serves 1/245 calories
2.5 fat units/9.0 grams fibre

Egg with Mushroom Sauce and Rice

You could use a larger or smaller egg for this recipe if you wish — the largest, size 1, will cost 15 calories more than size 3, and the smaller size 5, just 10 calories less. For other egg calories see our chart.

40g/1½oz long-grain brown rice
    or white
50g/2oz mushrooms
115ml/4floz skimmed milk
1 bay leaf

10ml/2 level teaspoons cornflour
Salt and pepper
1 egg, size 3

Boil the rice until tender. Drain and place in an ovenproof dish and keep warm. Chop the mushrooms and place in a small pan with most of the milk. Add the bay leaf, and seasoning and cover the pan. Simmer for 2-3 minutes. Blend the cornflour with the remaining milk, then stir into the sauce. Bring back to the boil, stirring all the time, and simmer for 1-2 minutes. Discard the bay leaf. Poach the egg and place on top of the rice. Cover with the sauce and serve.

Serves 1/	cals.	fat units	grams fibre
white rice	310	2	2.1
brown rice	305	2.5	3.4

Spaghetti with Tomato and Mushroom Sauce

It is easiest to cook with a tiny quantity of fat if you use a non-stick pan. Onions usually need a slightly longer cooking time than other vegetables and this is why they are often pre fried. As fat is a slimmer's enemy, always use the minimum amount.

1 small onion
5ml/1 teaspoon oil
¼ red or green pepper
50g/2oz mushrooms
227g/8oz can tomatoes
Good pinch dried oregano or mixed herbs
Salt and pepper
50g/2oz spaghetti

Finely chop the onion and place in a small saucepan with the oil. Cook over a moderate heat, stirring frequently until soft. Discard the pith and seeds from the pepper and dice the flesh. Slice the mushrooms. Roughly chop the tomatoes and add to the pan with their juice, the pepper, mushrooms and oregano or mixed herbs. Season and simmer uncovered for 10-15 minutes, or until most of the liquid has evaporated. Boil the spaghetti until tender. Drain and serve the sauce on top.

Serves 1/	cals.	fat units	grams fibre
wholewheat	285	2.5	10.1
white	305	2	6.2

Sweetcorn and Pickle Stuffed Potato
(see picture page 85)

1 potato, 200g/7oz
15ml/1 tablespoon skimmed milk
75g/3oz canned sweetcorn
Salt and pepper
30ml/2 level tablespoons sweet pickle
Strips of red or green pepper to garnish, optional

Scrub and prick the potato and bake in its jacket for about 45 minutes, or until soft when pinched. Cut in half lengthways or cut a slice off one end as shown in the picture. Carefully scoop out the flesh, leaving the shell intact. Mash the flesh with the milk, then stir in the sweetcorn. Season with salt and pepper. Pile back into the potato case and reheat in the oven for 10 minutes. Make a hollow in the middle. Fill this with the pickle and garnish with pepper slices, if used.

Serves 1/290 calories
0 fat units/10.4 grams fibre

Cheese and Asparagus Custard

6 spears canned or cooked asparagus, drained
1 egg, size 3
50g/2oz cottage cheese with chives
50ml/2floz skimmed milk
Salt and pepper
25g/1oz mature Cheddar cheese

Place the asparagus in an ovenproof dish. Lightly beat together the egg, cottage cheese and milk. Season with salt and pepper and pour over the asparagus. Grate the Cheddar and sprinkle on top. Stand the dish in a roasting tin containing enough hot water to come halfway up the dish. Bake at 180°C/350°F/gas mark 4 for about 35 minutes, or until just set.

Serves 1/305 calories
6.5 fat units/2.4 grams fibre

Egg and Vegetable Stuffed Potato
(see picture page 85)

1 potato, 200g/7oz
1 egg, size 3
75g/3oz frozen mixed vegetables
15ml/1 tablespoon skimmed milk
Salt and pepper
Sprig of parsley, optional

Scrub and prick the potato and bake in its jacket at 200°C/400°F/gas mark 6 for about 45 minutes, or until soft when pinched. While the potato is cooking, hard-boil the egg for 8 minutes, then cool in cold water. Shell and reserve one slice from the middle to garnish. Chop the rest. Boil the mixed vegetables as instructed on the packet. Drain, rinse in cold water and drain again. Either cut the potato in half lengthways or cut a slice from one end. Carefully scoop all the flesh into a basin leaving the shell intact. Add the milk to the flesh and mix well with a fork. Season and add the egg and vegetables. Pile back into the potato case and reheat in the oven for 10 minutes. Garnish with the reserved egg slice and parsley, if used.

Serves 1/305 calories
2 fat units/9.8 grams fibre

Summer Vegetable Pie

75g/3oz carrots
115g/4oz broad beans, frozen, canned
    or fresh, weighed shelled
50g/2oz button mushrooms
15ml/1 level tablespoon cornflour
30ml/2 level tablespoons skimmed milk
    powder
15ml/1 level tablespoon chopped parsley
25g/1oz mature Cheddar cheese
30ml/2 level tablespoons fresh
    breadcrumbs
Salt and pepper

Slice the carrots and cook with the fresh broad beans (add frozen or canned later) for 15 minutes in boiling salted water. Add the mushrooms and frozen or canned broad beans if used, and cook for another 5 minutes. Drain and reserve 150ml/¼ pint water. Blend the cornflour and powdered skimmed milk with 30ml/2 tablespoons cold water to make a smooth paste. Stir in the vegetable water, then return to the pan. Bring to the boil, stirring all the time, then simmer for 1 minute. Add the vegetables and parsley. Heat through on a low heat. Turn into an ovenproof dish. Grate the cheese and mix with the breadcrumbs. Sprinkle on top and grill until the cheese melts.

Serves 1/285 calories
3.5 fat units/9.0 grams fibre

Waldorf Salad

2 medium eating apples
Squeeze lemon juice
4 small or 2 large sticks celery
25g/1oz walnuts
30ml/2 level tablespoons natural
    yoghurt
15ml/1 level tablespoon low-calorie
    salad cream
Salt and pepper

Core and cube the apples, but do not peel. Toss in a little lemon juice to prevent them turning brown. Slice the celery and roughly chop the walnuts. Mix all the ingredients together and season with salt and pepper.

Serves 1/315 calories
6 fat units/8.9 grams fibre

Fruit and Nut Slaw

This salad is very satisfying with a crunchy texture. Ideally, buy and serve really fresh vegetables for the best taste and prepare as little in advance as possible to ensure minimum loss of vitamins.

75g/3oz white cabbage
50g/2oz carrot
1 stick celery
2 rings pineapple canned in natural
    juice, drained
25g/1oz dry roasted or roasted
    salted peanuts
30ml/2 level tablespoons low-calorie
    salad cream
15ml/1 level tablespoon raisins or
    sultanas
15ml/1 tablespoon pineapple juice
Salt and pepper

Shred the cabbage, grate the carrot and slice the celery. Cut the pineapple rings into small pieces. Mix all the ingredients together and season with salt and pepper.

Serves 1/315 calories
6 fat units/8.9 grams fibre

Cottage Cheese and Fruit Salad

115g/4oz cottage cheese with pineapple
15ml/1 level tablespoon low-calorie
    salad cream
50g/2oz black grapes
1 kiwi fruit
1 small banana
1 small pear
Squeeze lemon juice
Few lettuce leaves

Mix the cottage cheese with low-calorie salad cream. Halve and pip the grapes. Peel and slice the kiwi fruit and banana. Core and slice the pear but do not peel it. Toss the banana and pear in a little lemon juice to prevent them browning. Arrange the lettuce on a plate and pile the cheese mixture in the middle. Arrange the fruit around the cheese and serve

Serves 1/285 calories
2.5 fat units/6.5 grams fibre

Fennel and Celery in Cheese Sauce

Fennel has a mild aniseed flavour which goes well with both celery and cheese. To prepare fennel, cut off the roots and stems, and then slice the bulb.

2 small or 1 large stick celery
115g/4oz Florence fennel
45ml/3 level tablespoons skimmed
    milk powder
15ml/1 level tablespoon cornflour
Pinch dry mustard
40g/1½oz mature Cheddar cheese
Salt and pepper
45ml/3 level tablespoons fresh wholemeal
    breadcrumbs

Thickly slice the celery and fennel. Cook in boiling salted water for 20-30 minutes or

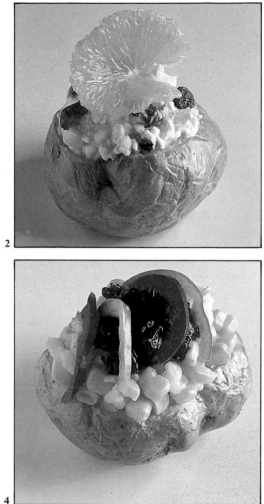

until tender. Drain and reserve 150ml/¼ pint liquid. Place vegetables in an ovenproof dish and keep warm. Allow the liquid to cool slightly, then whisk in the skimmed milk powder. Blend the cornflour with a little of the liquid until smooth, then add the remaining liquid. Pour into a saucepan and bring to the boil, whisking all the time. Simmer for 1-2 minutes. Whisk in the mustard and about two-thirds of the cheese. Season with salt and pepper. Pour over the vegetables and sprinkle the remaining cheese and breadcrumbs on top. Cook under a low grill until the cheese melts and the crumbs start to brown.

Serves 1/325 calories
5 fat units/2.2 grams fibre

Cottage Cheese and Raisin Stuffed Potato
(see picture page 85)

1 potato, 200g/7oz
75g/3oz cottage cheese
15ml/1 tablespoon unsweetened orange
*   juice*
½ stick celery
25g/1oz onion
25g/1oz raisins
Salt and pepper
1 slice orange to garnish, optional

A baked potato with a delicious savoury topping makes a light vegetarian meal: 1 Egg and Vegetable Stuffed Potato (recipe page 83); 2 Cottage Cheese and Raisin Stuffed Potato (recipe page 85); 3 Cottage Cheese and Walnut Stuffed Potato (recipe page 87); and 4 Sweetcorn and Pickle Stuffed Potato (recipe page 83)

Scrub and prick the potato and bake in its jacket until soft when pinched. Cut in half lengthways or cut a slice off one end as shown in the picture. Carefully scoop out the flesh into a basin, leaving the shell intact. Mash the flesh with the cottage cheese and orange juice. Chop the celery and add to the potato with the raisins. Season lightly with salt and pepper and pile back into the potato cases. Reheat in the oven for 10 minutes. Garnish with an orange slice.

Serves 1/335 calories
2 fat units/7.5 grams fibre

Cauliflower in Blue Cheese Sauce

225g/8oz cauliflower, fresh or frozen
50g/2oz Blue Cheshire cheese
150ml/5floz skimmed milk
15ml/1 level tablespoon cornflour
Salt and pepper

If using fresh cauliflower, discard any tough

outer leaves or stalks, then cut into four pieces. Boil in salted water until tender — about 15 minutes. If using frozen cauliflower, boil according to the instructions on the packet. Drain the cauliflower and keep warm. Grate the cheese. Blend 30ml/2 tablespoons milk with the cornflour until smooth. Heat the remaining milk to boiling point, then pour onto the cornflour mixture, stirring all the time. Return to the pan and bring to the boil, stirring continuously. Simmer for 1 minute. Remove from the heat, stir in the cheese and season with salt and pepper. Pour over the cauliflower and serve.

Serves 1/335 calories
6 fat units/5.1 grams fibre

Spicy Rice Pilaf with Peas

Although this pilaf has an authentic Indian spicy taste, it is not very hot. If you use white rice — the Indian Basmati rice is excellent — cook it for only 25 minutes and add the dried fruit and peas after 15 minutes.

1 small onion
4 cardamom pods
2.5ml/½ level teaspoon ground coriander
5ml/1 level teaspoon cumin seeds
Small piece stick cinnamon
3 cloves
1.25ml/¼ level teaspoon chilli powder
1.25ml/¼ level teaspoon salt
Pepper
50g/2oz long-grain brown rice
200ml/7floz water
30ml/2 level tablespoons sultanas or raisins
115g/4oz frozen peas

Finely chop the onion. Bruise the cardamom pods by pressing them with a heavy knife. Place in a pan with all the other ingredients except the sultanas or raisins and peas. Bring to the boil, stir once to mix, then cover the pan and simmer gently for 35 minutes. Add the sultanas or raisins and peas. Bring to the boil, cover again and simmer for another 10 minutes. Check frequently while cooking that the rice does not stick because too much liquid has evaporated. If necessary, add a little extra water. When cooked, the rice should be tender, the peas cooked and all the liquid should be absorbed. Discard the cardamom pods, cinnamon and cloves before serving.

Serves 1/315 calories
1 fat unit/13.0 grams fibre

Cheese and Fennel Coleslaw

An attractive looking salad combining three shades of red from the cabbage, cheese and apple. The slightly aniseed flavour of the fennel gives this coleslaw an unusual taste which is well worth sampling.

50g/2oz red cabbage
50g/2oz Florence fennel
1 medium apple, preferably red-skinned
50g/2oz Red Windsor or Cheddar cheese
15ml/1 tablespoon oil-free French dressing
15ml/1 level tablespoon low-calorie salad cream

Shred the cabbage and coarsely grate the fennel. Core and slice the apple but do not peel. Cut the cheese into small cubes. Mix all the ingredients together and serve.

Serves 1/340 calories
8 fat units/4.7 grams fibre

Rice Fruit and Nut Salad

Do not be tempted to use pineapple canned in syrup instead of the canned in natural juice varieties. Each ring in syrup wll cost you 15 extra calories and taste less like the fresh fruit.

50g/2oz long-grain brown rice
¼ red or green pepper
2 rings pineapple, canned in natural juice, drained
25g/1oz roasted or dry roasted cashew nuts
30ml/2 level tablespoons raisins or sultanas
15ml/1 tablespoon pineapple juice from can
15ml/1 tablespoon oil-free French dressing
5ml/1 teaspoon soya sauce
Salt and pepper

Cook the rice in boiling salted water until tender — about 25 minutes. Drain in a sieve and rinse in cold water. Drain well. Discard the pith and seeds from the pepper and dice the flesh. Cut the pineapple into small pieces. Mix all the ingredients together and season with salt and pepper. Chill before serving.

Serves1/470 calories
5.5 fat units/9.1 grams fibre

Macaroni in Broccoli and Cheese Sauce

Broccoli goes particularly well with macaroni cheese and its low-calorie value means that you get a nice big portion on your plate. You can make up this recipe until the stage when you mix the broccoli and macaroni with the cheese sauce, and then keep it in the refrigerator for up to 24 hours. When ready to eat, reheat in a saucepan, turn into a serving dish and follow the remaining instructions.

Leeks in Celery and Cheese Sauce (page 89)

115g/4oz broccoli, fresh or frozen
25g/1oz wholewheat macaroni
40g/1½oz mature Cheddar cheese
15ml/1 level tablespoon cornflour
150ml/5floz skimmed milk
Very small amount dry mustard
Salt and pepper
15g/½oz fresh breadcrumbs

Boil the broccoli in salted water until just tender. Drain, rinse under cold water and drain again. Cut into small pieces. Boil the macaroni in plenty of salted water for 10 minutes or until just tender. Drain, rinse under cold water and drain again. Grate the cheese. Blend the cornflour with a little of the milk to make a smooth paste. Heat the remaining milk to boiling point, then pour onto the blended mixture, stirring continuously. Return to the pan and bring to the boil, stirring all the time. Simmer for 1-2 minutes. Remove from the heat and add most of the cheese and the mustard. Season with salt and pepper. Stir in the broccoli and macaroni and reheat gently. Turn into a serving dish and sprinkle with the remaining cheese and the breadcrumbs. Grill until the cheese melts and the crumbs start to brown.

Serves 1/415 calories
5.5 fat units/8.1 grams fibre

Cottage Cheese and Walnut Stuffed Potato
(see picture page 85)

1 potato, 200g/7oz
115g/4oz cottage cheese with chives
4 walnut halves
Salt and pepper
Few fresh chives or pinch dried chives
   to garnish, optional

Scrub and prick the potato and bake in its jacket at 200°C/400°F/gas mark 6 for about 45 minutes, or until soft when pinched. Either cut in half lengthways or cut a slice from one end as shown in the picture. Carefully scoop

out the flesh leaving the shell intact. Mash the flesh with the cottage cheese. Reserve a small piece of walnut for the top and chop the rest. Add to the potato and season with salt and pepper. Pile back into the potato case and reheat in the oven for 10 minutes. Garnish with the reserved walnut and chives.

Serves 1/340 calories
3.5 fat units/5.4 grams fibre

Greek Salad
(see picture page 91)

3 medium tomatoes
50g/2oz cucumber
25g/1oz black olives
30ml/2 tablespoons oil-free French dressing
Lettuce
50g/2oz Fetta cheese

Cut the tomatoes into segments, chop the cucumber and stone the olives. Mix together with the dressing and place on a bed of shredded lettuce. Crumble the cheese over the salad.

Serves 1/170 calories
4 fat units/4.4 grams fibre

Fiesta Rice
(see picture page 90)

25g/1oz brown rice
30ml/2 tablespoons oil-free French dressing
75g/3oz sweetcorn, frozen or canned
50g/2oz cucumber
¼ red pepper
5ml/1 level teaspoon chopped mixed nuts

Cook the rice in boiling, salted water. Drain and mix with the oil-free French dressing. Leave to cool. If using frozen sweetcorn, cook in boiling, salted water. Rinse in cold water and drain. Chop the cucumber and red pepper. Mix all ingredients together.

Serves 1/200 calories
0.5 fat units/6.9 grams fibre

Meals to Share

These recipes are best made for two people so share them with your family or friends.

Stuffed Aubergine
(see picture page 16)

1 large aubergine
1 small onion
50g/2oz mushrooms
7g/¼oz butter or margarine
25g/1oz fresh white breadcrumbs
1 egg, size 3, beaten
25g/1oz mature Cheddar cheese, grated
15ml/1 level tablespoon chopped parsley
Salt and pepper
15ml/1 level tablespoon tomato ketchup

Halve the aubergine lengthwise and scoop

out the flesh leaving the shell intact. Place the shells on a baking dish. Chop the aubergine flesh, onion and mushrooms, then cook in the butter until soft. Add most of the breadcrumbs, the beaten egg, half the grated cheese, the parsley, salt and pepper and tomato ketchup. Fill the aubergine cases with the mixture. Sprinkle the remaining cheese and breadcrumbs on top. Bake at 180°C/350°F/gas mark 4 for 40 minutes.

Serves 2/190 calories
1.5 fat units/9.6 grams fibre per portion

Spicy Lentil and Egg Bake

Lentils take time to prepare, so if you wish you can soak and cook your lentils for this recipe in advance and keep them up to 48 hours in the refrigerator.

50g/2oz brown or green lentils
150ml/¼ pint water
1 small onion
5ml/1 teaspoon oil
7g/¼oz butter
2.5ml/½ level teaspoon curry powder
2.5ml/½ level teaspoon cumin seeds
2.5ml/½ level teaspoon ground
  coriander
2 eggs, size 3
2 tomatoes
Salt and pepper

Wash the lentils in a sieve under running cold water. Drain, place in a container and cover with cold water. Leave to soak for at least 4 hours. Drain again and place in a saucepan. Add 150ml/¼ pint water. Cover the pan, bring to the boil and simmer gently until tender — about 45 minutes. Drain off any excess water. Finely chop the onion. Melt the butter and oil in a small pan and add the onion. Cook over a moderate heat, stirring frequently until soft. Stir in the curry powder, cumin seeds and ground coriander. Cook over a low heat for 1-2 minutes, stirring all the time. Add the lentils and mix well. Hard-boil the eggs and then leave in cold water until cool enough to handle. Shell and chop. Stir gently into the lentil dish and season with salt and pepper. Turn into an ovenproof dish and level the top. Slice the tomatoes and arrange on top. Bake at 190°C/375°F/gas mark 5 for 20 minutes.

Serves 2/210 calories
4 fat units/4.3 grams fibre per portion

Lentil Stuffed Mushrooms

For a substantial main meal serve these stuffed mushrooms with a small jacket potato and another vegetable. You could also serve them on their own as a starter — one mushroom per person would be plenty.

50g/2oz small, brown lentils (Chinese
  lentils)
1 small clove garlic
1 bay leaf
1 bouquet garni
5ml/1 teaspoon tomato purée
2.5ml/½ level teaspoon yeast extract
150ml/¼ pint water
Salt and pepper
4 large open mushrooms, approximately
  225g/8oz altogether
50g/2oz Lancashire or Cheshire cheese

Wash the lentils in a sieve under cold running water. Drain, place in a container and cover with cold water. Leave to soak for at least 4 hours. Drain in a sieve and place in a small saucepan. Crush the garlic and add to the lentils with the bay leaf, bouquet garni, tomato purée, yeast extract and water. Cover the pan, bring to the boil and simmer gently for about 40 minutes, or until tender. When cooked there should be a little liquid left in the pan. Drain this off and reserve. If all the liquid evaporates before the lentils are cooked add a little extra water. Discard the bay leaf and bouquet garni and season the lentils with salt and pepper. Cut the stems off the mushrooms and chop them finely. Mix with the lentils. Arrange the mushrooms, dark side up, in a single layer in a shallow ovenproof dish. Pile the lentil mixture on top. Grate the cheese and sprinkle over the lentils. Pour the reserved liquid and some water into the dish to come halfway up the sides of the mushrooms. The liquid must not touch the stuffing. Bake at 200°C/400°F/gas mark 6 for 15 minutes. Carefully lift out and serve.

Serves 2/215 calories
3 fat units/6.1 grams fibre per portion

Spicy Lentil Rissoles

These spicy little rissoles are delicious. You could make up the cakes in advance and keep them in the refrigerator, but do not coat them until you are ready to cook. They can also be frozen uncooked.

115g/4oz split red lentils
225ml/8floz water
10ml/2 level teaspoons butter
2.5ml/½ level teaspoon ground cumin
2.5ml/½ level teaspoon ground
  coriander
2.5ml/½ level teaspoon ground turmeric
1.25ml/¼ level teapoon chilli powder
Salt and pepper
1 egg, size 3
40g/1½oz fresh wholemeal breadcrumbs

Wash the lentils in a sieve under cold running water. Drain and place in a small saucepan with the water. Cover the pan, bring to the boil and simmer very gently for 30 minutes or until the lentils are tender and the water has all been absorbed. Check frequently while cooking to make sure that the water does not evaporate too quickly and make the lentils burn. If necessary, add a little extra water. If there is any excess water after 30 minutes, cook uncovered for a few minutes longer, stirring all the time. Melt the butter in a small pan over a low heat. Stir in the cumin, coriander, turmeric and chilli powder and cook, stirring, for 1-2 minutes. Stir in the lentils and season with salt and pepper. Cool slightly. Separate the egg and add the yolk to the lentils. Leave until cold. Divide into four and shape into four cakes. Brush the cakes with egg white and then press on the breadcrumbs. Place on a baking sheet and bake at 200°C/400°F/gas mark 6 for 15 minutes.

Serves 2/290 calories
2.5 fat units/8.4 grams fibre per portion

Cheese Pudding

75g/3oz bread, thinly sliced
15ml/1 level tablespoon yeast extract
75g/3oz mature Cheddar cheese
1 egg, size 3
150ml/¼ pint skimmed milk
Salt and pepper

Spread half the slices of bread with yeast extract. Grate the cheese and use two-thirds to make into sandwiches with the bread. Cut the sandwiches into four pieces and place in an ovenproof dish. Lightly beat the egg and milk together. Season with salt and pepper. Pour over the bread. Leave to soak for 15 minutes. Sprinkle the remaining cheese on top. Bake at 180°C/350°F/gas mark 4 for 30 minutes.

Serves 2/	cals.	fat units	grams fibre
white bread	360	6.5	1.1
brown bread	355	6.5	2.2
wholemeal bread	350	6.5	3.6

Family Meals for Four

Most of these recipes take too much time to prepare to make them worth cooking for one person. But some will freeze if you do not have people to share with you.

Leeks in Celery and Cheese Sauce
(see picture page 87)

675g/1½lb leeks, weighed trimmed
553g/19½oz can celery hearts
60ml/4 level tablespoons skimmed milk powder
75g/3oz mature Cheddar cheese, grated
Pepper

Discard the roots and tough green leaves from the leeks before weighing. Clean well, then boil in salted water until tender. Drain and place on kitchen paper to absorb any excess water. Keep warm. Purée the contents of the can of celery hearts in a liquidiser or food processor until smooth. Add the powdered milk and blend until smooth again. Alternatively, sieve the canned celery, then whisk in the milk. Season with pepper — you will not need salt. Turn into a saucepan and heat to boiling point. Remove from the heat and add most of the cheese. Stir until melted. Pour over the leeks and sprinkle the remaining cheese on top. Grill until the cheese melts.

Serves 4/170 calories
2.5 fat units/6.8 grams fibre per portion

Red Kidney Beans in Chilli Sauce

This recipe has all the flavour of a chilli con carne, but contains no meat. For a mild chilli flavour, use just 5ml/1 level teaspoon chilli powder; for a spicy, hot flavour, use 10ml/2 level teaspoons. This recipe freezes successfully.

225g/8oz red kidney beans
575ml/1 pint water
575g/1lb 4oz can tomatoes
1 red or green pepper
1 medium onion
1 clove garlic
15ml/1 level tablespoon tomato purée
5-10ml/1-2 level teaspoons chilli powder
2.5ml/½ level teaspoon ground cumin
2.5ml/½ level teaspoon ground coriander
15ml/1 level tablespoon soft brown sugar
Salt and pepper
15ml/1 level tablespoon cornflour

Place the beans in a colander and rinse under cold water. Drain and place in a container. Add the water, cover and soak overnight or for at least 6 hours. Turn into a saucepan with the soaking liquid and bring to the boil. Boil for 10 minutes, then cover and simmer for 45 minutes. Drain off any excess liquid. Drain the tomatoes and add the juice to the beans. Roughly chop the tomatoes and add to the pan. Discard the white pith and seeds from the pepper and dice the flesh. Chop the onion and crush the garlic. Add all the ingredients except the cornflour to the pan. Season with salt and pepper. Cover and heat to simmering point. Simmer gently for 1 hour, or until the beans are tender. Blend the cornflour with a little cold water, then stir into the beans. Simmer for 1-2 minutes.

Serves 4/205 calories
0 fat units/15.9 grams fibre per portion

Aduki Bean, Cheese and Rice Salad

You could happily serve this colourful and attractive salad to guests — vegetarian or not. If you do not have time to soak the beans overnight, use the method described in the introduction to Aduki Bean Pilaf.

115g/4oz aduki beans
Water
115g/4oz long-grain brown rice
45ml/3 tablespoons oil-free French
    dressing
2 sticks celery
2 spring onions/scallions
115g/4oz Lancashire cheese
227g/8oz can pineapple in natural juice
Salt and pepper

Fiesta Rice (recipe page 87)

Rinse the beans in a colander under cold water. Drain and place in a container with 575ml/1 pint cold water. Cover and leave to soak for at least 6 hours or overnight. Turn into a pan with the soaking liquid. Cover, bring to the boil and simmer for 1 hour. Drain if necessary — most of the liquid will have been absorbed. While the beans are cooking, boil the rice in salted water until tender — about 25 minutes. Turn into a sieve and rinse in cold water. Drain well and mix with the beans. Immediately add the oil-free French dressing and stir gently to mix. Chop the celery and the bulbs of the spring onions. Cut the cheese into small cubes and do not worry if it crumbles a bit — just add the crumbs. Drain the pineapple and add 30ml/2 tablespoons of juice to the rice and beans. If the pineapple is in rings cut them into small pieces. Add the celery, spring onions, cheese and pineapple to the salad and mix together gently. Season with salt and pepper.

Serves 4/335 calories
3 fat units/9.3 grams fibre per portion

Aduki Bean Pilaf

These dark red tiny beans have a pleasant, almost sweet flavour and go particularly well with rice. If you do not have time to soak them overnight, this quick method takes 2 hours. Place the beans in a pan with the water and boil. Cover and simmer for 2 minutes, then stand, covered, for 1 hour. Heat until boiling again and simmer for 30 minutes. This recipe can be frozen.

115g/4oz aduki beans
850ml/1½ pints water
225g/8oz tomatoes
115g/4oz long-grain brown rice
1 medium onion
5ml/1 level teaspoon ground coriander
5ml/1 level teaspoon ground cumin

5ml/1 level teaspoon ground
    cinnamon
2.5ml/½ level teaspoon salt

Place the beans in a colander and rinse well under cold water. Drain and place in a container with 575ml/1 pint of the water. Leave to soak for at least 6 hours or overnight. Turn into a saucepan with the soaking liquid and bring to the boil. Cover the pan and simmer very gently for 30 minutes. Chop the onion. Skin and chop the tomatoes. Add all the ingredients to the beans including the extra 275ml/½ pint water and bring back to the boil. Cover the pan and simmer gently for 45 minutes. When cooked, the rice and beans should be tender and all the liquid absorbed. If there is too much liquid left, leave the lid off for a few minutes to allow it to evaporate. Check occasionally during the last 15 minutes, cooking time that the rice and beans are not sticking because the liquid has evaporated too quickly; add more water if necessary.

Serves 4/205 calories
0 fat units/9.3 grams fibre per portion.

Spinach Pancakes

Unfilled pancakes can be frozen or will keep for a week in a plastic bag in the refrigerator. You can use ready-grated Parmesan cheese for this recipe, but if you grate your own you will probably find it more flavoursome.

115g/4oz plain flour
Pinch of salt
1 egg, size 3
275ml/½ pint skimmed milk
2.5ml/½ teaspoon oil
225g/8oz frozen chopped spinach
225g/8oz curd cheese
25g/1oz Parmesan cheese
Salt and pepper
1 small onion
½ red or green pepper or 50g/2oz
    frozen diced peppers

Greek Salad (recipe page 87)

397g/14oz can tomatoes
1 bay leaf
2.5ml/½ level teaspoon oregano
5ml/1 level teaspoon sugar
5ml/1 teaspoon vinegar
10ml/2 level teaspoons cornflour

Make a batter with the flour, salt, egg and milk. Either place all the ingredients in a liquidiser or food processor and blend until smooth or sieve the flour and salt into a bowl and make a well in the centre. Break the egg into the well and add half of the milk. Gradually beat in the flour to make a smooth, thick batter. Beat in the remaining milk. Brush a small non-stick omelet pan or frying pan with a little oil. Heat the pan and pour in just enough batter to thinly coat the base of the pan. Cook until the underneath is set and bubbles form on top. Toss or flick over and cook the other side. Slide onto a plate. Repeat with the remaining batter. You should have twelve very small or eight fairly small pancakes.

Cook the spinach as instructed on the packet. Drain in a sieve and press lightly with the back of a spoon to remove any excess moisture. Turn into a bowl and mix with the curd cheese. Grate the Parmesan if it is not already grated and stir into the spinach. Season with salt and pepper. Spread this mixture on the pancakes and roll up. Arrange side by side in a single layer in a shallow ovenproof dish. Chop the onion and green or red pepper. Place in a pan with the tomatoes, bay leaf, oregano, sugar and vinegar. Season with salt and pepper. Cover the pan, bring to the boil and simmer for 15 minutes. Purée in a liquidiser or food processor, or rub through a sieve. Blend the cornflour with a little cold water to make a smooth paste, then mix with the puréed tomatoes. Return to the pan and bring to the boil, stirring all the time. Simmer for 1 minute. Reheat the pancakes in the oven at 200°C/400°F/gas mark 6 for 10 minutes. Reheat the sauce in a saucepan and serve separately.

Serves 4/330 calories
3.5 fat units/5.6 grams fibre per portion

Wholemeal Vegetable Pizza

Pizzas freeze well so it is often worth making a batch for the freezer all at the same time. This recipe is for a large pizza that can be divided into four, but you could make four small individual pizzas. Allow the cooked pizza to go cold before wrapping and freezing. To serve from frozen, reheat the pizza for about 20 minutes.

7g/¼oz fresh yeast or 5ml/1 level
  teaspoon dried yeast
150ml/¼ pint tepid water
2.5ml/½ level teaspoon sugar
225g/8oz strong plain wholemeal flour
5ml/1 level teaspoon salt
7g/¼oz butter
5ml/1 teaspoon oil
1 large onion
397g/14oz can tomatoes
2.5ml/½ level teaspoon dried basil
2.5ml/½ level teaspoon dried mixed herbs
Salt and pepper
50g/2oz mushrooms
198g/7oz can sweetcorn with peppers
75g/3oz Edam cheese

Cream the yeast with one-third of the water in a basin, then stir in the sugar and sprinkle on 1 heaped tablespoon flour. Leave in a warm place until frothy. Stir the salt into the remaining flour and rub in the butter. Add the yeast liquid and the remaining water and mix well. Knead on a lightly floured board for about 10 minutes until smooth and elastic. If you have a food processor you can mix and knead the dough in this, following the manufacturer's instruc-tions. Place half the oil in a large polythene bag and rub well until all the inside is coated with oil. Place the dough in the bag and leave in a warm place until doubled in size.

Meanwhile, prepare the topping. Finely chop the onion and place in a saucepan with the tomatoes and their juice, basil and mixed herbs. Season with salt and pepper. Cook uncovered until the juice has evaporated and the sauce is thick. Stir frequently as it cooks, and break up the tomatoes with the spoon. Slice the mushrooms and stir into the tomato sauce with the sweetcorn. When the dough is ready, knead it again for a few minutes, then roll it into a 25cm/10 in round. Grease a baking tray or a shallow flan tin with the remaining oil. Place the dough on the tin and spread the sauce on top. Thinly slice the cheese and arrange on top. Leave in a warm place to rise for about 30 minutes. Bake in a preheated oven at 220°C/425°F/gas mark 7 for about 20 minutes.

Serves 4/330 calories
3.5 fat units/9 grams fibre per portion

Biscuits: 100 calories.
50g/2oz Stilton cheese: 260 calories

Ham steak with pineapple: 140 calories.
Melted cheese: 120 calories

CHEESE

90g/3½ oz slice cheese
and onion flan: 340 calories

What makes most cheese such a potential dieting disaster is that it is easy to eat, easy to pick at and makes an ideal snack that needs no preparing. Many a dieter still believes that having cheese-and-biscuits instead of pudding, or Cheddar chunks (120 calories per 25g/1oz) and an apple for lunch are virtuous acts. Do not be fooled. And do not cling to the old idea of automatically labelling cheese as a 'protein' food: many types (but not the cottage and curd kinds) are more accurately considered as 'high-fat'. Many slimmers see cheese dishes as light snacks, rather than the substantial meals their calorie contents proclaim them to be. There's nothing 'wrong' with any of the items you see here as long as you count them into a daily calorie allowance. But do not kid yourself that, in calorie terms, you are eating on the cheap.

Bread and butter: 305 calories.
Cheese: 240 calories

Toast: 100 calories.
Grilled Cheddar cheese: 300 calories

Hamburger and bun: 280 calories:
Cheese: 50 calories

Cauliflower: 30 calories.
Cheese sauce: 490 calories

Apple: 50 calories. 65g/2½oz Leicester cheese: 250 calories

165g/5½oz slice cheesccake:
485 calories

Salad: 30 calories. 75g/3oz grated Cheddar cheese: 360 calories

93

Snacks

Remarkably few people get through the day without eating at least some extra calories in the form of snacks. You may have a biscuit with your mid-morning coffee or nibble your way through a bag of nuts while watching television. Or you may eat a snack to reward yourself for having completed a wearisome task or eat anything to hand because you are tired or bored. Whatever your snack-eating tendency your best diet plan is to allow some of your calories each day to satisfy snack urges. Vow not to indulge and you could end up not only eating the forbidden snack but launching on a guilty binge. When you eat a snack which is planned as part of your diet you do not feel that terrible sense of guilt and failure which can lead to the collapse of your dieting campaign.

We probably all have experienced those evenings when the TV programmes are not too good, we somehow cannot get into the

Salads make tasty and filling snacks when you are on a diet. They are very versatile and include:
1 traditional mixed salad which is very low in calories; 2 Tangy Salmon Salad Snack; 3 Nutty Cottage Cheese Salad Snack; 4 Rollmop and Apple Salad Snack; 5 Ham and Asparagus Rolls; 6 Curried Chicken and Peach Salad Snack; and 7 Egg and Prawn Salad Snack (all recipes on pages 96-98)

book we planned to read, we have finished the magazines, we feel a bit weary and fatigued but not quite ready for bed and generally do not know what to do with ourselves. So we end up pacing about and, if we are not careful, opening the fridge door and taking out a snack just to give us something to do. If your snack eating is due to boredom the first thing you should do is find a way to alleviate this. Finding an absorbing hobby can stop you feeling bored and help you to relax. Make a positive effort to unwind as you arrive home tired after a shopping expedition or a hard day at work. Take a little break and make yourself a cup of coffee or tea or sip a low-calorie drink. Sit down and relax before you even think about food. When we are tired our willpower is at its lowest ebb. Conversely our ability to control our behaviour tends to be at its peak when we are feeling well rested, vigorous and in good health. So many people's most dangerous snack-eating time tends to be in the evening when they come home from work or sit down after a day of domestic disasters.

When realistically planning your daily dieting, keep in mind not only the fact that you will be tempted to eat a snack, but also what sort of snack you will be tempted to eat. Some research has shown that the kinds of foods a slimmer enjoys in the evening often differ from those enjoyed during the day. Yoghurt, for instance, is nearly always eaten early in the day and much less frequently during or after the evening meal. There is no point in keeping an apple for an evening snack if what you usually desire is a warming bowl of soup at that time. Some people, perhaps because of a life-time habit, do find it difficult to get off to sleep without a little something to eat before they go to bed. If this is your most vulnerable snack-eating time, experiment to discover just how little that snack can be and still have the desired effect.

What tends to separate the slim from the overweight is that a slim person eats snacks rather less frequently than an overweight person. It is quite normal to want to eat a snack, but when you are slimming you must make sure that the snacks you eat fit into your dieting allowance. In this chapter you will find lots of low-calorie snacks that will satisfy both sweet and savoury cravings. If you tend to snack frequently during the day, try one of our 'munch box' recipes. Make up your munch box at the beginning of the day then dip into it whenever you feel the urge. We have taken into account that you probably will not want to spend a lot of time preparing snacks, so all the recipes here are very simple to make. If you are particularly fond of soup snacks, there are other recipes in the Soups and Starters chapter which could be frozen and reheated as a snack. Cereals also make good snack meals and you may like to choose one of the recipes from the Breakfast and Brunch section.

Make it a golden rule while you are dieting to keep any high-calorie snackable foods right out of your kitchen. Make leftovers into a meal to freeze or throw them away — yes, you really can do it if you steel yourself! The following snacks are the ones that can save rather than sabotage your diet.

95

Salad Snacks

Any of the following recipes can be served with a mixed salad to make a light snack for between 175 and 275 calories. Count about 25 calories on top of the figures given for a mixed green salad without dressing, or 30 calories with oil-free French dressing. There are no fat units in salad vegetables, but for fibre counts you will need to check the chart at the back of the book.

Tuna and Olive Salad Snack

Tuna in brine is considerably lower in calories than tuna canned in oil. Even if you drain off all the oil you would still be left with 195 calories from a 100g/3½oz can of tuna in oil — tuna in brine is just 110 calories for the same amount.

100g/3½oz can tuna in brine
15ml/1 level tablespoon tomato chutney
5ml/1 teaspoon oil-free French dressing
1 tomato
1 stuffed olive
Salt and pepper

Drain and flake the tuna, then mix with the tomato chutney and oil-free French dressing. Chop the tomato and olive and add to the tuna. Season. Serve with salad.

Serves 1/150 calories
0.5 fat units/1.3 grams fibre

Nutty Cottage Cheese Salad Snack
(see picture page 94)

This snack has a sweet-savoury flavour and the nuts add crunch. You could turn this into a light meal by doubling up the quantities.

25g/1oz lean cooked ham
4 walnut halves
50g/2oz cottage cheese with pineapple

Discard all visible fat from the ham and dice. Chop the nuts and mix with the cottage cheese and ham. Serve with salad.

Serves 1/160 calories
3.5 fat units/0.4 grams fibre

Blue Cheese and Pear Salad Snack

Because of its strong taste, a little blue cheese goes a long way. The dressing for the pear could also be served on jacket potatoes and costs 125 calories/3 fat units/0 grams fibre on its own.

25g/1oz Danish Blue or Roquefort cheese
30ml/2 level tablespoons natural yoghurt
Squeeze lemon juice
1 medium pear

Place the cheese in a basin with the yoghurt and lemon juice. Mix with a fork until fairly smooth. Core and dice the pear and stir into the dressing. Serve with salad.

Serves 1	cals.	fat units	grams fibre
Danish blue	165	3	5.2
Roquefort	150	2.5	5.2

Tangy Salmon Salad Snack
(see picture page 94)

100g/3½oz can red salmon
3 small or 1 large gherkin
10ml/2 level teaspoons low-calorie salad cream
5ml/1 level teaspoon tomato ketchup

Flake the salmon and chop the gherkins. Mix with the low-calorie salad cream and tomato ketchup. Serve with salad.

Serves 1/175 calories
4 fat units/0 grams fibre

Egg and Prawn Salad Snack
(see picture page 94)

The seafood sauce that goes with the prawns and eggs is just 40 calories/0.5 fat units/0 grams fibre and is ideal for serving with all shellfish and fish salads or for using in seafood cocktails.

1 egg, size 3
50g/2oz shelled prawns
15ml/1 level tablespoon low-calorie salad cream
10ml/2 level teaspoons natural yoghurt
10ml/2 level teaspoons tomato ketchup
Salt and pepper

Hard-boil the egg, then cool in cold water. Shell and chop roughly. Mix together the low-calorie salad cream, yoghurt and tomato ketchup and season lightly. Stir in the egg and prawns. Serve with salad.

Serves 1/180 calories
3.5 fat units/0 grams fibre

Curried Chicken and Peach Salad Snack
(see picture page 94)

A spicy dish can make a particularly satisfying snack. Although this recipe is best with a fresh peach, you could use an equivalent amount of peach slices in natural juice.

75g/3oz cooked chicken or turkey
1 small fresh peach
45ml/3 level tablespoons natural low-fat yoghurt
1.25ml/¼ level teaspoon curry paste or powder
Few drops Tabasco sauce, optional
Salt and pepper

Discard any skin from the chicken or turkey

and cut the flesh into bite-sized pieces. Stone and dice the peach. Mix the yoghurt with the curry paste or powder and Tabasco. Season with salt and pepper. Stir in the chicken and peach. Serve with salad.

Serves 1/185 calories
1.5 fat units/1.2 grams fibre

Ham and Asparagus Rolls
(see picture page 94)

40g/1½oz lean cooked ham, thinly sliced
45ml/3 level tablespoons curd cheese
Little mustard
Salt and pepper
3 canned or cooked asparagus spears,
   drained

You can keep a munch box at home or take it to work to dip into during the day: **1** *Herby Carrot and Cauliflower Munch Box;* **2** *Red Cabbage and Leek Munch Box;* **3** *Vegetable Munch Box;* **4** *Grapefruit and Celery Munch;* **5** *Apricot Cornflake Munch;* and **6** *Crunchy Fruit Munch (all recipes are on pages 98/99)*

Discard all visible fat from the ham and cut into 3 even slices. Mix the curd cheese with the mustard and then spread on the ham. Season. Place the asparagus on top and roll up. Serve with salad if wished.

Serves 1/165 calories
2 fat units/1.2 grams fibre

Rollmop and Apple Salad Snack
(see picture page 95)

1 rollmop herring
50g/2oz cucumber
1 small apple
5ml/1 teaspoon lemon juice
15ml/1 level tablespoon low-calorie salad
   cream
15ml/1 level tablespoon natural low-fat
   yoghurt
Salt and pepper

Cut the rollmop herring into small pieces. Dice the cucumber and apple, but do not peel them. Toss the apple in lemon juice. Mix all the ingredients together and season with salt and pepper. Serve with salad.

Serves 1/190 calories
3.5 fat units/1.8 grams fibre

Crispbread Snacks

Crispbread calories vary from 15 to 55 each, so check the packet information before you eat. The following snacks have been based on an average 25 calories/0 fat units/0.6 grams fibre per crispbread.

Apple and Raisin Crispbread
(see picture page 100)

1 crispbread
5ml/1 level teaspoon honey
½ medium apple
10ml/2 level teaspoons raisins

Spread the crispbread with the honey. Discard the core from the apple, then cut into 4 wedges. Place on the crispbread with the raisins.

Serves 1/85 calories
0.5 fat units/2.3 grams fibre

Peanut Butter Crunch Crispbread

1 crispbread
10ml/2 level teaspoons peanut butter,
   smooth or crunchy
1 small tomato
Few slices cucumber

Spread the crispbread with peanut butter. Slice the tomato and arrange on top with the cucumber.

Serves 1/100 calories
2 fat units/2.0 grams fibre

Prawn and Cheese Crispbread
(see picture page 100)

If you wish you can eat extra cucumber sticks with your crispbread snack. Half a cucumber would only be about 30 calories/0 fat units and would contribute 1.0 grams fibre to your day's total.

1 crispbread
15g/½oz shrimp-flavoured cheese spread
Few slices cucumber
25g/1oz peeled prawns

Spread the crispbread with the cheese. Arrange the cucumber on top and cover with the prawns.

Serves 1/100 calories
1 fat unit/0.6 grams fibre

Apricot and Curd Crispbread

1 crispbread
25g/1oz curd cheese
5ml/1 level teaspoon strawberry jam
Half 227g/8oz can apricots in low-calorie
   syrup

Spread the crispbread with curd cheese, then with the jam. Drain the apricots and arrange on top.

Serves 1/150 calories
1.0 fat units/2.1 grams fibre

Chocolate Nut Crispbread
(see picture page 100)

1 crispbread
10ml/2 level teaspoons chocolate spread
5ml/1 level teaspoon chopped nuts

Spread the crispbread with chocolate spread. Sprinkle the nuts on top.

Serves 1/75 calories
1 fat unit/0.9 grams fibre

Herby Carrot and Cauliflower Munch Box
(see picture page 97)

115g/4oz raw carrot
115g/4oz raw cauliflower
45ml/3 tablespoons oil-free French dressing
10ml/2 level teaspoons chopped fresh herbs
   or 2.5ml/½ level teaspoon mixed dried
   herbs
Salt and pepper

Cut the carrot into small sticks and the cauliflower into small sprigs. Blend the oil-free French dressing with the herbs. Mix with the vegetables and season. Keep in the refrigerator.

Serves 1/50 calories
0 fat units/5.6 grams fibre

Red Cabbage and Leek Munch Box
(see picture page 97)

150g/5oz red cabbage
1 medium carrot
2 medium leeks
30ml/2 tablespoons oil-free French dressing
15ml/1 tablespoon low-calorie salad cream
Salt and pepper

Shred the red cabbage. Grate the carrot. Discard the roots and tough green leaves from the leek, then slice thinly. Mix all the vegetables with the salad dressing and season with salt and pepper. Keep in the refrigerator to nibble during the day.

Serves 1/125 calories
0.5 fat units/11.6 grams fibre

Vegetable Munch Box
(see picture page 97)

115g/4oz frozen peas
75g/3oz frozen French beans or haricot verts
115g/4oz canned sweetcorn
¼ red or green pepper
30ml/2 tablespoons oil-free French dressing
Salt and pepper

Cook the frozen vegetables as instructed on the packets. Drain in a colander and rinse in cold water. Drain the sweetcorn. Discard the pith and seeds from the pepper and dice the flesh. Mix with the cooked vegetables and oil-free French dressing. Season. Place in a plastic container with a lid and keep in the refrigerator to nibble at throughout the day.

Serves 1/200 calories
0 fat units/18.2 grams fibre

Grapefruit and Celery Munch
(see picture page 97)

2 medium grapefruits
2 sticks celery
25g/1oz raisins or sultanas
30ml/2 level tablespoons flaked almonds

Peel and segment the grapefruit. Chop the celery. Mix all the ingredients and keep in the refrigerator to nibble during the day.

Serves 1/210 calories
2.5 fat units/7.7 grams fibre

Apricot Cornflake Munch
(see picture page 97)

25g/1oz dried apricots
25g/1oz raisins or sultanas
40g/1½oz cornflakes

Chop the dried apricots and mix with the raisins or sultanas and cornflakes.

Serves 1/270 calories
1 fat unit/9.8 grams fibre

Crunchy Fruit Munch
(see picture page 97)

1 small banana
1 large apple
5ml/1 teaspoon lemon juice
50g/2oz crunchy breakfast cereal (e.g. Jordans Original Crunchy)

Peel and slice the banana. Core and dice the apple. Toss both fruits in the lemon juice. Mix with the cereal. Keep in the refrigerator to nibble during the day.

Serves 1/360 calories
3 fat units/7.0 grams fibre

Supper Snacks

Many slimmers find that their most dangerous time of the day is the evening when they sit down to relax or watch television. If you are an evening eater, plan a supper snack into your calorie allowance for the day.

Two-Minute Spicy Tomato Soup
(see picture page 100)

This simple soup takes just two minutes to make because it uses tomato juice as its base and there are no vegetables to prepare or cook. It is good served on its own or with bread or twiglets as shown. Eight small twiglets cost 20 calories.

225ml/8floz tomato juice
5ml/1 teaspoon Worcestershire sauce
½ chicken stock cube
2.5ml/½ level teaspoon sugar
Pinch chilli powder
Salt and pepper
10ml/2 level teaspoons cornflour

Place most of the tomato juice in a saucepan with the Worcestershire sauce, stock cube, and chilli powder. Season and heat until boiling. Blend the cornflour and sugar with the remaining juice until smooth. Pour on the boiling juice, stirring all the time. Return to the pan and simmer for 1 minute, stirring. Serve hot.

Serves 1/90 calories
0 fat units/0 grams fibre

Chicken Noodle Soup
(see picture page 101)

A good suppertime soup that can be made if you have a little leftover roast chicken from lunch. All sorts of pasta cost the same calories and fat units but you will need to use small shapes or thin noodles for this recipe so that they cook quickly.

1 small spring onion/scallion
25g/1oz cooked chicken
½ chicken stock cube
2.5ml/½ teaspoon soya sauce
225ml/8floz water
Salt and pepper
15ml/1 level tablespoon small pasta shapes or thin noodles
5ml/1 level teaspoon cornflour

Chop the bulb of the spring onion. Discard any skin from the chicken and chop the flesh. Place the onion and chicken in a pan with the stock cube, soya sauce and most of the water. Season. Bring to the boil and then sprinkle in the pasta shapes. Simmer for 10 minutes. Blend the cornflour with the remaining water and then stir into the pan. Simmer for a minute and serve.

Serves 1/105 calories
0.5 fat units/0.4 grams fibre

Creamed Mushrooms on Toast
(see picture page 101)

¼ chicken stock cube
115ml/4floz water
115g/4oz button mushrooms
30ml/2 level tablespoons skimmed milk
powder
10ml/2 level teaspoons cornflour
Salt and pepper
1 small slice bread, 25g/1oz

Crumble the stock cube into 75ml/3floz water in a small saucepan. Add the mushrooms, cover and simmer for 5 minutes. Blend the remaining cold water with the skimmed milk powder and cornflour. Add to the pan, stirring all the time. Simmer for 1-2 minutes, stirring continuously. Season. Toast the bread and serve the mushrooms on top.

Serves 1/	cals.	fat units	grams fibre
white bread	145	0	3.8
brown bread	145	0	4.4
wholemeal bread	140	0	5.4

Cottage Cheese and Celery Sticks

A very low-calorie suppertime nibble — in fact, you could easily afford to eat several of these if you budget your daily calories to allow for them.

1 stick celery
Little yeast extract
15ml/1 level tablespoon cottage cheese

Scrub the celery and spread the hollow with a little yeast extract. Fill with cottage cheese.

Serves 1/25 calories
0 fat units/1 gram fibre

Simple Onion Soup with Toasted Croutons
(see picture page 101)

Onion soup is very easy to make and the croutons and cheese make this soup a little more substantial.

50g/2oz onion
½ beef stock cube
225ml/8floz water
1 bay leaf
Salt and pepper
10ml/2 level teaspoons cornflour
1 small slice bread, 25g/1oz
5ml/1 level teaspoon grated Parmesan
cheese

Finely chop the onion and place in a saucepan with the stock cube, water and bay leaf. Season. Cover the pan, bring to the boil and

1 *Apple and Raisin Crispbread (p.98);* **2** *Chocolate Nut Crispbread (p.98);* **3** *Cheese, Tomato and Pickle Toast (p.101);* **4** *Creamed Mushrooms on Toast (p.100);* **5** *Prawn and Cheese Crispbread (p.98);* **6** *Two Minute Spicy Tomato Soup (page 99);* **7** *Chicken Noodle Soup (p.99);* **8** *Simple Onion Soup (p.100);* **9** *Sardine and Tomato Toast (p.101)*

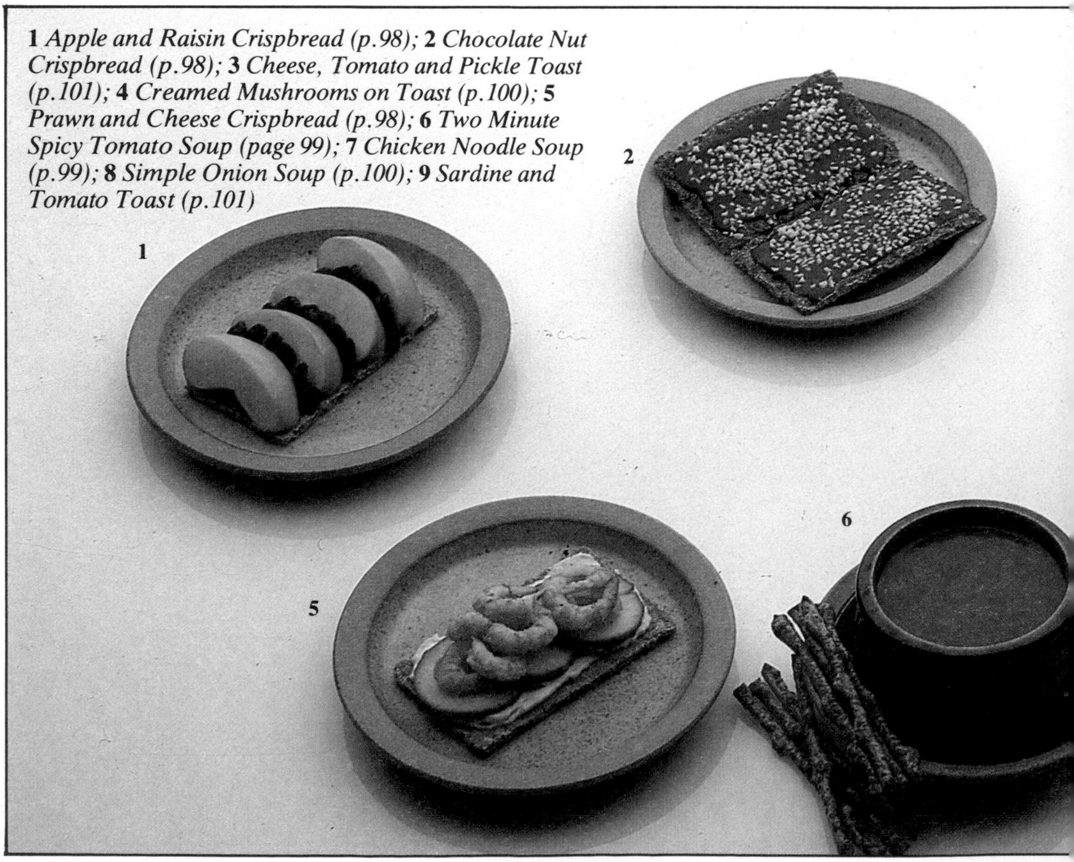

simmer for 15 minutes. Blend the cornflour with a little cold water until smooth and then add to the pan, stirring all the time. Simmer for a minute. Toast the bread and cut into squares. Pour the soup into a bowl. Float the toast on top and sprinkle with the grated cheese.

Serves 1/	cals.	fat units	grams fibre
white bread	125	0.5	1.8
brown bread	125	0.5	2.4
wholemeal bread	120	0.5	3.4

Blue Cheese and Celery Stick

A far lower calorie nibble than a couple of crackers and a hunk of blue cheese. That could easily amount to 275 calories/7 fat units.

7g/¼oz Danish blue cheese
15ml/1 level tablespoon cottage cheese
1 stick celery

Mash the blue cheese with a fork, then mix with the cottage cheese. Scrub the celery and fill the hollow with the cheese.

Serves 1/45 calories
1 fat unit/1 gram fibre

Cheese, Tomato and Pickle Toast
(see picture page 101)

If you are still automatically buttering the untoasted side of bread before you place on a topping, make a resolution to stop right now. A 15g/½oz of butter — an amount easily soaked up on hot toast — will add an extra 105 calories/4 fat units to your snack.

1 small slice bread, 25g/1oz
1 tomato
15ml/1 level tablespoon piccalilli
25g/1oz Edam cheese

Toast the bread on one side only. Slice the tomato and place on the untoasted side. Top with the piccalilli and grill until hot. Grate the cheese, sprinkle on top and grill until melted.

Serves 1/	cals.	fat units	grams fibre
white bread	170	2.5	1.9
brown bread	170	2.5	2.6
wholemeal bread	165	2.5	3.5

Sardine and Tomato Toast
(see picture page 101)

1 small slice bread, 25g/1oz
2 sardines, canned in tomato sauce, drained
5ml/1 level teaspoon finely chopped onion
1 tomato, sliced

Toast the bread. Mash the sardines and mix with the onion. Spread on the toast. Put the sliced tomato on top. Grill until hot.

Serves 1/	cals.	fat units	grams fibre
white bread	175	2	1.6
brown bread	175	2	2.3
wholemeal bread	170	2	3.2

Things on toast: how low can you go?

Grilled Cheddar Cheese *515 calories*
Surveys show most people cut guesswork slices off the cheese hunk, slap them on toast, then grill. There is 75g/3oz here and at 120 calories per 25g/1oz it totalled 360 calories. Grated cheese goes further. Lowest cost for 40g/1½oz grated Cheddar on buttered toast is 335.

Creamed Mushrooms *440 calories*
Made the high-calorie way with butter, double cream, flour and milk, this snack costs 440 calories. The lowest calorie count is for mushrooms poached in stock and creamed with 30ml/2 tablespoons powdered skim milk and 10ml/2 teaspoons cornflour: not bad for a filling light meal at 240 calories.

Peanut Butter *295 calories*
Smooth or crunchy, peanut butter is a wicked 177 calories per 25g/1oz. The amount shown here is 20ml/2 rounded teaspoons/140 calories. The smooth sort spreads thinner and gives better calorie control. Lowest cost, if you use 5ml/1 level teaspoon is 190 calories.

Baked Beans in Tomato Sauce *265 calories*
We show the contents of a 150g/5.3oz can. Even if you are starving and go for the medium size 7.9oz can, you still only add 50 calories to the total. Baked beans always come in tomato sauce so you do not need to butter the toast. Lowest count (without butter and using small size can) is 210 calories.

Sardines in Tomato Sauce *260 calories*
Sardines which are canned in tomato sauce come cheaper than those canned in oil — about 15 calories less per sardine. The lowest-calorie cost for half a 130g/4½oz can of sardines in tomato sauce served on buttered toast is shown here. Use the canned-in-oil kind and you will pay around 275 calories.

Poached Egg *235 calories*
Poaching in water adds no calories; if you lightly grease a poacher you add about 5. Even if you fry, you will not add more than about 20 calories. Calorie values differ with the size of the egg. Smallest is 70 calories, biggest is 95 calories. We used a standard size 3 at 80 calories.

Calorie counts include a toasted 40g/1½oz slice white bread (100 calories) and 7g/¼oz butter (55 calories).

Cottage Cheese *210 calories*
This faithful slimmer's friend makes an ideal snack on toast. Because of its knobbly texture, you tend to pile it on — which does not matter because it is so low in calories (27 per 25g/1oz for natural and with chives or herbs). Serve 50g/2oz on butterless toast and pay just 155 calories.

Cheese Spread *195 calories*
Cheese spread is about 80 calories for 25g/1oz but you only need 15g/½oz to cover a toast slice. Cheese triangles have the advantage of being portion-controlled, but if you are using a tube or tub take 15ml/1 level tablespoon as 50 calories. Butterless toast plus 15g/½oz spread is lowest at 140 calories.

Honey *195 calories*
Whether thick, clear, gathered by bees from exclusive flowers or labelled 'blended', honey is 20 calories for each teaspoonful and there are two on the above slice. It's easier to measure thick honey, but you can spread clear honey much thinner if you are strong-willed.

Jam *185 calories*
Jam lovers come in two kinds; those who spread a rounded teaspoon (amount shown here) carefully over the slice and those who use twice as much. With jam or marmalade at 30 calories per rounded teaspoon it pays to be mean. Artificially sweetened jams save about 10 calories per rounded teaspoon.

Tomatoes *170 calories*
At 4 calories per 25g/1oz (only 3 for canned) tomatoes are the perfect toast toppers for a light snack. Grill if fresh or gently heat the canned kind. Frying is fatal — each tomato leaves the pan 30 calories higher than it went in. Add butter when grilling and the count soars to 50 calories each tomato.

Yeast Extract *165 calories*
Marmite, Bovril and yeast extract all make excellent toast toppers because their strong flavour means a little goes a very long way. A level teaspoon (10 calories) is just right to cover a toast slice. You achieve a lower count only if you omit to spread the toast with butter which saves 55 calories.

Desserts

Below are some delicious summer desserts and a refreshing punch: **1** Blackcurrant Brulée (recipe page 110); **2** Banana and Chocolate Custard (recipe page 114); **3** Caribbean Rum Punch (recipe page 151); **4** Apricot Condé (recipe page 112); and **5** Raspberry Russe (recipe page 114)

If you are a sweet-toothed slimmer, do not despair, for there are lots of delicious desserts that are low enough in calories to be included in a diet. Not only that, a swap from traditional puddings to these low-sugar, low-fat alternatives will be of great benefit to your health — and that of your family if you invite them to share.

Before you automatically include a dessert in your dieting menu, though, pause for thought. Are you eating dessert because you have just got into the habit of having a portion of what you serve to the family? Or do you get a lot of pleasure from a sweet ending to a meal? The next time a hostess or waiter offers you a dessert, stop and ask yourself if you are still hungry, or if you just want a different taste sensation. It is the anticipation of this rather than a desire to eat more food, which often persuades you to swallow a load of additional calories on top of those you have already eaten. We would like to bet that in the past you have eaten so much of a main course that you felt another morsel could not be entertained, but along came the offer of a dessert and suddenly not only did you find room for it, but it also slipped down surprisingly easily.

If you are simply eating a pudding out of habit then your best plan is to break that

104

habit right now and spend your calories on something you really enjoy eating. If you would feel deprived if you did not eat something sweet, though, it is best to include one of these desserts in your daily menu plan. And if eating a dessert is a top priority, choose it first, and then plan a savoury course from the calories you have left.

A dessert-lover needs to take special care when visiting a restaurant but accept that you are likely to be tempted by a display of gorgeous creations and decide on a plan of action in advance. If you know that you are not going to be able to resist a portion of something very naughty, make sure that your other courses are low-calorie; choosing,

perhaps, a melon starter and plain grilled fish with vegetables. The picture guide that follows this chapter shows eating-out best buys and also the desserts better avoided.

When you are preparing desserts at home it is unwise to make more portions than will be eaten in one meal unless they will freeze. You may think that you will keep a portion in the fridge to eat tomorrow, but you will have to struggle with temptation each time you open the door — best not risk it. You will find here desserts that are easy to make for one person, and others to share with up to six people. Some are hot, some are cold, but all of them are the very best low-calorie, low-fat desserts that you could make.

Cold desserts for one

When you are eating alone the easiest cold dessert is, of course, a piece of fresh fruit. You will find these listed in the chart at the back of the book. But if you feel like treating yourself to something a little special, try one of these desserts which can cost as little as 90 calories and no more than 205 calories maximum.

Strawberry and Grapefruit Cups
(see picture page 108)

½ medium grapefruit
50g/2oz strawberries, fresh or frozen
50g/2oz white grapes
5ml/1 level teaspoon caster sugar
5ml/1 teaspoon sweet sherry or
*   orange liqueur, optional*

Cut around the grapefruit between the flesh and pith and between the segments — a grapefruit knife is ideal for this job. Lift out the segments and place in a bowl. Discard the pith and membranes but reserve the grapefruit shell. Hull the strawberries and set one aside. Quarter the rest. Pip the grapes. Add the strawberries, grapes, sugar and sherry or liqueur to the grapefruit and mix gently. Spoon into the grapefruit shell and decorate with the reserved strawberry. Chill for at least half an hour before serving.

Serves 1/90 calories with sherry:
100 calories with liqueur
0 fat units/2.2 grams fibre

Orange Poached Pear with Ice-cream
(see picture page 107)

You can use apple instead of orange juice for this recipe if you happen to have a carton of this already open. When cooking small amounts of food you need to use a pan with a tight-fitting lid to prevent too much moisture evaporating. If you find that the juice disappears before the pear is cooked, add a little water. The pear must be simmered for at least 20 minutes in order that the flavours may penetrate, and to prevent the pear from going brown in the centre. If after this time you find that you have more than a couple of tablespoons of juice left in the pan, remove the pear and boil the juice uncovered until it reduces.

1 medium-sized hard pear
115ml/4floz unsweetened orange juice
5ml/1 level teaspoon honey
40g/1½oz vanilla ice-cream

Peel the pear but leave the stalk intact. Place in a small saucepan with the orange juice and honey. Cover the pan and simmer very gently for 20-30 minutes, or until the

pear is tender when pierced with a knife. Turn the pear over 2 or 3 times while cooking. At the end you should have about 30ml/2 tablespoons of juice left. Chill. Cut the ice-cream into cubes and serve the pear on top.

Serves 1/170 calories
1.5 fat units/2.3 grams fibre

Rhubarb Mallow
(see picture page 111)

115g/4oz rhubarb
30ml/2 tablespoons water
Artificial liquid sweetener
4 marshmallows
Squeeze lemon juice

Cut the rhubarb into short lengths. Place in a small pan with the water; cover and simmer very gently until tender. Place in a bowl and sweeten to taste with artificial liquid sweetener. Pour the juice back into a pan and add 3 marshmallows. Heat gently until almost melted, then add a good squeeze of lemon juice and pour back over the rhubarb. Chill. Before serving, cut the remaining marshmallow into small pieces and sprinkle on top.

Serves 1/110 calories
1 fat unit/2.9 grams fibre

Banana, Nut and Yoghurt Dessert

15g/½oz toasted hazelnuts
1 small banana
1 small carton natural low-fat yoghurt
*   150g/5oz*

Roughly chop the hazelnuts. Peel and slice the banana and mix with the yoghurt and nuts. Serve immediately.

Serves 1/205 calories
2 fat units/3 grams fibre

Hot Desserts for One

None of these desserts is difficult to make and they are all well worth making just for one. Calories start at 70, and because fruit contains no fat, there are a number of fruity puddings that you can eat freely if you are following a low-fat diet.

Baked Peach
(see picture page 107)

1 large ripe peach
2 sponge finger biscuits
30ml/2 tablespoons unsweetened orange juice
Squeeze of lemon juice
15ml/1 level tablespoon ground almonds,
*   optional*

Plunge the peach into boiling water for 1 minute, then put into a bowl of cold water for 5 minutes. Lift out and remove the skin — it should peel easily now. Halve and stone the peach and place, rounded side down, in a small ovenproof dish. Crumble the sponge fingers into a small basin; add the orange and lemon juice. Mix in the ground almonds, if used. Pile into the peach cavities and bake at 180°C/350°F/ gas mark 4, for 15 minutes. Baste once or twice while cooking with any juices that run out, and serve hot.

Serves 1/	cals.	fat units	grams fibre
with ground almonds	135	1	2.9
without ground almonds	105	0	2.1

Baked Apple with Sultanas

1 medium cooking apple
30ml/2 level tablespoons sultanas or raisins
5ml/1 level teaspoon sugar, preferably brown

Core the apple and make a cut through the skin around the middle. Place the apple in a small ovenproof dish and fill the centre with sultanas or raisins and sugar. Pour enough water into the dish to come 6mm/¼ in up

These slimming desserts taste as good as they look: **1** *Banana Sherbert (recipe page 114);* **2** *Blackcurrant Yoghurt Dessert (recipe page 108);* **3** *Baked Peach (recipe page 106); and* **4** *Orange Poached Pear with Ice-cream (recipe page 106)*

the sides of the apple. Bake at 190°C/375°F/ gas mark 5, for 25-35 minutes or until soft. Serve hot.

Serves 1/145 calories
0.5 fat unit/5.7 grams fibre

Choc-bar with Tangy Orange Sauce

15ml/ 1 tablespoon unsweetened
*   orange juice*
15ml/1 level tablespoon orange marmalade
1 vanilla choc-ice or choc-bar

Heat the orange juice and marmalade in a small saucepan and stir until evenly mixed. Simmer for 1 minute, watching carefully to make sure it does not burn. Pour over the choc-bar and serve immediately.

Serves 1/185 calories
3.5 fat units/0.1 grams fibre

Baked Banana with Rum

1 medium banana
15ml/1 tablespoon unsweetened orange
or pineapple juice
5ml/1 level teaspoon caster sugar
5ml/1 teaspoon rum

Peel the banana and place on a piece of foil which is sufficiently large to completely enclose it. Sprinkle with the fruit juice, caster sugar and rum. Wrap up to make a loose parcel. Place on a baking tray and cook for 15 minutes at 190°C/375°F/ gas mark 5. Serve immediately.

Serves 1/115 calories
0 fat units/3.4 grams fibre

Cold Desserts For Two

These desserts are ideal to make for sharing with someone else. If you feel that you could safely keep a portion in the refrigerator for the next day, you could make up both portions for yourself.

Blackcurrant Yoghurt Dessert
(See picture page 107)

If you have to rub blackcurrants through a sieve to make the purée you will reduce the fibre content of this dessert, as most of the blackcurrants' fibre content is in the pips. You could also make this recipe using blackberries — the calories and fat units would be the same but the fibre count would come down to 8.2 grams.

225g/8oz blackcurrants, fresh or frozen
Sprig of mint
150ml/¼ pint water
10ml/2 level teaspoons gelatine
150g/5oz carton natural low-fat yoghurt
Artificial liquid sweetener
Mint leaves to decorate, optional

Place the blackcurrants, mint and all but 30ml/2 tablespoons of the water in a small saucepan. Cover the pan, bring to the boil and simmer gently until tender. Reserve a few blackcurrants for decoration. Discard the mint. Purée the remainder in a blender or rub through a sieve. Make the purée up to 115ml/4floz with water if necessary. Sprinkle the gelatine onto the remaining 30ml/2 tablespoons water in a cup and leave to soak for 5 minutes. Place the cup in a pan containing a little simmering water and leave until dissolved. Stir into the blackcurrant purée and leave until cold. Stir in the yoghurt and sweeten to taste with artificial sweetener. Pour into 2 serving dishes and chill until set. Decorate with blackcurrants and mint.

Serves 2/90 calories
0 fat units/9.8 grams fibre per portion

Strawberry and Grapefruit Cup (recipe page 106)

Semolina Mandarin Pudding
(see picture page 111)

30ml/2 level tablespoons semolina
225ml/8floz skimmed milk
15ml/1 level tablespoon sugar
75g/3oz canned mandarin oranges, drained
1 glacé cherry

Mix the semolina with a little skimmed milk in a small non-stick pan. Add the remaining milk and bring to the boil, stirring all the time. Simmer for 5 minutes, stirring frequently to make sure that the semolina does not stick to the pan. Stir in the sugar and divide between individual moulds or 2 serving dishes. Leave until cold. If using moulds, turn them out onto plates. Top with the mandarin oranges and the halved cherry.

Serves 2/130 calories
0 fat units/0.4 grams fibre per portion

Apricot Snow
(see picture page 17)

115g/4oz dried apricots
150ml/¼ pint water
¼ lemon
Liquid artificial sweetener, optional
2 egg whites, size 3

Soak the apricots in the water overnight or for several hours. Put them in a small pan with the soaking water and grated rind and juice of the lemon. Simmer gently for about 30 minutes. Purée in a blender or rub through a sieve and leave to cool. Stir in artificial sweetener to taste. Whisk the egg whites until stiff, then whisk into the apricot purée. Turn into two glasses and chill.

Serves 2/120 calories
1 fat unit/13.6 grams fibre per portion

Grapes with Raspberry Whip
(see picture page 111)

When jelly is whipped with evaporated milk it becomes rather mousse-like. It is important to chill the evaporated milk before you whisk it or otherwise it will not thicken.

¼ packet raspberry-flavoured jelly
Boiling water
115g/4oz white grapes
60ml/4 tablespoons evaporated milk, chilled

Place the jelly in a measuring jug and make up to 75ml/3floz with boiling water. Stir until dissolved. Leave in a cold place until it is on the point of setting. Reserve 6 grapes for decoration. Halve and deseed the remainder and place in 2 serving glasses. Place the evaporated milk in a small basin and whisk until thick. Add the jelly and whisk until thick. Pour over the grapes and then chill until set. Decorate with the reserved grapes.

Serves 2/120 calories
1 fat unit/0.5 grams fibre per portion

Hot Desserts For Two

If you would like to serve any of these puddings to more than one other person, you can easily double up the quantities.

Chocolate Ground Rice Pudding

15ml/1 level tablespoon cocoa
30ml/2 level tablespoons drinking chocolate powder
225ml/8floz skimmed milk
30ml/2 level tablespoons ground rice
Artificial liquid sweetener

Blend the cocoa and drinking chocolate powder with a little skimmed milk until smooth. Add the remaining milk, then pour into a non-stick pan and heat until simmering. Sprinkle on the ground rice and stir well. Simmer for 2-3 minutes, stirring all the time. Remove from the heat and leave for 2 minutes. Add the artificial sweetener to taste and turn into 2 serving dishes.

Serves 2/120 calories
0.5 fat unit/0.2 grams fibre per portion

Baked Bananas with Sultanas and Nuts

350g/12oz bananas
30ml/2 tablespoons unsweetened pineapple or orange juice
25g/1oz sultanas
15g/½oz hazelnuts

Peel the bananas and cut into thick slices. Place in an ovenproof dish with the fruit juice and sultanas. Toss together gently so that all the pieces are coated in juice — take care not to damage the banana. Cover the dish with a lid or foil and bake at 180°C/ 350°F/gas mark 4, for 20 minutes. Place the hazelnuts on a small baking sheet and cook alongside the bananas until golden-brown. Watch that they do not burn. Rub the skins off, using a piece of kitchen paper and chop roughly. Sprinkle over the bananas and serve.

Serves 2/150 calories
1.0 fat unit/4.8 grams fibre per portion

Coffee Custard Meringue
(see picture page 111)

150ml/¼ pint semi-skimmed milk
5ml/1 level teaspoon instant coffee
1 egg, size 3, plus 1 extra egg white
10ml/2 level teaspoons brown sugar
30ml/2 level tablespoons caster sugar

Heat the milk but do not allow it to boil. Stir in the coffee. Lightly whisk together the whole egg and the brown sugar. Pour on the milk, whisking all the time. Divide between two ovenproof dishes, then stand the dishes in a small roasting tin filled with enough water to come halfway up the sides. Bake at 180°C/350°F/ gas mark 4, for 15-20 minutes, or until set. Whisk the egg white until stiff. Add the caster sugar and whisk until stiff again. Pile on top of the custards, making sure that the meringue goes right to the edge of the dishes. Cook for another 10 minutes, or until the meringue browns on top. Serve warm or cold.

Serves 2/155 calories
2 fat units/0 grams fibre per portion

Cold Desserts for Four

Do not worry about serving a low-calorie dessert to guests or your family; it is unlikely that they will notice. Some of these desserts are rather special, whereas others are quick and easy to prepare. All of them are under 180 calories.

Tipsy Strawberries

450g/1lb fresh strawberries
1 medium orange
4 sugar lumps
60ml/4 tablespoons brandy

Hull the strawberries and rinse them in cold water. Pat dry gently with kitchen paper, then place in a bowl. Rinse the orange in cold water and dry with kitchen paper. Rub the sugar lumps over the skin of the orange until they are saturated with the zest. Place them in a basin and crush with a wooden spoon. Squeeze the orange and add the juice to the sugar lumps with the brandy. Pour over the strawberries, cover with cling-film and chill for 2-3 hours. Divide the strawberries and brandy syrup between 4 individual glasses and serve.

Serves 4/90 calories
0.5 fat unit/2.5 grams fibre per portion

Pears in Red Wine
(see picture page 113)

4 medium-sized pears
115ml/4floz red wine
115ml/4 floz water
Strips of lemon rind
7.5ml/1½ level teaspoons arrowroot or
*   cornflour*
Liquid artificial sweetener
4 small pieces angelica, optional

Peel the pears but leave the stems on. Place them in a saucepan large enough to hold them in one layer. Add the wine, water and lemon rind. Cover the pan, bring to the boil and simmer very gently for 30 minutes. Turn the pears gently once or twice while cooking. Lift them out and stand upright in a shallow dish. Blend the arrowroot or cornflour with a little cold water until smooth. Strain the wine mixture, then pour onto the arrowroot or cornflour, stirring all the time. Return to the saucepan and bring to the boil, stirring all the time. Simmer for 1-2 minutes. Sweeten to taste with artificial sweetener. Pour over the pears and chill. Decorate with angelica leaves before serving.

Serves 4/65 calories
0 fat units/2.3 grams fibre per portion

Apple Snow with Hazelnuts
(see picture page 113)

450g/1lb cooking apples, preferably
*   Bramley, weighed peeled and cored*
1 clove
5ml/1 level teaspoon finely grated lemon
*   rind*
30ml/2 tablespoons water
15ml/1 level tablespoon honey
Few drops liquid artificial sweetener, optional
2 egg whites
15g/½oz toasted hazelnuts

Slice the apples and place in a saucepan with the clove, lemon rind and water. Cover

and cook over a low heat until soft and pulpy. Discard the clove. Stir in the honey. Taste and sweeten with a few drops of artificial sweetener, if liked. Leave until cold. Whisk the egg whites until stiff. Fold into the apple purée, then whisk again until fluffy. Divide between 4 serving dishes. Roughly chop the hazelnuts and sprinkle on top. Serve within an hour.

Serves 4/75 calories
0.5 fat unit/2.9 grams fibre per portion

Blackcurrant Brulée
(see picture page 104)

275g/10oz blackcurrants, fresh or frozen
120ml/8 tablespoons water
10ml/2 level teaspoons cornflour
Artificial sweetener to taste
150g/5oz carton blackcurrant yoghurt
20ml/4 level teaspoons soft light brown
*   sugar*
15g/½oz flaked almonds

Place the blackcurrants and water in a saucepan. Cover and cook gently until soft. Blend the cornflour with a little extra water to make a smooth paste. Add to the blackcurrants and bring to the boil, stirring continuously. Cook for 1-2 minutes. Sweeten to taste with the sweetener. Divide between 4 small heatproof dishes and leave until cold. Spread the yoghurt over the blackcurrants and chill. Sprinkle the sugar and almonds on top and grill for a few minutes until the sugar melts and the almonds turn brown. Serve immediately.

Serves 4/95 calories
0.5 fat units/6.4 grams fibre per portion

Summer Pudding

This dessert needs to be prepared the day before you intend to eat it. It can be frozen after it has been refrigerated with a weight on top for 24 hours. Although you can use brown or wholemeal bread, white is really best because part of the charm of the dish is the colour of the juice-soaked bread.

225g/8oz mixed blackcurrants, redcurrants,
*   and blackberries*
30ml/2 tablespoons water
50g/2oz fruit sugar (fructose)
115g/4oz raspberries
115g/4oz thinly sliced crustless bread

Place the blackcurrants, redcurrants, and blackberries in a saucepan. You can use a mixture of all three or just one variety of fruit as long as the total weight is 225g/8oz. Add the water and fruit sugar. Cover the

1
2
3
4

pan and simmer for 10 minutes. Remove from the heat and stir in the raspberries. Turn into a bowl and leave to cool. While the fruit is cooling, cut up the bread. You will need a basin or soufflé dish that will hold 425ml/¾ pint. Cut 3 circles of bread — one to fit the bottom, one to fit the middle and another to fit the top of the basin or dish. Cut the remaining bread to fit the sides — it should completely cover the sides but only overlap at the joins by a tiny amount.

Turn the fruit into a sieve over a bowl and leave to stand for a few minutes so that the juice drains out. Dip the pieces of bread in the juice and line the base and sides of the dish. Half-fill with fruit and place a slice of bread on top. Fill with the rest of the fruit and cover with the remaining bread. Sprinkle on any remaining juice. Cover with a piece of greaseproof paper, and then place a saucer on top — it should fit inside the rim of the basin or dish. Place a 450g/1lb weight or a heavy can of food on top. Refrigerate overnight. Turn out to serve.

Serves 4		fat	grams
per portion	cals.	units	fibre
white bread	140	0.5	7.4
brown bread	140	0.5	8.1
wholemeal bread	135	0.5	9.0

All these desserts are easy to make and could be served to guests: **1** *Rhubarb Mallow (recipe page 106);* **2** *Grapes with Raspberry Whip (recipe page 109);* **3** *Semolina Mandarin Pudding (recipe page 108); and* **4** *Coffee Custard Meringue (recipe page 109)*

Peaches Cardinal

575g/1¼ lbs ripe peaches
450g/1lb raspberries, fresh or frozen
25g/1oz icing sugar
30ml/2 level tablespoons flaked almonds

Plunge the peaches into boiling water for one minute and then plunge into cold water. Cut them in half and ease out the stones, taking care not to bruise the flesh. Peel them and place in a glass bowl. Rub the raspberries through a nylon sieve to remove the pips. Stir in the icing sugar and pour over the peaches. Chill. Toast the almonds until golden-brown, watching carefully that they do not burn, and scatter on top just before serving.

Serves 4/115 calories
0.5 fat units/2.1 grams fibre per portion

Tropical Fruit Salad

1 medium-sized ripe mango
1 medium-sized ripe paw-paw
2 passion fruit
2 kiwi fruit
175ml/6floz unsweetened apple or orange
*   juice*
1 large banana

Cut the mango into three parts horizontally, making one cut just above the stone and one just below. Discard the stone and skin. Cube the flesh and place in a bowl. Cut the paw-paw in half horizontally and scoop out and discard the black seeds. Peel and cube the flesh. Add to the mango. Cut the passion fruit in half, scoop out the flesh and mix with the paw-paw and mango. Peel and slice the kiwi fruit and add to the prepared fruits with the juice. Cover and chill for at least 1 hour. Just before serving, peel and slice the banana and mix with the other fruits.

Serves 4/110 calories
0 fat units per portion

Individual Autumn Puddings

Unsliced bread is less doughy in texture than sliced and is best for any Summer Pudding (page 110). Cut your bread circles and weigh them, making up the weight with pieces cut to fit the sides. These puddings freeze well although you must weight them down for 24 hours first. If you serve each pudding with 30ml/2 tablespoons half cream as we have done in the picture, it will add 40 calories/1 fat unit/0 grams fibre.

225g/8oz cooking apples, weighed peeled,
*   cored and sliced*
175g/6oz blackberries
30ml/2 tablespoons water
50g/2oz fruit sugar (fructose)
115g/4oz thinly sliced crustless bread

Peel and slice the apples and place in a saucepan with the blackberries, water and fruit sugar. Cover the pan and cook gently until soft but not mushy. Turn into a bowl and leave to cool. Cut 8 circles of bread to fit the bases of 4 individual basins or soufflé dishes, and 8 circles to fit the top of the dishes. Cut the rest to fit the sides. Turn the fruit into a sieve over a bowl and leave to drain for a few minutes. Soak the bread in the juice and place a circle in the base of each individual dish, and then line the sides. Fill with the fruit and place the remaining circles of bread on top. Cover each dish with a piece of greaseproof paper and stack on top of each other. Place a 225g/8oz weight inside another dish or a cup and place on top. Refrigerate overnight. Turn out and serve.

Serves 4 per portion	cals.	fat units	grams fibre
white bread	150	0	5.2
brown bread	150	0.5	5.9
wholemeal bread	145	0.5	6.8

Apricot Mousse
(see picture page 157)

115g/4oz dried apricots
Cold water
10ml/2 level teaspoons gelatine
150ml/¼ pint unsweetened orange juice
25g/1oz powdered skimmed milk
10ml/2 level teaspoons honey
1 egg white
30ml/2 level tablespoons flaked almonds

Soak the dried apriots in 150ml/¼ pint water for at least 4 hours or overnight. Place in a saucepan with the soaking liquid and another 150ml/¼ pint water. Cover the pan and simmer for 30 minutes. Turn into a basin with the cooking liquid and leave to cool. Place another 30ml/2 tablespoons water in a small basin and sprinkle the gelatine on top and leave to soak for 5 minutes. Stand the basin in a pan containing a little simmering water and leave until dissolved. Place the apricots with their cooking liquid, orange juice, powdered skimmed milk and honey in a liquidiser or food processor and blend until smooth. Add the gelatine and blend again for a few seconds. Turn into a basin. Whisk the egg white and fold in gently. Pour into 4 serving dishes and chill until set. Toast the flaked almonds until golden-brown and sprinkle on top just before serving.

Serves 4/125 calories
1 fat unit/7.2 grams fibre per portion

Apricot Condé
(see picture page 105)

50g/2oz pudding or round-grain rice
570ml/1 pint skimmed milk
5ml/1 level teaspoon custard powder
15ml/1 tablespoon water
Artificial liquid sweetener to taste
227g/8oz canned apricots in apple juice
*   or low-calorie syrup*
75ml/3floz apple juice
5ml/1 level teaspoon powdered gelatine

Place the rice and milk in a basin wedged over a pan of water. Cover and simmer for 45 minutes. Remove the lid and cook for 1 hour, stirring every 15 minutes. Blend the custard powder with the water and add to the rice. Place in a non-stick saucepan and bring to the boil, stirring. Cook for 1 minute, then add the sweetener to taste. Cool and divide between 4 sundae glasses. Arrange the drained apricots on top of the rice. Mix the

Apple Snow with Hazelnuts (recipe page 110)

Apple and Apricot Meringue (recipe page 114)

Pears in Red Wine (recipe page 110)

Apple Charlotte (recipe page 114)

juice from the apricots with the apple juice and make up to 150ml/¼ pint with water. Place in a basin with the gelatine and stand in a pan of simmering water until the gelatine dissolves. Leave until cold but not set, and spoon over the apricots. Chill until set.

Serves 4/140 calories
0 fat units/1.0 grams fibre per portion

Rhubarb and Orange Fluff
450g/1lb rhubarb
150ml/¼ pint water
1 packet orange jelly
1 individual carton orange yoghurt,
*   150g/5oz*
25g/1oz skimmed milk powder

Cut the rhubarb into short lengths and place in a saucepan with the water. Cover the pan and cook over a low heat until tender. Remove the pan from the heat and add the jelly. Stir until dissolved. Place in a liquidiser or food processor with the yoghurt and skimmed milk powder, and blend until smooth. If no liquidiser or food processor is available, rub the rhubarb through a sieve, then whisk in the remaining ingredients. Chill until on the point of setting, then whisk until fluffy. Turn into one large or four small serving dishes and chill until set.

Serves 4/150 calories
0 fat units/2.9 grams fibre per portion

Coffee Hazelnut Cream
1 egg, size 3
1 egg yolk, size 3
25g/1oz soft brown sugar
30ml/2 level tablespoons plain flour
30ml/2 level tablespoons cornflour
350ml/12floz skimmed milk
15ml/1 level tablespoon instant coffee
25g/1oz toasted hazelnuts

Separate the eggs and place both yolks in a basin. Add about one-third of the sugar, the flour, cornflour and a little of the milk. Mix to a smooth cream. Heat the remaining milk, preferably in a non-stick pan, but do not allow it to boil. Stir in the coffee, then pour onto the yolk mixture, stirring all the time. Pour back into the pan and cook over a gentle heat, stirring continuously until it boils and thickens. Pour into a basin and cover the surface with a piece of damp greaseproof paper to prevent a skin forming. Leave to cool. Whisk one egg white until stiff. Add the remaining sugar, half at a time, and whisk after each addition until stiff again. Fold into the coffee cream. Reserve four nuts for decoration and roughly chop the rest. Fold into the cream and divide between four serving dishes or glasses. Chill. Decorate with nuts before serving.

Serves 4/155 calories
2 fat units/0.6 grams fibre per portion

DESSERTS

Hot Desserts For Four

Whether you choose a homely rice pudding or a more glamorous meringue, all these desserts are good enough to share and none will cost more than 180 calories.

Spicy Apple and Orange Compôte

3 medium-sized oranges
30ml/2 level tablespoons orange marmalade
30ml/2 level tablespoons sugar
1 small stick cinnamon
450g/1lb eating apples

Grate 5ml/1 level teaspoon of rind from 1 orange and then squeeze out the juice. Make the juice up to 220ml/7floz with water and place in a wide-bottomed saucepan. Add the grated orange rind, marmalade, sugar and cinnamon. Heat gently until the sugar has dissolved. Stir well. Peel and core the apples, and then cut each into 8 wedges. Place in the pan and baste well with the juices. Cover the pan and simmer gently until the apples are tender but not mushy. Peel and segment the remaining 2 oranges and add to the compôte. Discard the cinnamon and turn into a bowl.

Serves 4/130 calories
0.5 fat unit/3.4 grams fibre per portion

Apple Charlotte
(see picture page 113)

5ml/1 level teaspoon low-fat spread
450g/1lb cooking apples, weighed
  peeled and cored
60ml/4 tablespoons honey
75g/3oz fresh wholemeal breadcrumbs
60ml/4 tablespoons apple juice
1.25ml/¼ level teaspoon ground ginger

Lightly grease a large ovenproof dish or four individual ovenproof dishes with low-fat spread. Slice the apples and arrange half in the dish, or dishes. Top with half the honey and sprinkle on half the breadcrumbs. Repeat the layers. Sprinkle on the apple juice and ginger. Cook at 180°C/350°F/ gas mark 4 for about 1 hour or until the apples are tender and the topping is crisp.

Serves 4/155 calories
1 fat unit/4.5 grams fibre per portion

Apple and Apricot Meringue
(see picture page 113)

115g/4oz dried apricots
450g/1lb cooking apples
Few drops liquid artificial sweetener
2 egg whites
50g/2oz caster sugar

Wash the apricots, then soak in cold water for at least 4 hours, or overnight. Drain and reserve 60ml/4 tablespoons liquid. Peel, core and slice the apples and place in a saucepan with the apricots and reserved liquid. Cover the pan and simmer until the fruits are soft. Sweeten to taste with artificial sweetener. Turn into an ovenproof dish or 4 individual ovenproof dishes. Whisk the egg whites until stiff. Add half the sugar and whisk until stiff again. Repeat with the remaining sugar. Pile on top of the fruit, making sure that the meringue goes right to the edge of the dish. Bake at 190°C/375°F/ gas mark 5 for 10-15 minutes, or until the top of the meringue starts to brown. Serve warm.

Serves 4/155 calories
1 fat unit/7.6 grams fibre per portion

Banana and Chocolate Custard
(see picture page 104)

You only need to add a tiny amount of sweetener to this recipe as it is naturally sweet. If you wish to substitute sugar, add 30ml/2 level teaspoons to the custard powder. This will add 25 calories to each portion.

570ml/1 pint skimmed milk
60ml/4 level tablespoons custard powder
50g/2oz drinking chocolate
Artificial liquid sweetener to taste
2 medium bananas
Lemon juice

Blend a little of the milk with the custard powder and drinking chocolate. Heat the rest of the milk to boiling point. Pour onto the custard powder, stirring all the time. Return to the pan, bring to the boil, stirring, and cook for 1-2 minutes. Sweeten to taste. Pour into a basin — cover the top with wet greaseproof paper to prevent a skin forming. Allow to cool. Slice the bananas and reserve 12 slices. Brush these with lemon juice. Divide the rest between 4 glasses and spoon the custard over. Decorate with the reserved slices.

Serves 4/175 calories
0.5 fat units/1.7 grams fibre per portion

Cold Desserts for Six

With the exception of the cheesecake and the raspberry russe, all the desserts in this section are frozen and can be taken from the freezer a portion at a time.

Banana Sherbert
(see picture page 107)

A very refreshing ice which is slightly more milky than a sorbet but not as rich as ice-cream, it keeps in the freezer for up to six weeks and is a great favourite with children.

114

If you do not intend to serve the sherbert to six people, freeze it in individual portions after the egg white has been added.

350g/12oz bananas
30ml/2 tablespoons lemon juice
225ml/8floz unsweetened orange juice
30ml/2 level tablespoons clear honey
50ml/2floz skimmed milk
1 egg white
1 small orange to decorate, optional

Purée the bananas in a liquidiser or food processor with the lemon juice, orange juice and honey. Alternatively, mash the bananas well with the lemon juice, then stir in the orange juice, honey and skimmed milk. Pour into a shallow container, cover and freeze until almost firm. Whisk the egg white until stiff but not dry. Turn the sherbert into a chilled bowl and whisk to break down the ice crystals. Fold in the egg white and pour back into the container. Freeze until firm. Remove from the freezer and place in the main part of the fridge 30 minutes before serving. Spoon into glasses and decorate with orange slices.

Serves 6/65 calories
0 fat units/1.1 grams fibre per portion

Orange Cheesecake
(see picture page 141)

50g/2oz digestive biscuits
25g/1oz butter
20ml/4 level teaspoons powdered gelatine
45ml/3 tablespoons water
2 medium-sized oranges
225g/8oz cottage cheese
115g/4oz curd cheese
150g/5oz natural yoghurt
Artificial liquid sweetener to taste
1 egg white
115g/4oz black grapes or 2 kiwi fruit

Crush the biscuits. Melt the butter and mix with the biscuit crumbs. Press into the base of a loose-based 15cm/6in cake tin. Chill while you prepare the topping. Sprinkle the gelatine onto the water in a cup and leave to soak for 5-10 minutes. Meanwhile, finely grate enough orange rind to give 10ml/2 level teaspoons. Cut a slice from the middle of one orange and save for decoration. Squeeze the juice from both oranges and make up to 150ml/¼ pint with water. Stand the gelatine cup in a pan containing a little simmering water and leave until dissolved. Place in a blender or food processor with the orange juice and rind, cottage cheese, curd cheese and yoghurt. Run the machine until well blended. Alternatively, sieve the cottage cheese and mix together all the ingredients in a bowl. Add some artificial sweetener to taste — add this gradually, tasting as you go, as the cheesecake should not be too sweet.

Whisk the egg white and fold in gently. Pour on top of the biscuit base and chill until set. Halve and pip the grapes or slice the kiwi fruits and use to decorate the cheesecake with the orange slice.

Serves 6/205 calories
3 fat units/0.5 grams fibre per portion

Blackcurrant Sorbet
(see picture page 130)

350ml/12floz water
115g/4oz caster sugar
225g/8oz blackcurrants, fresh or frozen
5ml/1 teaspoon lemon juice
2 egg whites
Mint sprigs to decorate, optional

Dissolve the sugar in 275ml/½ pint water over a low heat, stirring all the time. Boil gently for 10 minutes without stirring. Leave to cool. Cook the blackcurrants in the remaining water over a low heat for 10 minutes. Rub through a sieve and add the purée to the syrup. Add enough water to make 550ml/1 pint. Leave until completely cold. Add the lemon juice and turn into a shallow plastic container. Cover and freeze until almost firm. Whisk the egg whites until stiff but not dry. Turn the sorbet into a chilled bowl and whisk to break down the ice crystals. Fold in the egg whites. Return to the freezer and freeze until firm. Half an hour before serving, place in the main part of the refrigerator. Spoon into glasses and decorate with mint sprigs.

Serves 6/90 calories
0.5 fat units per portion

Raspberry Russe
(see picture page 105)

1 envelope powdered gelatine
45ml/3 tablespoons water
350g/12oz raspberries
150ml/¼ pint unsweetened orange juice
50g/2oz powdered skimmed milk
Artificial liquid sweetener to taste
11 sponge finger biscuits

Sprinkle the gelatine onto the water in a small basin and leave to stand for 5 minutes. Stand the basin in a pan of simmering water until the gelatine has dissolved. Place 225g/8oz raspberries, the orange juice and powdered skimmed milk in a liquidiser and blend until smooth. Sweeten to taste. Stir in the dissolved gelatine. Pour the mixture into a 15cm/6in straight-sided dish or tin and refrigerate until set. Turn out onto a plate. Cut each sponge finger in half and arrange them around the russe, rounded side up. Decorate with the remaining raspberries.

Serves 6/95 calories
0 fat units/4.2 grams fibre per portion

115

Desserts: how low can you go?

Chocolate Profiteroles *600 calories*

This is just about the most fattening pudding you can choose. Profiteroles combine choux pastry with a figure-fatal mix of double cream and sweet sauce often made with real chocolate. Count 150 calories for each profiterole with sauce.

Apple Pie *420 calories*

This top favourite is not as goody-goody as it sounds. Whether you pack it with fruit or not, those layers of pastry do the damage. You cannot roll the pastry too thin or the fruit will spoil it; the thicker the pastry, the higher the calories will be.

Cheesecake *410 calories*

Recipes for cheesecake vary enormously. High-calorie toppings are made with double cream and cream cheese; lower-calorie varieties with cottage or curd cheese. A slice from a patisserie could cost over 500 calories. This slice was made with cream and curd cheese.

Black Forest Gâteau *350 calories*

This gâteau is not always as wicked as it looks. A lot of air is whipped into its low-fat sponge cake base; the cream is whipped, too, so a little goes a long way. But beware: some restaurants are lavish with additional cream and more generous with portions.

Chocolate Mousse *265 calories*

This classic recipe is a rich mix of eggs and plain chocolate. If a restaurant is generous with the cream, you could find this simple dessert costs up to 300 calories. Individual frozen chocolate mousses usually cost only around 100 calories each.

Crème Caramel *200 calories*

Although the sugar, eggs and milk from which this pudding is made are all rather high-calorie, it is usually baked in individual dishes. Even in expensive restaurants, you are unlikely to pay more than 235 calories. Frozen or chilled crème caramel costs about half the calories.

That pudding can cost as few as 30 calories or as many as 600. Calories are
for portions shown — all 115g/4oz unless otherwise stated.

Rice Pudding *160 calories*
The surprise is that creamy canned rice
pudding (175g/6oz shown here) is at least 10
calories an ounce less than the standard
home-made version. Canned rice puddings tend
to be more runny than home-made puddings
and are not usually baked in a greased dish.

Plain Ice-cream *155 calories*
Despite its name, ice-cream — even the dairy
variety — is much lower in fat than many
people imagine. And the ingredients are
whisked to trap in lots of no-calorie air! Ice-
cream averages out at around 50 calories per
25g/1oz. A wafer adds 5 calories.

Fresh Fruit Salad *130 calories*
Although fruit salad on its own is never high,
sugar or syrup bases add calories to the
otherwise innocent fruit. At home, you can
mix fruit with apple juice, but restaurants
usually drown it in syrup — for sweetness and
to prevent browning.

Stewed Apple *115 calories*
Even cooked with sugar, stewed apple is
reasonably low — and the calorie count does
not vary much. If you use custard, the average
dollop will add 100 calories to the cost of this
175g/6oz portion. If you like cream, it is hard
to add less than 125 calories.

Lemon Sorbet *50 calories*
A sorbet is merely iced water with flavouring
and a little sugar, so it is a safe choice wherever
you are eating. A small restaurant scoop gives
you just 40g/1½oz — a mere 50 calories' worth.
At this rate, you can even afford the two
scoops served in some restaurants.

Fresh Berries *30 calories*
When they are at their sweetest, fresh berries
— strawberries, raspberries, blackberries —
are the best buy. You get a whole luxurious-
looking bowl holding a full 115g/4oz for only
30 calories. And they taste so delicious you
can resist adding sugar and cream.

Baking

These are the best cakes and breads you can bake while you are dieting, but we have to urge you to bake as little as possible. When you are in the kitchen surrounded by tempting aromas, it would take a saint to resist sampling them. When you are down to your target you will be able to afford to bake a little more often and it is worth swapping these recipes for any high-fat, high-sugar alternatives you would normally bake. If you never bake, do not start now! But if your family and friends insist on home-made cakes, these are the healthiest sort you can make.

Beware, though, of the 'I'm just making this cake for them' syndrome. The next time you bake a cake, note exactly how much is eaten by you and how much is eaten by them. Many people who have tried this have had a bit of a shock. Quite often they have discovered that the score worked out something like 'two-thirds to me and one-third to them'. Another good test is to bake something that others enjoy but you dislike. If you have difficulty in doing this, then you are not baking for them alone.

Most of the cakes in this chapter will freeze. A large cake can provide considerable temptation if it is left sitting in your kitchen for days. Do not bake one of the unfreezable large cakes, unless you have lots of people with whom to share it. With other large cakes, cut as much as you need for one meal and freeze the rest.

In modern dieting the emphasis has moved away from banning certain foods towards

A slice of Nutty Apricot Teabread (recipe page 120) makes a real teatime treat when you are on a slimming diet

stricter fat control and more freedom with some carbohydrates. The common tendency among many overweight people is to eat certain foods only in private — the ones identified as being particularly fattening. Many overweight people feel self-conscious about eating sugary or starchy foods when others are watching. For when they are seen eating a slice of cake or indulging in the occasional biscuit they may well get the response: "I thought you were supposed to be dieting."

Eating certain foods in guilty solitude can easily turn into secret bingeing. When you are eating with others you become positively saintly — you do not touch cream or cakes and refuse all offers of sugar and biscuits. "I just don't understand why I'm not losing weight," you say to friends. "I barely eat anything." But later, alone in your kitchen, you stuff down all those goodies you have been refusing in public.

Your dieting campaign stands much more chance of success if you come out into the open. Shed all your shyness about eating certain foods in public and explain to your friends and family that you have counted these items into your calorie allowance. A diet can contain many foods that uninformed people may consider to be 'banned'. Firmly tell anyone who may infuriate you into out-of-control eating that they will be seeing you eating these foods as part of your weight loss plan. As they see your excess weight disappearing, they will know you are telling the truth.

Plan a portion of whatever you are baking into your daily calorie allowance. Sit and eat it with everyone else, slowly savouring every mouthful — it will taste much better that way than gulped down behind closed doors — and then make sure all left-overs are disposed of. That way your baking day will not turn into a guilt-ridden eating orgy.

Fruit Cakes and Teabreads

These are the highest-fibre cakes you can make. Unless you want a whole loaf or cake to decorate a tea-table, cut your cake or teabread into slices before freezing. Then you can take just the number of slices you want from the freezer when you are ready to serve them.

Nutty Apricot Teabread
(see picture page 118)

The nuts on top of this loaf make it look and taste really special, but they add quite a few calories and fat units. For a lower-calorie version, omit them and reduce each slice to 210 calories/2.5 fat units/4 grams fibre.

1.25ml/¼ teaspoon oil
115g/4oz dried apricots
Grated rind 1 medium orange
75ml/3floz unsweetened orange juice
75g/3oz glacé cherries
350g/12oz white self-raising flour
Pinch salt
50g/2oz butter or margarine
115g/4oz sultanas or raisins
2 eggs, size 2
Artificial liquid sweetener equivalent to 75g/3oz sugar
175ml/6floz skimmed milk
15g/½oz hazelnuts
25g/1oz walnut halves
15g/½oz whole blanched almonds
25g/1oz Brazil nuts

Preheat the oven to 170°C/325°F/gas mark 3. Line a 1kg/2lb loaf tin and brush with the oil. Chop the apricots and place in a small saucepan with the orange juice and rind. Cover the pan and simmer for 5 minutes. Turn into a basin and leave to cool slightly. Rinse the cherries in hot water, then halve them. Pat dry with kitchen paper. Sieve the flour and salt into a basin and rub in the butter or margarine. Add the sultanas, cherries and apricots with their juices. Lightly beat together the eggs, artificial sweetener and milk. Add to the dry ingredients and stir until evenly mixed — do not over-beat. Turn into the prepared

tin and level the top. Arrange the nuts on top, pressing them into the surface. Bake for 1¼-1½ hours, or until a skewer inserted in the centre comes out clean.

Makes 12 slices/250 calories
3.5 fat units/4.5 grams fibre per slice

Carrot and Date Cake

Granary flour is 6 calories per 25g/1oz more than wheatmeal but only makes a slight difference in calories per slice for this cake. Granary flour owes its coarse texture to the fact that the wheatmeal flour is mixed with malted wheat flakes. This cake can be frozen or will keep in an airtight tin for up to one week.

1.25ml/¼ teaspoon oil
50g/2oz butter or margarine
90ml/6 level tablespoons honey
115g/4oz peeled carrots
115g/4oz stoned dates
175g/6oz plain granary or wheatmeal flour
5ml/1 level teaspoon bicarbonate of soda
2.5ml/½ level teaspoon baking powder
2.5ml/½ level teaspoon cinnamon
1 egg, size 3
115ml/4floz skimmed milk
45ml/3 tablespoons unsweetened orange juice

Preheat the oven to 180°C/350°F/gas mark 4. Line a 15cm/6in square tin with grease-proof paper or non-stick baking paper and brush with oil. Place the butter or margarine and honey in a small pan and warm until the butter melts. Stir to mix and set aside. Finely grate the carrots and roughly chop the dates. Mix the flour with the bicarbonate of soda, baking powder and cinnamon. Beat the egg with the milk and orange juice until evenly blended. Add to the honey and butter mixture. Stir all the ingredients together until well mixed — do not over-beat. Pour into the tin and bake for 1 hour. Cool on a wire rack.

Makes 16 slices/ per slice	cals.	fat units	grams fibre
granary	115	1.5	1.6
wheatmeal	110	1.5	1.6

Old-fashioned Teabread

This teabread is best eaten after being stored in an airtight tin or wrapped in foil for two or three days. It will keep this way for up to a week and can also be frozen. You can use raisins instead of sultanas and currants if you wish, or you could use all sultanas or all currants. The values will remain the same.

115g/4oz sultanas
115g/4oz currants
150ml/¼ pint hot tea

30ml/2 level tablespoons runny honey
1 egg, size 3
45ml/3 level tablespoons orange marmalade
225g/8oz white or wheatmeal self-raising
*   flour*
1.25ml/¼ teaspoon oil

Place the sultanas and currants in a basin and pour over the tea. Stir in the honey. Cover and leave to soak overnight or for at least 6 hours. Preheat the oven to 180°C/350°F/gas mark 4. Line a 1kg/2lb loaf tin and brush with the oil. Lightly beat the egg and stir into the tea mixture with the marmalade. Stir in the flour and turn into the tin. Bake in the preheated oven for about 1 hour, or until a skewer inserted in the centre comes out clean.

Makes 12 slices/		fat	grams
per slice:	cals.	units	fibre
white flour	140	1	1.9
wheatmeal flour	140	1	2.7

Bran and Sultana Teabread

75g/3oz All-Bran
225g/8oz sultanas
115g/4oz caster sugar
275ml/½ pint skimmed milk
175g/6oz white self-raising flour
5ml/1 level teaspoon baking powder
1.25ml/¼ teaspoon oil

Place the All-Bran, sultanas, caster sugar and milk in a basin. Stir to mix, then cover and refrigerate for several hours or overnight. Sieve together the flour and baking powder and stir into the soaked mixture. Line a 1kg/2lb loaf tin and brush with the oil. Turn the loaf mixture into the tin and level the top. Bake at 190°C/375°F/gas mark 5 for about 1¼ hours, or until a skewer inserted in the centre comes out clean. Cool on a wire rack.

Makes 12 slices/160 calories
1 fat unit/3.7 grams fibre per slice

Variations:

Bran and Apricot Teabread
Replace the sultanas with 200g/7oz chopped dried apricots.
145 calories/1 fat unit
6.4 grams fibre per slice

Date and Walnut Bran Teabread
Replace the sultanas with 175g/6oz chopped, stoned dates and 50g/2oz chopped walnuts.
170 calories/1.5 fat units
4 grams fibre per slice

Sponges

The lowest-calorie way to make a sponge is by the whisking method. Sponges that require you to cream together butter and sugar are far higher in calories and fat.

Sponges are quite low in fibre unless you add a high-fibre filling.

Sponge Sandwich Cake

2.5ml/½ teaspoon oil
75g/3oz plain white flour + 10ml/2 level
*   teaspoons*
3 eggs, size 3
115g/4oz caster sugar
45ml/3 level tablespoons jam

Preheat the oven to 190°C/375°F, gas mark 5. Line the base of two 17.5cm/7in sandwich tins with greaseproof paper or non-stick baking paper. Brush the insides with oil and dust with 10ml/2 level teaspoons flour. Place the eggs and sugar in a large basin and stand it over a pan of simmering water. The bottom of the basin should not touch the water. Whisk until light and fluffy. When the whisk is lifted out it should leave an impression which holds for a few seconds. Remove the basin from the pan. Sieve the flour over the surface of the mixture and then fold in very gently. Turn into the prepared tins. Bake in the preheated oven for about 25 minutes, or until well-risen and springy. Cool on a wire rack. Sandwich together with the jam.

Makes 8 slices/145 calories
1.5 fat units/0.5 grams fibre per slice

Variation:

Chocolate Sandwich Cake
Replace 15g/½oz flour with 15g/½oz cocoa. Omit the jam and fill with 45ml/3 level tablespoons chocolate spread.
145 calories/1.5 fat units
0.4 grams fibre per slice

Lemon Cheese Swiss Roll

2.5ml/½ teaspoon oil
115g/4oz plain white flour + 5ml/1 level
*   teaspoon*
3 eggs, size 3
Grated rind 1 lemon
115g/4oz caster sugar + 15ml/1 level
*   tablespoon*
15ml/1 tablespoon hot water
225g/8oz carton skimmed milk soft cheese
*   or quark*
60ml/4 level tablespoons lemon curd

Preheat the oven to 210°C/425°F/gas mark 7. Line a swiss roll tin (22.5cm/9in by 30cm/12in) with greaseproof paper and brush with oil. Dust the surface with 5ml/1 level teaspoon flour. Place the eggs in a large bowl with the lemon rind and 115g/4oz caster sugar. Stand the basin over a pan of simmering water (the bottom of the basin should not touch the water) and whisk until thick and creamy. When lifted out, the whisk should leave an impression for a few seconds. Remove the basin from the pan. Sieve the flour over the surface and fold in gently with the water, using a metal spoon. Pour into the prepared tin and tilt until the mixture covers the whole surface. Bake in the preheated oven for 7-10 minutes on a shelf just above the centre, until risen and firm. Meanwhile, lay a sheet of greaseproof paper on a working surface and sprinkle with 15ml/1 level tablespoon caster sugar. As soon as the cake is cooked, turn it out onto the paper and trim off the crisp edges. Immediately roll up with the paper inside. Leave to cool on a wire rack. Unroll gently and spread with the skimmed milk soft cheese and lemon curd. Roll up again and place in an airtight tin. If possible, serve within 24 hours.

Makes 8 slices/195 calories
1.5 fat units/0.5 grams fibre per slice

Variations:

Orange Cheese Swiss Roll
Replace the lemon rind with the rind of 1 small orange. Replace the lemon curd with orange curd.
195 calories/1.5 fat units
0.5 grams fibre per slice

Chocolate Cherry Roll
Omit the lemon rind. Replace 15g/½oz flour with 15g/½oz cocoa. Omit the lemon curd from the filling. Fill with 60ml/4 level tablespoons black cherry jam and the cheese.
195 calories/1.5 fat units
0.4 grams fibre per slice

Jam Swiss Roll
Omit the lemon rind, lemon curd and cheese. Spread with 60ml/4 level tablespoons warm jam while still hot. Roll up, leaving paper outside, and leave to cool.
170 calories/1.5 fat units
0.5 grams fibre per slice

Strawberry Chocolate Roll
(see picture page 127)
This cake is best eaten on the day it is made and it is not suitable for freezing. If you make it ahead of the time when it is to be eaten, keep it in the refrigerator until you are ready.

2.5ml/½ teaspoon oil
3 eggs, size 2
60ml/4 level tablespoons Hermesetas
  Sprinkle Sweet
40g/1½oz white self-raising flour
30ml/2 level tablespoons drinking chocolate
  powder
15ml/1 level tablespoon cocoa
30ml/2 tablespoons hot water
225g/8oz skimmed milk soft cheese
60ml/4 level tablespoons strawberry jam
115g/4oz fresh strawberries

Preheat the oven to 200°C/400°F/gas mark 6. Line a swiss roll tin (20cm/8in by 28cm/11in) and brush with the oil. Separate the eggs and whisk the yolks with 45ml/3 level tablespoons Sprinkle Sweet until light and creamy. Sieve together the flour, drinking chocolate and cocoa. Fold into the yolk mixture with the water. Whisk the egg whites until stiff but not dry, then fold in gently. Immediately turn into the prepared tin and bake for 12-15 minutes or until the cake springs back when lightly pressed. Turn out onto a sheet of greaseproof paper and cut off the crisp edges. Roll up with the paper inside. Leave to cool. Unroll gently and spread with the skimmed milk soft cheese and jam. Slice half the strawberries and place on the jam. Roll up again and place on a serving dish. Slice one or two more strawberries and place on top. Arrange the rest around the edge. Sprinkle the remaining Sprinkle Sweet on top just before serving.

Makes 8 slices/120 calories
1.5 fat units/0.6 grams fibre per slice

Variation: Lemon and Pineapple Roll
(see picture page 123)
Add the grated rind of one lemon to the yolk and sugar. Omit the drinking chocolate and cocoa; replace with an extra 15g/½oz self-raising flour. Omit the skimmed milk, cheese and strawberries for the filling. Replace with 60ml/4 level tablespoons lemon curd and 4 rings pineapple canned in natural juice, drained and chopped.
95 calories/1 fat unit
0.5 grams fibre per slice

Apple Nut Sponge

Once you have filled this sponge with apple purée you will need to eat it within 2 hours. The unfilled sponges can be kept in an airtight tin for up to 24 hours, or frozen.

2.5ml/½ teaspoon oil
3 eggs, size 3
115g/4oz caster sugar
15ml/1 tablespoon coffee essence
75g/3oz plain white flour
50g/2oz ground hazelnuts
450g/1lb eating apples, preferably Coxes or
  Sturmer Pippins

Preheat the oven to 190°C/375°F/gas mark 5. Line the base of two 17.5cm/7in tins with greaseproof paper or non-stick baking paper. Brush the insides lightly with oil. Place the eggs and sugar in a basin standing over a pan of simmering water. Whisk until thick and light. When the mixture is ready, the whisk should leave a trail which lasts a few seconds. Whisk in the coffee essence. Remove from the pan. Sieve the flour over the surface, then fold in gently with the ground hazelnuts. Turn into the prepared tins and bake for about 25 minutes until well risen and springy. Cool on a wire rack. Meanwhile, peel, core and slice the apples. Place in a thick-based pan, cover and cook over a low heat until soft. Add a little water if necessary to prevent sticking but make sure that you do not make the mixture too wet. Mash with a fork and leave to cool. Sandwich the cakes together with the apple purée.

Makes 8 slices/175 calories
2.5 fat units/1.6 grams fibre per slice

Chocolate Pear Upside-down Cake
(see picture page 124)

125g/4¼oz butter or margarine
425g/15oz can pears in natural juice
3 glacé cherries
60ml/4 level tablespoons Hermesetas Sprinkle Sweet
3 eggs, size 2
115g/4oz white self-raising flour
25g/1oz drinking chocolate powder
30ml/2 tablespoons hot water

Preheat the oven to 180°C/350°F/gas mark 4. Grease a 20-23cm/8-9in tin with 7g/¼oz butter or margarine. Drain the pears and arrange in the tin, hollow sides down. Halve the cherries and slip one half in the hollow of each pear. Place the remaining cherry half in the centre of the tin. Cream together the remaining 115g/4oz butter or margarine and the Sprinkle Sweet. Beat in the eggs, one at a time, beating well between each addition and adding 30ml/1 rounded tablespoon flour with the last one. Fold in the remaining flour. Mix the drinking chocolate powder with the hot water and add to the mixture. Place in the tin and spread evenly over the pears, taking care not to disturb them. Bake for about 35 minutes, or until the sponge springs back when lightly pressed. Turn out onto a serving plate and serve warm or cold.

Makes 8 slices/235 calories
5.5 fat units/1.4 grams fibre per slice

Muffins and Buns

Bran and Raisin Muffins

These muffins are high in fibre and can be eaten as a cake or served topped with cottage cheese. A muffin topped with 50g/2oz cottage cheese with pineapple, for example, would come to 140 calories, so you could afford two of these for a light lunch.

20g/¾oz lard
50g/2oz bran
225ml/8floz skimmed milk
25g/1oz butter or margarine
25g/1oz caster sugar
1 egg, size 3
115g/4oz plain white flour
2.5ml/½ level teaspoon salt
15ml/3 level teaspoons baking powder
50g/2oz raisins

Grease 16 deep patty tins (6.5cm/2½in in diameter) really thoroughly with the lard. Preheat the oven to 190°C/375°F, gas mark 5. Place the bran and milk in a basin and leave to soak for 5 minutes. Melt the butter or margarine in a pan. Remove from the heat and stir in the sugar and the bran mixture. Lightly beat the egg and add. Sieve

Lemon and Pineapple Roll (recipe page 122)

123

together the flour, salt and baking powder. Add the raisins. Make a well in the centre and pour in the bran mixture. Mix together until evenly blended — stop as soon as you reach this point. Divide between the patty tins and bake for 20-25 minutes, until firm and brown on top. Cool on a wire rack.

Makes 16/85 calories
1.5 fat units/2.0 grams fibre per muffin

Spicy Currant Buns

For any yeast recipes you need to use a strong flour. This is sometimes labelled as being specifically suitable for bread making. These flours have a high gluten content which means that the dough becomes elastic when kneaded, and this is what gives buns and bread a good texture. It is best to eat these buns within 24 hours unless you freeze them. Serve them split and toasted if you wish.

Buns are drier than cakes and teabreads and you may find it necessary to spread them with a little low-fat spread. Count 15 calories/…fat units/0 grams fibre for every level teaspoon of low-fat spread you use.

200-225ml/7-8floz skimmed milk
25g/1oz caster sugar
10ml/2 level teaspoons dried yeast
115g/4oz strong plain white flour
225g/8oz strong plain wholemeal flour
5ml/1 level teaspoon salt
25g/1oz butter or margarine
5ml/1 level teaspoon ground mixed spice
115g/4oz currants
5ml/1 teaspoon oil

Chocolate Pear Upside-down Cake (recipe page 123) can be served warm as a delicious dessert or cold as a teatime cake. It is an American recipe traditionally made in a frying pan

Glaze:
10ml/2 teaspoons milk (full fat)
10ml/2 teaspoons caster sugar

Heat the milk to blood heat, then pour 150ml/¼ pint into a basin. Whisk in the sugar and the yeast. Sprinkle on 15ml/1 tablespoon flour and leave in a warm place until frothy. Mix the remaining flours together with salt and spice. Rub in the butter or margarine. Add the yeast liquid, extra milk and currants and mix to a fairly soft dough. Knead well for about 5 minutes, on a lightly floured surface. (This could be done in a food processor.) Place about a third of the oil in a large polythene bag and rub until the sides are well coated. Place the dough in the bag and leave in a warm place until doubled in size. Turn onto a floured board and knead for a further 2-3 minutes. Divide into 14 equal pieces and shape into rolls. Lightly grease one or two baking sheets with some of the oil. Arrange the buns on the sheets, placing them well apart. Either split open the polythene bag or oil a piece of cling film and use to loosely cover the buns. Preheat the oven to 220°C/425°F, gas mark 7. Leave the buns in a warm place until doubled in size. Uncover them and bake for about 15 minutes. While they are cooking, warm the milk for the glaze and dissolve the sugar in it. Place the cooked buns on a cooling rack and brush with the glaze. Leave to cool.

Makes 14/135 calories
1.5 fat units/2.3 grams fibre per bun

Scones and Cobblers

An ordinary plain scone bought from your local baker will cost about 210 calories and that's before you add any butter and jam

Apple and Blackberry Cobbler (recipe page 126) makes a change from ordinary fruit pie and is at least 200 calories per portion less than a slice of Apple and Blackberry Pie

topping. These scone recipes are lower in calories. The scone cobblers could be served as a dessert.

Slimmer's Scones

1.25ml/¼ teaspoon oil
225g/8oz plain flour (white or wheatmeal or wholemeal or granary) + 30ml/2 level tablespoons
20ml/4 level teaspoons baking powder
Pinch salt
25g/1oz butter or hard margarine
150ml/¼ pint skimmed milk
Liquid artificial sweetener equivalent to 25g/1oz sugar

Preheat the oven to 230°C/450°F/gas mark 8. Lightly grease a baking tray with the oil. If white flour is used, sieve 225g/8oz with the baking powder and salt. Mix 225g/8oz other flours with baking powder and salt. Rub in the butter or margarine. Reserve 15ml/1 tablespoon milk. Mix the remainder with the sweetener, and then add to the dry ingredients. Mix with a round bladed knife to make a fairly soft dough. Sprinkle the remaining flour on a working surface and then knead the dough on it very lightly. You should only knead with the fingertips, not knuckles, and stop as soon as the dough is smooth. Pat or roll out into a round, 1.2-1.9cm/½-¾in thick. Cut into 10 wedges. Alternatively, cut into 5cm/2in rounds with a cutter. Place on the baking sheet and brush the tops with the reserved milk. Bake for about 10 minutes until well risen and light brown. Cool. Eat warm or cold.

Makes 10 per scone	cals.	fat units	grams fibre
wholemeal flour	100	1	2.1
wheatmeal flour	100	1	1.6
granary flour	105	1	1.6
white flour	105	1	0.8

Variation:

Fruit Scone
Add 50g/2oz raisins or sultanas to the dry ingredients, before adding the milk. This will add 15 calories/0 fat units/0.4 grams fibre to each scone.

Apple and Blackberry Cobbler
(see picture page 125)

450g/1lb cooking apples, preferably Bramleys
225g/8oz blackberries, fresh or frozen
30ml/2 tablespoons water
Artificial sweetener (powdered or liquid) equivalent to 50g/2oz sugar
One quantity of scone dough (see above)

Peel, core and slice the apples. Place in a saucepan with the blackberries and water.

Cover the pan and cook the fruit over a low heat until tender. If necessary, add a little more water to prevent the fruit sticking. Drain off any liquid and mix with the sweetener. Pour back over the fruit and mix well. Turn into an ovenproof dish. Heat the oven to 210°C/425°F/gas mark 7. Make up the scone dough as directed. Roll out to 1.2cm/½in thick and cut into 5cm/2in rounds. Place in a slightly over-lapping circle over the edge of the fruit. Brush with milk. Bake in the oven for about 15 minutes or until the scones are well risen and golden-brown.

Serves 6/ per portion	cals.	fat units	grams fibre
wholemeal scones	170	1.5	7.5
wheatmeal scones	170	1.5	6.7
white scones	180	1.5	5.2
granary scones	180	1.5	6.7

Apple Scones

All scones are best eaten within 24 hours but they will freeze very well.

115g/4oz plain white flour + 15ml/1 level tablespoon
20ml/4 level teaspoons baking powder
1.25ml/¼ level teaspoon ground cinnamon
1.25ml/¼ level teaspoon ground mixed spice
Pinch salt
115g/4oz plain wholemeal flour
50g/2oz caster sugar
25g/1oz butter
225g/8oz cooking apples
115ml/4floz skimmed milk
1.25ml/¼ teaspoon oil

Preheat the oven to 220°C/425°F, gas mark 7. Sieve together 115g/4oz white flour, baking powder, cinnamon, mixed spice and salt. Stir in the wholemeal flour and sugar. Rub in the butter. Peel, core and grate the apple and then stir into the flour mixture with the milk to make a soft but not sticky dough. Roll out to a round, 2.5cm/½in thick and then cut into 8 wedges. Brush a baking sheet with the oil and arrange the scones on it. Bake in the preheated oven for 10-15 minutes or until well risen and golden-brown. Cool on a wire rack.

Makes 8/170 calories
1.5 fat units/2.3 grams fibre per scone.

Variation:
Apple and Ginger Scones
Replace the cinnamon and mixed spice with 2.5ml/½ level teaspoon ground ginger.
170 calories/1.5 fat units
2.3 grams fibre per scone.

Bread

A word of warning before you start baking bread — it is very much more temptingly

Strawberry Chocolate Roll (recipe page 122) makes a special cake when fresh strawberries are in season. It is only 120 calories per slice

delicious than manufactured breads. But here are a couple of recipes that you will not find in your local shop and which might be worth risking when you have enough calories to spare for a special treat.

High Fibre Bread

This recipe just makes a small loaf but if you did go mad and polish off the lot it would cost you 1,250 calories/9.5 fat units. Be careful what you top your bread slices with. You could use any of the sandwich fillings or toast toppings which are given in other chapters of this book.

15g/½oz fresh yeast or 10ml/2 level
    teaspoons dried yeast
275ml/½ pint tepid water
2.5ml/½ level teaspoon sugar
350g/12oz strong plain wholemeal flour
15g/½oz soya flour
5ml/1 level teaspoon salt
20g/¾oz bran
5ml/1 teaspoon oil

If using dried yeast, whisk it into the water with the sugar. Leave in a warm place until frothy — about 15 minutes. Blend the fresh yeast with the water, then stir in the sugar. Mix the wholemeal flour, soya flour, salt and bran in a large bowl. Stir in the bran. Make a well in the centre and pour in the yeast liquid and mix to a soft dough. Knead by hand for 10 minutes or in a food processor for the time suggested in the instruction book. Place a little of the oil in a large polythene bag and rub the sides until the inside is coated with oil. Place the dough in the bag and leave in a warm place until doubled in size — about 45 minutes. Remove

from the bag and knead for another 10 minutes. Preheat the oven to 230°C/450°F, gas mark 8. Grease a 1kg/2lb loaf tin or baking tray with the remaining oil. Either shape into a round loaf and place on a baking sheet or shape into an oblong and then fit into the loaf tin. Alternatively, shape into 12 rolls and place on a baking sheet. Cover loosely with the split open polythene bag or a piece of cling film and leave in a warm place until doubled in size again — about 30 minutes. Uncover and bake in the preheated oven. For the loaf, cook for 15 minutes and then reduce the temperature to 200°C/400°F/gas mark 6, and cook for another 15-20 minutes. When cooked, the loaf should sound hollow if tapped. For the rolls, cook for about 15 minutes only.

Makes 1 small loaf/55 calories
0.5 fat units/2.0 grams fibre per 25g/1oz slice

Sage Bread Rolls

Sage rolls are delicious served with curd cheese or ham. Freeze them individually so that you can take them from the freezer one at a time as you want to use them.

115g/4oz strong plain white flour
115g/4oz strong wholemeal plain flour
2.5ml/½ level teaspoon salt
5ml/1 level teaspoon celery seeds
2.5ml/½ level teaspoon ground allspice
10ml/2 level teaspoons dried sage
15g/½oz butter or margarine
7g/¼oz fresh yeast or 5ml/1 level teaspoon
    dried yeast
150ml/¼ pint skimmed milk
5ml/1 level teaspoon sugar
2.5ml/½ teaspoon oil

Warm the milk to blood heat, then stir in the sugar. Cream the fresh yeast with a little of the milk, then mix with the remaining milk; or whisk the dried yeast into the milk. Sprinkle on 15ml/1 tablespoon flour and leave until frothy. Meanwhile mix the rest of the flours with the salt, celery seeds, allspice and sage. Rub in the butter or margarine. Add the yeast mixture and beat to make a soft but not sticky dough. Knead for a few minutes. Place the oil in a polythene bag and rub until the insides of the bag are coated. Place the dough in the bag and leave in a warm place until doubled in size. Knock the dough down and knead again for a few minutes. Divide into 10 and shape into 10 rolls. Place well apart on a baking sheet and cover loosely with a damp cloth. Heat the oven to 220°C/425°F/gas mark 7. Leave the rolls in a warm place until doubled in size. Uncover the rolls and place in the oven. Cook for 10-15 minutes. Cool on a wire rack or eat warm.

Makes 10/95 calories
0.5 fat units/1.4 grams fibre per roll

Know your potatoes

At just 25 calories for 25g/1oz, potatoes are reasonably low in calories. But the spud is a rather weighty vegetable, which means that the medium 165g/5½oz one above costs 140 calories; the big 350g/12oz one 300 calories.

Two potato cakes make a low-calorie snack for just 145 calories. We made up 90ml/6 level tablespoons instant mash potato with 150ml/¼ pint water and 15ml/1 level tablespoon flour, then seasoned. We shaped the mixture into two cakes and baked for 20 minutes at 200°C/400°F/gas mark 6.

There are 105 calories in these two small new potatoes. And precisely the same number of calories in the little 15g/½oz knob of butter. Go very easy on butter and margarine additions to potato. The same amount of low-fat spread would cost half the calories.

Because it absorbs more fat in frying, this 25g/1oz portion of frozen crinkle-cut chips costs as many calories — 80 — as the 50g/2oz portion of thick cut chips. Calories per 25g/1oz for other chips are: thin cut 85; medium cut 70; chip-shop bought 65; oven chips 60.

This average 150g/5oz restaurant portion of sauté potatoes totals 200 calories, which makes it an expensive addition to a main course. If you must eat fried potato, though, sauté potatoes are half the calories of the crinkle-cut chips which are usually served in restaurants.

Roast potatoes vary in calorie value and the saving secret is to cut them in big chunks to put less surface in contact with fat. The halved 175g/6oz roasted potato above costs 240 calories. If you cut a same weight potato into four pieces before roasting, you could add 60 calories or more!

Light and airy instant mash fluffs up to give you the biggest potato helping at the lowest calorie cost. These two heaped tablespoons total a modest 115 calories. Like all potato, instant mash contains a useful amount of fibre — 5.1 grams for a 150g/5oz portion.

This 200g/7oz potato was baked in its jacket, then split in half. Each half was then topped with 15ml/1 level tablespoon piccalilli, 7g/¼oz Edam, sprinkled with paprika, then reheated in the oven until the cheese melted. Makes a very filling lunch for just 235 calories.

Entertaining

For a special dinner party, try Menu 1 on page 132: **1** *Salmon and Cottage Cheese Mousse (recipe page 61);* **2** *Blackcurrant Sorbet (recipe page 115);* **3** *a crisp green salad of lettuce, cucumber and watercress; and* **4** *Chicken Marengo (recipe page 132)*

Now you have got into a healthily low-fat way of eating it does not make sense to suddenly start pouring pints of cream into sauces or buttering up vegetables when you invite guests to join you for a meal. Many of your friends may be as weight-and-health-conscious as you are, but even if they are not they are unlikely to have any complaints about being served one of the delicious menus in this chapter. By all means, put butter and cream on the table so that anyone who wants can add them to their meal, but the new eating etiquette requires you to allow your guests a choice of whether they indulge or not.

Assuming that you do not entertain every other day of the week, these are occasions when you should not have to bother with counting every single calorie, fat unit or fibre gram. In the recipes that follow, we

have given you these values for your information, but whichever menu you choose you can relax in the knowledge that, while you may not actually lose weight on a day when you entertain, it is highly unlikely that you will gain.

Trying to be too virtuous when you are entertaining can end in disaster. Mrs Saintly Eater serves her guests all her favourite most fattening foods, then piles her plate with raw celery and carrot sticks. When friends ask why she is not sampling the pâté with buttered toast or the tempting game pie, she admits it is because she is on a diet. Faced with the prospect of dining with an unhappy martyr, friends will use the most persuasive arguments they can think of to get Mrs Saintly Eater to join them. So she gives in and has just the tiniest portion of everything. Later, alone in the kitchen, she is overcome with feelings of guilt and remorse, coupled with a resentment that everyone else is now feeling nicely full while she has only whetted her appetite for more. It is not surprising when Mrs Saintly Eater turns into Mrs Sinner and secretly scoops up any left-overs. Guilt and depression from binges such as this have heralded the end of many a dieting campaign.

So first rule for entertaining is serve something you can enjoy and indulge in without feeling guilty. Having a relaxed meal with friends can, according to some researchers, be a good way to cut calorie consumption. Chatting while you eat, unless you are rude enough to speak with your mouth full, should entail much less swallowing, and conviviality and human warmth brought to the dinner table means that all pleasure is not derived from the food alone. When you are eating on your own, play a record or the radio as you eat and this can help you relax and eat more slowly. But avoid eating while watching the television because if you do this you are more likely to eat 'mindlessly', getting little conscious pleasure from food and maybe absentmindedly eating extra.

In the following menus we have suggested a selection of vegetables to accompany your main course. If you wish to serve a different combination, by all means do so. We do not give quantities because these are foods which you can eat as much of as you wish. If the number of guests you are entertaining is different from the numbers we give, recipes can usually be adapted accordingly.

MENU 1

Serves 4

Salmon and Cottage Cheese Mousse
(recipe page 61: see picture page 130)

Chicken Marengo
(recipe below: see picture page 131)

Green Salad

Boiled New Potatoes
or Jacket Baked Potatoes

Blackcurrant Sorbet
(recipe page 115: see picture page 130)

Chicken Marengo

4 chicken leg joints, 225g/8oz each
227g/8oz can tomatoes
1 small onion
2 carrots
64g/2¼oz can tomato purée
1 chicken stock cube
425ml/¾ pint boiling water
15ml/1 level tablespoon cornflour

45ml/3 tablespoons dry or medium sherry
Salt and pepper
115g/4oz button mushrooms

Skin the chicken joints and set aside. Roughly chop the tomatoes and place in a saucepan with their juice. Finely chop the onion and carrots and add to the pan. Cover and simmer for 8 minutes. Stir in the tomato purée, stock cube and boiling water and simmer for another 10 minutes. Rub through a sieve and then return to a clean pan. Blend the cornflour with a little cold water until smooth. Stir into the sauce with the sherry. Bring to the boil, stirring all the time, and simmer for 2 minutes. Season with salt and pepper. Place the chicken joints in the pan and spoon over the sauce so that they are all completely coated. Cover the pan and bring back to simmering point. Simmer for 30 minutes. Add the mushrooms and simmer for a further 15 minutes, or until the chicken is tender. Arrange the chicken on a serving

dish and spoon the sauce over the top.

Serves 4/225 calories
2 fat units/1.9 grams fibre per portion

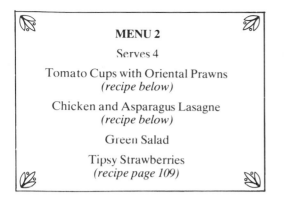

MENU 2

Serves 4

Tomato Cups with Oriental Prawns
(recipe below)

Chicken and Asparagus Lasagne
(recipe below)

Green Salad

Tipsy Strawberries
(recipe page 109)

Tomato Cups with Oriental Prawns

4 large tomatoes, 115g/4oz each
75g/3oz peeled prawns
2 rings pineapple, canned in natural juice,
  drained
4cm/1½in piece cucumber

30ml/2 level tablespoons low-calorie salad
  cream
Few lettuce leaves

Cut the tops off the tomatoes and carefully
scoop out the insides, using a grapefruit
spoon or small teaspoon. Turn upside-down
and leave to drain while you are preparing
the filling. The insides can be saved and
used in a casserole or they can be discarded.
Chop the pineapple and dice the cucumber.
Mix with the prawns and salad dressing.
Pile into the tomatoes and chill for at least
30 minutes. Shred the lettuce and arrange
on 4 individual plates or 1 large plate. Serve
the tomato cups on top.

Serves 4/65 calories
0.5 fat units/1.9 grams fibre per portion

*Pizza Alla Francesca (recipe page 140) is ideal for
a buffet party with a pizza theme (see Menu 10).
You can serve these pizzas whole, or cut them into
more manageable slices for your guests*

Chicken and Asparagus Lasagne

2 part-boned chicken breasts, 200g/7oz each
1 small onion
1 small carrot
1 chicken stock cube
1 bay leaf
1 bouquet garni
115g/4oz lasagne, preferably green
115g/4oz button mushrooms
340g/12oz can asparagus spears
35g/1¼oz skimmed milk powder
50g/2oz low-fat spread
50g/2oz flour
Salt and pepper
75g/3oz Lancashire cheese

Skin the chicken breasts, then place in a saucepan. Thickly slice the carrot and onion and add to the pan with the stock cube, bay leaf and bouquet garni. Add enough water to just cover the chicken and bring to the boil. Cover the pan and simmer gently for 25 minutes. While the chicken is cooking, boil the lasagne in plenty of salted water until *just* tender. Look at the packet for the exact time required but check 5 minutes before it is meant to be ready. Do not overcook as it will be cooked a little more in the sauce — it should still have a bite to it. Drain in a colander and rinse under the cold tap. Lay out on kitchen paper to dry. Slice the mushrooms and add to the chicken. Cook for another 10 minutes. Drain, and reserve the stock. Discard the onion, carrot, bay leaf and bouquet garni. Discard the bones from the chicken and chop the flesh into small pieces. Set the chicken and mushrooms aside. Drain the liquid from the asparagus into a measuring jug and make up to 575ml/1 pint with chicken stock. Place in a saucepan with the skimmed milk powder, low-fat spread and flour. Bring to the boil, whisking all the time, and then simmer for 2 minutes. Taste and season with salt and pepper. Stir in the chicken and mushrooms. Spread one-third of the sauce over the base of a fairly shallow ovenproof dish and cover with half of the lasagne. Spread on another third of the sauce and arrange half the asparagus on top. Cover with the remaining lasagne, followed by the sauce and asparagus. Crumble the cheese and sprinkle on top. Bake at 190°C/375°F/gas mark 5 for 30 minutes.

Serves 4/420 calories
5 fat units/3.0 grams fibre per portion

MENU 3

Serves 4

Marinaded Mushrooms
(recipe page 64: see picture page 57)

Fish in Piquant Apple and Caper Sauce
(recipe below: see picture page 135)

New Potatoes or Jacket Baked Potatoes

Peas, Carrots

Summer Pudding
(recipe page 110)

Fish in Piquant Apple and Caper Sauce

675g/1½lb halibut, cod or haddock fillets,
    fresh or frozen
60ml/4 tablespoons lemon juice
Salt and pepper
1 small cooking apple
200g/7oz natural low-fat yoghurt
75g/3oz soured cream
2 eggs, size 3
12.5ml/2½ level teaspoons capers
Grated rind of a lemon
30ml/2 level tablespoons chopped parsley
4 thin lemon slices

Defrost the fish if frozen. Preheat the oven to 170°C/325°F/gas mark 3. Place the fish in a single layer in a shallow ovenproof dish. Sprinkle on the lemon juice and season lightly with salt and pepper. Cover with a lid or foil and cook in the preheated oven for 15 minutes. Meanwhile, peel, core and finely dice the apple. Beat the yoghurt, soured cream and eggs together and then stir in the apple, all but four capers, the lemon rind and parsley. Season and then pour over the fish, taking care to cover it completely. Return to the oven and cook, uncovered, for a further 40 minutes. Garnish with the reserved lemon slices and capers.

Serves 4/350 calories
4 fat units/0.5 grams fibre per portion

MENU 4

Serves 4

Melon Cocktail
(recipe below)

Sweetcorn and Mushroom Stuffed Plaice
(recipe below: see picture page 135)

French Beans, Carrots

Coffee Hazelnut Cream
(recipe page 113)

Melon Cocktail

450g/1lb honeydew or yellow melon
2 medium oranges
4 tomatoes
Few lettuce leaves
60ml/4 level tablespoons low-calorie salad
  cream
60ml/4 level tablespoons low-fat natural
  yoghurt
2.5ml/½ teaspoon lemon juice
1.25ml/¼ level teaspoon caster sugar
Paprika

Remove the seeds from the melon, and then either scoop out the flesh with a melon baller or discard the skin and cube the flesh. Cut away the rind and pith from the orange using a small sharp knife, then carefully cut out the segments. Peel and quarter the tomatoes. Mix together the melon, orange segments and tomato. Chill. Shred the lettuce and divide between 4 dishes. Place the melon mixture on top. Mix together the low-calorie salad cream, yoghurt, lemon juice and sugar. Pour over the cocktails and sprinkle with a little paprika.

Serves 4/90 calories
1 fat unit/3.4 grams fibre per portion

Sweetcorn and Mushroom Stuffed Plaice

8 small plaice fillets or similar flat white fish,
  fresh or frozen, about 115g/4oz each
115g/4oz mushrooms
2 × 198g/7oz cans sweetcorn with pepper
30ml/2 level tablespoons tomato purée

225ml/8floz dry or medium white wine
10ml/2 level teaspoons cornflour
Salt and pepper
Sprigs of parsley

Preheat the oven to 180°C/350°F/gas mark 4. If the plaice is frozen, defrost it at room temperature for 2-3 hours. Lay the fillets skin-side down on a board and make a slit down the centre of the flesh, taking care not to cut through the skin on the underside. With the point of a sharp knife, ease the flesh away from the skin on either side of the slit to make a small pocket for the stuffing. Finely chop the mushrooms and mix with half the sweetcorn and 10ml/2 level teaspoons tomato purée. Divide this stuffing into 8 equal portions and fill into the plaice 'pockets'. Arrange the fish in a single layer in a shallow ovenproof dish. Season with salt and pepper and pour on the wine. Cover the dish with a lid or foil and cook in the preheated oven for 20 minutes. Pour the cooking liquid into a small saucepan and keep the plaice warm. Blend the cornflour with a little cold water. Add to the liquid with the remaining tomato purée. Bring to the boil, stirring. Simmer 1-2 minutes. Garnish.

In the foreground are five ideas for entertaining using fish. Reading clockwise: Sweetcorn and Mushroom Stuffed Plaice (recipe page 135); Fish in Piquant Apple and Caper Sauce (recipe page 134); Florida Trout (recipe page 136); and an unusual first course of Oriental Smoked Mackerel Salad (recipe page 137)

the plaice with the remaining sweetcorn and parsley sprigs and serve the sauce separately.

Serves 4/340 calories
2.5 fat units/6.3 grams fibre per portion

MENU 5

Serves 4

Watercress Soup
(recipe page 57: see picture page 156)

Florida Trout
(recipe below: see picture page 135)

New Potatoes, Peas, Broccoli

Rosy Apples
(recipe below: see picture page 143)

Sponge Fingers

Florida Trout

4 trout, fresh or frozen, 200g/7oz each
425ml/¾ pint water
60ml/4 tablespoons lemon juice
Salt and pepper
8 sprigs parsley
20ml/4 level teaspoons cornflour
60ml/4 tablespoons frozen concentrated orange juice, thawed
30ml/2 level tablespoons flaked almonds
1 small orange

If frozen trout are used, defrost them at room temperature for 2-3 hours. Put the water, lemon juice, salt and pepper and 4 sprigs parsley in a large shallow saucepan or a deep frying pan. Bring to the boil. Put the trout into the boiling liquid. Reduce the heat until the liquid is *just* bubbling and simmer gently for 10 minutes. Carefully lift out the trout and keep warm on a serving dish. Strain the cooking liquid and reserve 225ml/8floz. Blend the cornflour and concentrated orange juice until smooth. Stir in the reserved stock. Place in a saucepan stirring all the time. Simmer for 2 minutes and then pour over the trout. Slice the orange and use to garnish the trout with the remaining parsley and almonds.

Serves 4/225 calories
2.5 fat units/0.5 grams fibre per portion

Rosy Apples

675g/1½lb cooking apples, preferably Bramleys
150ml/¼ pint undiluted blackcurrant cordial
15g/½oz powdered gelatine
50g/2oz skimmed milk powder
150g/5oz natural low-fat yoghurt

Peel, core and slice the apples, then place in a saucepan with the blackcurrant cordial. Cover and cook gently until soft. Purée in a liquidiser or food processor until smooth, or rub through a sieve. Place 45ml/3 tablespoons cold water in a small basin or cup and sprinkle on the gelatine. Leave to soak for 5 minutes, then stand the basin or cup in a pan containing a little simmering water. Leave until dissolved. Pour in a steady stream into the apple purée, stirring all the time. Leave to cool. Blend the skimmed milk powder with 275ml/½ pint cold water, then stir into the apple purée. Chill until on the point of setting. Divide between 4 glasses and swirl the yoghurt on top. Chill thoroughly until set.

Serves 4/180 calories
0 fat units/2.6 grams fibre per portion

MENU 6

Serves 4

Melon and Ham Gondola
(recipe page 62: see picture page 63)

Beef Stroganoff
(recipe below)

Noodles or Boiled Rice

Green Salad

Chocolate Liqueur Mousse
(recipe below)

Beef Stroganoff

450g/1lb fillet of beef
1 medium onion
115g/4oz small button mushrooms
10ml/2 teaspoons oil
25g/1oz butter
One third beef stock cube
150ml/¼ pint boiling water
5ml/1 level teaspoon tomato purée
90ml/6 level tablespoons soured cream
Salt and pepper

Discard all visible fat from the beef and then cut the lean into strips about the size of your little finger. Set aside. Finely slice the onion and slice the mushrooms. Heat half of the oil and half of the butter in a non-stick frying pan. Add the onion and cook over a low heat, stirring frequently, until soft and golden. Stir in the mushrooms. Dissolve the stock cube in the water. Stir in the tomato purée, then add to the pan. Boil rapidly until the liquid is reduced to about 60ml/4 tablespoons. Turn into a bowl and set aside. Take care to scrape up any sediment from the pan. Wash and dry the pan. Heat the remaining oil and butter in the pan, then add the meat. It should all fit in the pan easily in a single layer. If necessary, cook it in two batches. Cook over a fairly high heat until the outsides are browned but the insides of the strips are still pink — about 3 minutes on each side. Shake and toss the pan frequently as the meat cooks. Add the vegetable mixture and heat through. Add the soured cream and season. Heat through but do not allow to boil. Serve immediately.

Serves 4/275 calories
8.5 fat units/1.0 grams fibre per portion

Chocolate Liqueur Mousse

100g/3½oz plain dessert chocolate
3 eggs, size 3
10ml/2 teaspoons coffee essence, eg. Camp
20ml/4 teaspoons coffee liqueur,
*   eg. Tia Maria*
15ml/1 level tablespoon flaked almonds

Place the chocolate in a basin, then stand it over a pan of gently simmering water. The bottom of the basin should not touch the water. Take care that no water comes in contact with the chocolate. As soon as it is melted, remove from the heat. Immediately separate the eggs, then add the yolks to the chocolate mixture, one at a time. Stir well with each addition. Add the coffee essence and liqueur. Whisk the whites until stiff but not dry, then fold in gently. Divide between 4 serving dishes and chill. To decorate, toast the almonds until golden-brown, then leave to cool. Sprinkle on top of the mousses just before serving.

Serves 4/220 calories
3 fat units/0.2 grams fibre per portion

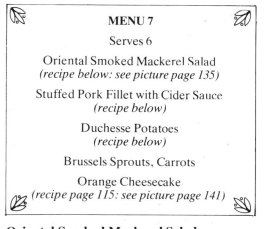

MENU 7

Serves 6

Oriental Smoked Mackerel Salad
(recipe below: see picture page 135)

Stuffed Pork Fillet with Cider Sauce
(recipe below)

Duchesse Potatoes
(recipe below)

Brussels Sprouts, Carrots

Orange Cheesecake
(recipe page 115: see picture page 141)

Oriental Smoked Mackerel Salad

350g/12oz smoked mackerel fillet
6 spring onions/scallions
115g/4oz button mushrooms
175g/6oz fresh beansprouts
45ml/3 tablespoons lemon juice
15ml/1 tablespoon Worcestershire sauce
5ml/1 teaspoon vinegar
5ml/1 teaspoon salad oil
Salt and pepper
½ bunch watercress

Discard the skin from the smoked mackerel and divide the flesh into large flakes. Discard the roots and tough green leaves from the spring onions, then slice the bulbs. Slice the mushrooms. Mix together the smoked mackerel, spring onions, mushrooms and beansprouts. Place the lemon juice, Worcestershire sauce, vinegar and salad oil in a screwtop jar. Season with salt and pepper, then shake well. Pour over the salad and toss well. Leave to stand in a cool place for half an hour. Divide the watercress into small sprigs. Just before serving, add to the salad and toss well.

Serves 6/165 calories
5.5 fat units/1.2 grams fibre per portion

Stuffed Pork Fillet with Cider Sauce

675g/1½lb whole pork tenderloin fillets
*   (3 small or 2 large fillets)*
25g/1oz toasted hazelnuts
1 medium eating apple
75g/3oz fresh wholemeal breadcrumbs
5ml/1 level teaspoon dried sage
30ml/2 level tablespoons sultanas
45ml/3 tablespoons unsweetened apple or
*   orange juice*
275ml/½ pint dry cider
15ml/1 level tablespoon cornflour

Trim any fat or sinew from the pork fillets. Cut them lengthways through the middle, almost all the way through, and open out like a book. Lay between double layers of greaseproof paper and beat out until flat, using a rolling pin or the base of a heavy saucepan to flatten them. You will need 3 pieces of about the same size, so if you have bought 2 large fillets cut a third off each. This broken layer can go in the middle. Roughly chop the hazelnuts. Peel, core and grate the apple. Mix together the hazelnuts, apple, breadcrumbs, sage, sultanas and fruit juice. Season with salt and pepper. Spread half of the stuffing over the middle of one whole piece of fillet. Cover with another piece (or 2 half pieces) and spread the remaining stuffing on top. Cover with the remaining piece of pork and tuck in the sides and ends to make a meat parcel. Tie in several places with string. Place in a roasting tin and pour over the cider. Cover loosely with foil and cook at 180°C/350°F/gas mark 4 for 1 hour. Remove the foil and cook for another 30 minutes. Carefully lift the pork out onto a serving dish and remove the string. Pour the cidery juices into a small pan. Blend the cornflour with a little cold water until smooth, then stir into the cider. Bring to the boil, stirring all the time, and simmer for 1-2 minutes. Pour a little sauce over the top of the pork and serve the rest separately.

Serves 6/260 calories
6 fat units/2.1 grams fibre per portion

Coq au Vin

1 medium onion
1 large carrot
1 clove garlic

275ml/½ pint dry red wine
2 cloves
1 bouquet garni
Salt and pepper
4 chicken leg joints, 225g/8oz each
75g/3oz streaky bacon rashers
115g/4oz button onions
115g/4oz button mushrooms
30ml/2 tablespoons brandy
275ml/½ pint water
1 chicken stock cube
15ml/1 level tablespoon cornflour
15ml/1 level tablespoon chopped parsley

Coarsely chop the onion and thickly slice the carrot. Crush the garlic. Stand a large polythene bag in a bowl for support and in it place the onion, carrot, garlic, red wine, cloves and bouquet garni. Season with pepper (do not add any salt at this stage).

Wipe the chicken joints and discard any pieces of fat; (remove the skin at this stage if you wish). Place in the marinade and turn so that they are completely coated. Cover the bowl or tie the ends of the bag. Leave in a cool place for at least 2 hours (they could be left overnight). Turn in the marinade occasionally. Remove the rind from the bacon rashers, then grill them until crisp. Cut into small pieces and place in the base of an ovenproof or flameproof dish. Peel the onions and wash the mushrooms. Remove the chicken joints from the marinade and place them in the casserole. Warm the brandy in a ladle, set it alight and pour it flaming over the chicken joints. When the flames have died down, add the marinade, onions and mushrooms, water

Coq au Vin is a traditional French dish of tasty chicken cooked in red wine. To reduce the calorie count, remove the chicken skin before cooking as indicated in the recipe

and crumbled stock cube. Season with salt and pepper: only use a little pepper as you have already added some to the marinade. Cover with a lid. If using a flameproof casserole, bring to the boil and simmer very gently for 45 minutes-1 hour, or until the chicken is tender. If using an ovenproof casserole dish, cook in the oven at 180°C/350°F/gas mark 4 for the same time. Lift out the chicken, mushrooms, onions and bacon and arrange them on a warm serving dish. Cover and keep warm. Strain the liquid into a saucepan and boil rapidly to reduce by half. Blend the cornflour with a little cold water, then stir into the liquid. Simmer, for 1-2 minutes. Pour the sauce over the chicken and sprinkle with parsley.

Serves 4/ per portion:	cals.	fat units	grams fibre
with chicken skin	550	7	1.2
without skin	305	4	1.2

Duchesse Potatoes

1kg/2lbs potatoes, weighed peeled
Salt and pepper
Pinch ground nutmeg
1 egg, size 3
1 egg yolk, size 3
1.25ml/¼ teaspoon oil

Boil the potatoes in salted water until tender. Drain well, then return to the pan and stand over a low heat for a few seconds to drive off any excess moisture. Remove from the heat and beat with an electric mixer to mash. If no electric mixer is available, use a wooden spoon. Season with salt, pepper and nutmeg. Beat the whole egg and yolk together, then beat into the potatoes. They should be very smooth and free from lumps. If an electric mixer is used, this is usually easy. If a wooden spoon is used and some lumps remain, press them through a sieve. Lightly grease a baking sheet with the oil, then pipe the potato onto it to make 12 pyramids. Bake at 200°C/400°F/gas mark 6 for about 15 minutes.

Serves 4-6/80 calories
0.5 fat unit/1.6 grams fibre per whirl

MENU 9

Serves 4

Cucumber Cups with Prawns
(recipe page 60: see picture page 59)

Beef in Red Wine
(recipe below)

Duchesse Potatoes
(recipe above)
or New Potatoes

Peas

Ice-cream

Beef in Red Wine

575g/1¼ lb topside of beef or lean, good
quality braising steak
1 medium onion
1 medium carrot
275ml/½ pint dry red wine
Salt and pepper
1 clove garlic
115g/4oz lean ham or bacon steak
½ beef stock cube
5ml/1 level teaspoon tomato purée
115ml/4floz boiling water
1 bay leaf
1 bouquet garni
115g/4oz button onions
115g/4oz button mushrooms
15ml/1 level tablespoon cornflour

Discard all visible fat from the beef and cut
into large cubes. Place in a bowl or a plastic
bag standing in a bowl for support. Thickly
slice the onion and carrot and add to the
bowl with the wine. Season with salt and
pepper and cover the bowl or tie the end of
the bag. Leave to marinade in a cool place
for at least 3 hours. It could be left in the
refrigerator overnight. Lift out the meat
and place in a casserole dish. Strain the
marinade over the meat. Crush the garlic
and add. Discard all visible fat from the
ham or bacon and cut the lean into small
cubes. Add to the beef with the bay leaf and
bouquet garni. Dissolve the stock cube and
tomato purée in the boiling water. Pour
over the meat and cover with a lid. Cook in
the oven at 150°C/300°F/gas mark 2 for 2
hours. Peel the button onions and wipe the
mushrooms. Add to the casserole and cook
for a further half hour. Blend the cornflour
with a little cold water until smooth. Stir
into the casserole and return to the oven for
another half an hour. Discard the bay leaf
and bouquet garni before serving.

Serves 4/280 calories
3.5 fat units/1.2 grams fibre per portion

MENU 10

Serves 12

Prawn Puffs
(recipe below: see picture page 142)

French Bread or French Toast

Pizza Francesca
(recipe below: see picture page 133)

Seafood Pizzas
(recipe below)

Party Coleslaw
(recipe below)

Pears in Wine
(recipe below)

Prawn Puffs

105g/3¾oz plain white flour (strong flour
for preference)
215ml/7½ floz water
75g/3oz low-fat spread
3 eggs, size 3
450g/1lb skimmed milk soft cheese
30ml/2 level tablespoons natural low-fat
yoghurt
225g/8oz peeled prawns
Salt and pepper
Paprika
½ cucumber
8 whole prawns in shells

First make the pastry. Preheat the oven to
220°C/425°F, gas mark 7. Sieve the flour.
Place the low-fat spread and water in a
saucepan. Bring to the boil over a moderate
heat. As soon as the low-fat spread melts
and the water boils, remove from the heat
and tip all the flour in at once. Beat with a
wooden spoon until the mixture leaves the
sides of the pan. Cool slightly. Lightly beat
the eggs together, then beat into the pan a
little at a time. If you have an electric hand
mixer use this, if not use a wooden spoon.
Dampen 2 baking sheets. Pipe or spoon the
mixture out to make 16 small puffs. Bake
for 15 minutes. Reduce the heat to 190°C/
375°F/gas mark 5 and cook for a further
10-15 minutes until the puffs are crisp and
golden-brown. Remove from the oven and
make a slit in the side of each to allow the
steam to escape. Cool on a wire rack. Mix
the skimmed milk soft cheese with the
yoghurt, then stir in the prawns. Season
with salt, pepper and a pinch of paprika.
Spoon into the choux puffs and pile up on a
plate. Garnish with slices of cucumber and
whole prawns.

Makes 16 puffs/100 calories
1 fat unit/0.2 grams fibre per puff

Pizza Alla Francesca

Pizza bases:
2.5ml/½ level teaspoon sugar
150ml/¼ pint tepid water
7g/¼oz fresh yeast or 5ml/1 level
teaspoon dried yeast
225g/8oz strong, plain flour
5ml/1 level teaspoon salt
7g/¼oz butter
5ml/1 teaspoon oil
Topping:
675g/24oz canned tomatoes
1 clove garlic
15ml/1 level tablespoon dried onion flakes
7.5ml/1½ level teaspoons dried oregano or
mixed herbs
6 processed Cheddar cheese slices

115g/4oz button mushrooms
50g/2oz anchovy fillets
50g/2oz black olives

Stir the sugar into the water. Blend the fresh yeast with the water or whisk the dried yeast into the water. In either case, sprinkle on 15ml/1 level tablespoon flour and leave in a warm place until frothy — about 10 minutes. Mix the flour and salt in a bowl and rub in the butter. Add the yeast liquid and mix to a firm dough that leaves the bowl clean. Remove the dough from the bowl and knead on a lightly floured surface until smooth and elastic — about 5 to 10 minutes. The kneading can be done in a food processor, in which case follow the manufacturer's instructions. Place half the oil in a large polythene bag and rub until the insides are completely coated in oil. Place the dough in the bag and leave in a warm place until doubled in size — about 45 minutes. While the dough is proving, prepare the topping. Place the tomatoes in a pan with their juice and mash them with a fork. Crush the garlic and add to the tomatoes with the onion flakes and oregano or mixed herbs. Bring to the boil and simmer until the sauce is thick and the excess liquid has evaporated — about 10 minutes. Leave

to cool slightly. Turn the risen dough out onto a board and knead again to knock out the air. Divide into 6 equal pieces and roll or press out to make 15cm/6in circles. Lightly grease 3 medium or 2 large baking trays with a little of the oil. Place the dough on the tins and place a processed cheese slice on each round. Slice the mushrooms and place on top. Cover with the tomato sauce. Rinse the anchovies in water and then pat dry with kitchen paper. Divide each fillet in half lengthwise and arrange on the pizzas in a lattice pattern. Garnish with the olives. Heat the oven to 220°C/425°F/gas mark 7 and leave to heat up for 10 minutes while the pizzas prove again. Cook for 15 minutes until the dough is cooked.

Serves 6/		fat	grams
per portion:	cals.	units	fibre
white flour	250	3.5	3.2
wheatmeal flour	245	3.5	4.6
granary flour	250	3.5	4.6
wholemeal flour	240	3.5	5.4

Orange Cheesecake (recipe page 115) is served with a colourful garnish of sliced kiwi fruits. If these are unavailable, however, you can use black grapes instead

141

Seafood Pizzas

Pizza base:
2.5ml/½ level teaspoon sugar
150ml/¼ pint tepid water
7g/¼oz fresh yeast or 5ml/1 level teaspoon
dried yeast
225g/8oz strong, plain flour
5ml/1 level teaspoon salt
7g/¼oz butter
5ml/1 teaspoon oil
Topping:
30ml/2 level tablespoons tomato ketchup
2 spring onions/scallions
175g/6oz tomatoes
2.5ml/½ level teaspoon dried oregano or
mixed herbs
100g/3½oz can tuna in brine
250g/9oz can mussels in brine
115g/4oz peeled prawns
75g/3oz Mozzarella cheese

Make the pizza bases as instructed for Pizza Francesca. Spread with tomato ketchup. Chop the bulbs of the spring onions and scatter on top. Slice the tomatoes and arrange on the bases. Sprinkle with herbs. Drain and flake the tuna. Drain the mussels. Place the tuna, prawns and mussels on the bases. Thinly slice the cheese and arrange on top. Heat the oven to 220°C/425°F/gas mark 7 while the pizzas are proving for 10 minutes.

Prawn Puffs (recipe page 140) are filled with a mixture of skimmed milk cheese, yoghurt and prawns to make a low-calorie buffet savoury

Cook the pizzas in the oven for 15 minutes until the dough is cooked.

Serves 6/ per portion:	cals.	fat units	grams fibre
white flour	270	2.5	1.5
wheatmeal flour	260	2.5	3.2
wholemeal flour	255	2.5	4.0

Party Coleslaw

675g/1½lb white cabbage
225g/8oz carrots
4 sticks celery
6 spring onions/scallions
298g/10½oz can mandarins in natural juice
75g/3oz seedless raisins
50g/2oz roasted cashew nuts
275g/10oz natural low-fat yoghurt
150ml/¼ pint low-calorie salad cream
Salt and pepper

Discard the tough stem and any damaged leaves from the cabbage, then shred the remainder. Place in a large bowl. Peel and grate the carrots. Finely slice the celery. Discard the tough green leaves and roots of the spring onions. Slice the remaining bulbs very finely. Drain the mandarins and add to

Farmer's Pancakes (recipe page 172) is suitable for entertaining. Rosy Apples (recipe page 136) makes an attractive dessert

2 strips lemon rind
1 small piece stick cinnamon
12 medium firm pears
25ml/5 level teaspoons arrowroot
12 small pieces angelica

Place the red wine and 115ml/4floz water in one wide-based pan with the white wine and 115ml/4floz water in another wide-based pan. Add half the sugar and a strip of lemon rind to each pan. Heat slowly, stirring frequently until the sugar is dissolved. Simmer for 2 minutes. Add the cinnamon to the red wine pan. Peel the pears but leave the stems on. Remove the 'eye' at the base. Place half the pears in a single layer in one pan and baste well with the wine. Repeat with the remaining pears and the other pan. Cover the pans and simmer very gently for 30 minutes. Turn and baste the pears occasionally while cooking. Lift out carefully and arrange on a serving dish. Arrange the pears so that the colours alternate. Discard the lemon rind and cinnamon. Blend half the arrowroot with a little cold water until smooth. Stir into one pan and then bring to the boil, stirring all the time. Simmer for 1-2 minutes. Repeat with the remaining arrowroot in the other pan. Leave the pears and sauces to cool. Decorate each pear with an angelica leaf. Serve the sauces separately.

Serves 12/165 calories
1 fat unit/2.3 grams fibre per portion

the cabbage with the carrot, celery, spring onions, raisins and cashews. Mix the yoghurt with the low-calorie salad cream and season. Stir into the coleslaw.

Serves 12/105 calories
1.5 fat units/3.6 grams fibre per portion

Pears in Wine

225ml/8floz medium or dry red wine
225ml/8floz white wine (Hock or Moselle or Riesling)
225ml/8floz water
275g/10oz sugar

There is no doubt that, on health grounds, too much sugar is bad. And one surefire way of zooming up your calorie count is consuming lots of sugary drinks or heaping spoonfuls of the stuff into cups of tea or coffee. Two heaped teaspoons would cost around 100 calories and that could easily add up to over 3,500 calories in a week if you drink five cuppas a day. It is virtually impossible to avoid refined sugar altogether as it is added to many commercially prepared foods, such as canned vegetables and cereals. But what turns sugar into a colossally high-calorie enemy is any get-together with fat. Once teamed with fat — in chocolates, toffees and cakes — sugar becomes a diet-wrecking monster.

1 *The sugar cubes by each of these items above represent the amount of sugar they contain. Muesli often has 55 calories' worth sugar in a 50g/2oz bowlful. The muesli helping above totals 210 calories. Rhubarb is a very low-calorie fruit — 10 calories' worth in the dish shown; but stewed with sugar your helping would soar to 145 calories.*
2 *Some sugar sweetshop buys are more fattening than others. There's the same 25g/1oz sugar in two tubes of fruit gums and the seven squares of chocolate. But the fatless fruit gums cost 110 calories. The chocolate, which has sugar and fat, costs 265 calories.*
3 *Sugary drinks, such as the cola above, could well contain over 25g/1oz sugar per can. An ordinary cola will cost about 140 calories, whereas a low-calorie version has just 5*

144

4 Sugar is added to many savoury foods; but there is no need to get neurotic about label-checking. This helping of baked beans has nearly 15g/½oz sugar but its nutritional content still gives good value for 160 calories a 225g/7.9oz can.

5 Both the slices of sponge cake contain 25g/1oz sugar in the sponge and jam filling, but the Victoria sponge slice is 305 calories while the fat-free whisked sponge is only 185 calories.

6 Virtually all the calories in an apple come from fructose — a natural sugar which, because it is combined with natural fibre and no-calorie water, is the healthiest way to satisfy a sweet tooth

145

A bowl of Cider Punch (recipe page 150) always goes down well at parties

Drinks

Order a drop of the hard stuff in a pub and you can depend on very strict portion control. A standard tot of spirits is normally one sixth gill in England and Wales and one fifth gill (or 1 floz) in Scotland. If either, surveyed with a sober eye, strikes you as a distinctly mean measure, it could be that you are carelessly pouring 'doubles' at home and counting only 'single' calories. Many a diet has gone west this way. The differing shapes of glasses can also make more look less — even, if you are lucky, vice versa.

To make a slimming campaign a success, you cannot afford guesswork. Measures can be bought from large department stores or you can use a fluid ounce measure. Spirits go far further, of course, if mixed, but steer clear of mixers that do not have a low-calorie label. They can be over 100 calories more than low-calorie versions.

Measure for measure, beer is lower in calories than wines or spirits; but beer, lagers, shandies and ciders are normally drunk in much larger quantities. Avoid strong beers and ciders, though, as these are higher in calories.

For a festive treat a liqueur can give you good value for the calories it costs. As most liqueurs are traditionally served from tiny glasses, even the minimum pub measure tends to last for quite some time. Just one glass savoured slowly can be very satisfying. It may even pay you to miss a stodgy dessert at a dinner and treat yourself to, say, a Tia Maria with your coffee.

If you are going to a party and are not sure what drink will be available, here are some tips to help you keep your calorie consumption down. Just plain thirsty when you arrive? Then start off by having a low-calorie mixer, if available, or even discreetly grab a glass of water. The point is do not quench your thirst expensively. When you are slimming keep calorie-laden drinks for savouring, not swallowing by the bucketful. If you cannot spot any low-calorie mixers, the next best thing would probably be a squash with soda or water. Make up your mind before you go to a party how many calories you can really afford to spend on drinks. When you near your limit, do not hang on to an empty glass, mutely inviting refills. Keep it brimming with low-calorie tonic and a slice of lemon and if out of a mistaken sense of generosity your host or hostess insists on ten-minute top-ups, sip away cautiously as if your drink is practically pure gin.

When you are entertaining at home, try some of the drinks given in this chapter and you can be sure exactly how many calories you are consuming.

Although many people are aware that alcohol needs to be limited on a diet, it is surprising how easily calories in other sorts of drinks are sometimes forgotten. A half pint of whole milk a day in excess of the food you need to maintain your weight could add up to a weight increase of 1st 4lb by the end of a year. Or if you are keeping to a strict dieting allowance and not counting in your milk calories it could be enough to prevent you losing a pound. Include all drinks calories in your allowance — you will find a chart at the back of this book.

Swapping to skimmed milk can cut your milk calories by half. If you find the taste of skimmed milk a little hard to swallow at first, try semi-skimmed milk initially. Eventually you will probably find that full cream milk loses its appeal. Using sugar in drinks is one of the easiest ways to boost your calorie total. If you usually drink six cups of tea or coffee a day and add two heaped teaspoons of sugar to each, that could add up to 4st 8lb more by the end of the year if you are already eating the correct number of calories.

Drinks do not satisfy in the same way as food and they slip down without giving any chewing satisfaction, either. It is not necessary to control your intake of water, black unsugared coffee or tea, however, as these are all calorie-free. You can also drink lots of low-calorie mixers and squashes as these are usually very low in calories — check the labels, for they vary a bit from manufacturer to manufacturer.

The recipes that follow are for some special slimmer's cocktails and hot drinks. There are fruity drinks, mulled wine, milk shakes and hot chocolate. Enjoy them as a treat, but remember to count them into your calorie allowance.

Non-alcoholic soft drinks

On a hot day you can consume a lot of unwanted calories without really realising you are doing so. Most ordinary soft drinks contain a lot of sugar and one long glassful could cost as much as 150 calories. Try one of these delicious cocktails instead.

Cola Float

If you are a cola fan, always keep a plentiful supply of the low-calorie type in the house. A Coca Cola costs 130 calories for a 330ml/ 11.6floz can. Pepsi Cola costs 140 calories for a can that is about half a fluid ounce more. Both do diet versions for under 5 calories a can.

Ice
1 can Diet Cola, chilled
25g/1oz vanilla ice-cream
Ice

Place some ice in a glass and pour in the Cola. Float the ice-cream on top.

Serves 1/50 calories
1 fat unit/0 grams fibre

Banana Milkshake

You will need to make this satisfying drink in two portions but it is one your family would probably be only too pleased to share with you.

1 medium banana
175ml/6floz skimmed milk, chilled
5ml/1 level teaspoon honey
2 ice cubes

Cut the banana into four pieces and place in a blender or food processor with the milk, honey and ice cubes. Blend until smooth and serve.

Serves 2/80 calories
0 fat units/1.7 grams fibre per drink

Raspberry Milkshake
(see picture page 157)

This creamy milkshake makes a super sweet treat and tastes much nicer than any synthetic milk shake mixture. For the same calorie count you could use strawberries and strawberry ice-cream.

150ml/¼ pint cold water
25g/1oz raspberries, fresh or frozen
45ml/3 level tablespoons skimmed milk
  powder
25g/1oz raspberry ripple or vanilla
  ice-cream

Place all the ingredients in a liquidizer and blend until frothy. Pour into a glass and serve immediately.

Serves 1/115 calories
1 fat unit/2.1 grams fibre

Strawberry Fizz
(see picture page 148)

This makes a really refreshing treat when strawberries are in season and is worth

Three refreshing cool drinks for a hot summer's day: 1 Citrus Gin Cooler (recipe page 150); 2 Orange Spritz (recipe page 150); and 3 Strawberry Fizz (recipe page 148)

making in two portions — if you do not have anyone to share with, the calories are so low you could afford to drink the second half yourself. If you use frozen strawberries do so when they are only half thawed so that they help chill the drink.

225g/8oz strawberries, fresh or frozen
10ml/2 teaspoons unsweetened orange juice
Liquid artificial sweetener
Ice
150ml/¼ pint sparkling mineral water
2 sprigs mint, optional

Purée the strawberries and lemon juice in a liquidiser or rub through a sieve. Sweeten to taste with artificial sweetener. Pour into two glasses, add ice and sparkling mineral water. Add a sprig of mint to decorate each glass if liked.

Serves 2/30 calories
0 fat units/2.5 grams fibre per drink

Raspberry Sparkle

This delicious and fruity cocktail could be served to guests without them even noticing you are watching your calories. Try it on a hot summer's day when you are sitting out in the garden — even nicer if you can go and gather yourself a helping of fresh raspberries.

50g/2oz raspberries, fresh or frozen
30ml/2 tablespoons unsweetened orange juice
5ml/1 teaspoon lemon juice
Liquid artificial sweetener (equivalent to 10ml/1 rounded teaspoon sugar)
175ml/6floz soda water
Ice

Purée the raspberries in a liquidiser with the orange and lemon juice. Sieve if you wish to remove the pips, or they can be left in. Sweeten to taste with artificial sweetener and pour into a glass. Add the ice and pour on the soda water.

Serves 1/25 calories
0 fat units/4.2 grams fibre

Strawberry Milk Shake

Provided that you have a liquidiser, this milk shake can be made in a minute and makes a refreshing but satisfying snack — try it instead of breakfast. It has a real fruit flavour which bears no relation to synthetic milk shake syrups and powders. If the mixture is not sweet enough for your taste, you could add no-calorie artificial sweetener or an extra 5ml/1 level teaspoon icing sugar (17 calories) before blending.

75g/3oz strawberries, fresh or frozen
150ml/¼ pint chilled skimmed milk
15ml/1 level tablespoon skimmed milk powder
5ml/1 level teaspoon icing sugar

Hull the strawberries if fresh. Place all the ingredients in a liquidiser and blend until smooth. Pour into a glass and serve.

Serves 1/105 calories
0.5 fat units/1.8 grams fibre

Pineapple Yoghurt Drink

This drink is satisfying enough to count as a snack. Pineapple juice is particularly good in this recipe but if you wish you could substitute unsweetened apple, grapefruit or orange juice — any of these would reduce the calories to 85.

75ml/3floz natural low-fat yoghurt, chilled
115ml/4floz unsweetened pineapple juice, chilled
Liquid artificial sweetener, optional

Whisk together the yoghurt and pineapple juice. Taste and sweeten with artificial sweetener. Pour into a glass and serve.

Serves 1/105 calories
0 fat units/0 grams fibre

Iced Coffee

This makes a very refreshing treat on a hot day. Traditionally iced coffee recipes require your glass to be topped up with whole milk, sugar and cream — that could cost you as high as 200 calories.

10ml/1 rounded teaspoon instant coffee
50ml/2floz boiling water
1 tablet artificial sweetener or liquid sweetener equivalent to 10ml/1 rounded teaspoon sugar
150ml/¼ pint skimmed milk, chilled
25g/1oz vanilla or coffee ice-cream

Dissolve the coffee in the boiling water and sweeten. Leave until cold. Mix with the milk and pour into a glass. Float the ice-cream on top and serve.

Serves 1/95 calories
1 fat unit/0 grams fibre

Alcoholic Cold Drinks

If you are fond of an occasional alcoholic drink, include some in your dieting menus. These clever cocktails make your calories go as far as possible as well as making your tipple a delicious treat.

Mint Sparkle

This pretty-looking drink could be drunk before dinner instead of having a starter. It will not fill you up in the same way, but it could give you a lot of pleasure.

10ml/2 teaspoons Crème de Menthe
2 cubes ice
150ml/5floz low-calorie bitter lemon
Mint sprig, optional

Place the Crème de Menthe in a glass with

the ice. Pour on the bitter lemon and decorate with mint.

Serves 1/35 calories
0.5 fat units/0 grams fibre

Orange Spritz
(see picture page 148)

This is 10 calories higher than a straight Spritz but it is a very refreshing drink.

75ml/3floz medium or dry white wine,
* chilled*
75ml/3floz unsweetened orange juice,
* chilled*
75ml/3floz sparkling mineral water,
* chilled*
Ice, optional

Mix together the wine, orange juice and water and pour in a glass. Add ice if desired. Serve immediately.

Serves 1/90 calories
0.5 fat units/0 grams fibre

Citrus Gin Cooler
(see picture page 148)

Tastes even nicer than an ordinary gin and bitter lemon. You could use orange juice instead of grapefruit — if you make sure it is unsweetened, calories will be 75 and fat units will stay the same.

Ice
15ml/1 tablespoon gin
115ml/4floz unsweetened grapefruit juice
115ml/4floz low-calorie bitter lemon

Place some ice in a glass and then add the gin, grapefruit juice and bitter lemon in that order.

Serves 1/65 calories
0.5 fat units/0 grams fibre

Cider Punch
(see picture page 146)

Serve this drink in a glass bowl or jug and it will look very attractive with the fruit floating on top. When you are counting your calories carefully, make sure that your glass holds about 150ml/¼ pint — measure it before the party starts. That way you can be sure you are pouring yourself no more than 50 calories per glass.

700ml/1¼ pints medium sweet cider,
* chilled*
700ml/1¼ pints low-calorie ginger ale,
* chilled*
150ml/¼ pint dry sherry
575ml/1 pint soda water, chilled
Liquid artificial sweetener (approximately
* equivalent to 25g/1oz sugar)*
1 small pineapple
450g/1lb strawberries, fresh or frozen

Pour the cider, ginger ale, sherry and soda water into a punch bowl or large jug. Sweeten to taste with artificial sweetener. Discard the skin and core from the pineapple and cut the flesh into chunks. Hull the strawberries. Add the fruit to the punch and serve.

Serves 15/50 calories
0.5 fat units/0.9 grams fibre

Apricot Cup

A refreshing and pretty party drink which you can dip into without feeling guilty.

2 × 425g/15oz cans apricots in natural juice
850ml/1½ pints medium sweet cider, chilled
425ml/¾ pint low-calorie tonic water,
* chilled*
1 orange
1 lemon
Ice

Purée the apricots and their juice in a liquidiser or food processor. Mix with the

Here are two warming drinks for bedtime to help you go to sleep:
1 *Hot Chocolate and Brandy Treat (recipe page 151); and* **2** *Hot Mocha Cup (recipe page 151)*

cider and tonic water and pour into a punch bowl or large jug. Slice the orange and lemon and add to the apricot cup with some ice.

Serves 15/50 calories
0 fat units/0.7 grams fibre per drink

Blackcurrant Wine Fizz

This is a low-calorie version of the traditional French drink Kir, which is made from a mixture of blackcurrant liqueur and white wine, without the addition of mineral water. Our version knocks 40 calories off the original recipe and you will get more in your glass too.

2 cubes ice
10ml/2 teaspoons Crème de Cassis
115ml/4floz dry or medium white wine
115ml/4floz sparkling mineral water

Place the ice and Crème de Cassis in a glass. Pour on the wine and stir to mix. Pour in the sparkling water and serve.

Serves 1/100 calories
1 fat unit/0 grams fibre

Caribbean Rum Punch
(see picture page 104)

If you visit Barbados you will find this kind of punch served in many hotels and bars. Sip it in the garden on a hot day and you could imagine you are in more exotic surroundings!

1 medium banana
227g/8oz can pineapple in natural juice, chilled
150ml/¼ pint unsweetened orange juice, chilled
283ml/½ pint low-calorie bitter lemon, chilled
90ml/6 tablespoons rum
30ml/2 tablespoons lime juice or lemon juice
Liquid artificial sweetener
4 ice cubes
1 lime or lemon
Mint sprigs, optional

Peel the banana and cut into four. Place in a liquidiser or food processor with the pineapple and its juice, orange juice, bitter lemon, rum, lime or lemon juice and ice cubes. Blend until smooth. Taste, then sweeten with a little artificial sweetener. Add it very carefully as you will not need much. Pour into a jug or six glasses and decorate with slices of lime or lemon and mint.

Serves 6/75 calories
0.5 fat units/0.9 grams fibre per portion

Spritz

If you like your wine light and sparkling, try this mixture. It makes a very refreshing drink on a hot day, too. If you are eating out, you could order a bottle of mineral water to add to your wine — many non-dieters do this

anyway. As water contains no calories, you will reduce the calories of each glassful.

115ml/4floz dry or medium white wine, chilled
115ml/4floz sparkling mineral water, chilled
Ice, optional

Pour the wine and water into a glass and add ice if desired. Serve immediately.

Serves 1/80 calories
1 fat unit/0 grams fibre

Hot Drinks

A mug of hot full-cream milk with a couple of spoons of bedtime beverage could come to 275 calories. Try one of these hot drink recipes instead — they turn a 'comfort' into a special treat.

Hot Mocha Cup
(see picture page 150)

A special suppertime drink which will cheer you up after a hard day. Much less expensive in calories than comforting yourself with a bar of chocolate.

175ml/6floz skimmed milk
75ml/3floz water
10ml/2 level teaspoons drinking chocolate
5ml/1 level teaspoon instant coffee
Artificial liquid sweetener
Pinch ground nutmeg, optional

Bring the milk and water to the boil in a non-stick pan. Stir in the drinking chocolate and simmer for 1 minute. Pour into a mug and stir in the coffee and sweetener to taste. Sprinkle the nutmeg on top and serve.

Serves 1/80 calories
0 fat units/0 grams fibre

Hot Chocolate and Brandy Treat
(see picture page 150)

A very special bedtime treat. If you feel that you cannot risk grating half a square of chocolate without scoffing what remains, you could omit the chocolate topping. This will cut calories to 130, fat units to 0.

175ml/6floz skimmed milk
20ml/2 rounded teaspoons drinking chocolate
15ml/1 tablespoon brandy
Artificial sweetener to taste
½ square plain chocolate, optional

Place the milk in a non-stick saucepan and heat. Stir in the drinking chocolate and simmer gently for 1 minute (take care that it does not boil over). Pour into a mug or heatproof glass and add the brandy and artificial sweetener. Grate the chocolate and sprinkle on top.

Serves 1/150 calories
0.5 fat units/0 grams fibre

Drinks: how low can you go?

Tequila Sunrise *210 calories*
This popular mix of Tequila (50 calories per single measure), Grenadine (70 calories for a fluid ounce) and orange juice serves as an awful warning about cocktails generally. Recipes are based on spirits plus (all too often) sugary juices and are invariably calorie-laden.

Rum and Coke *125 calories*
A $\frac{1}{6}$ gill single rum — light, dark or white — costs 50 calories at 70°proof (40% alcohol by volume). But rum at 100°proof (57% alcohol) could cost 80 calories for the same amount. Coke adds 75 calories for a small bottle unless you choose the low-calorie sort.

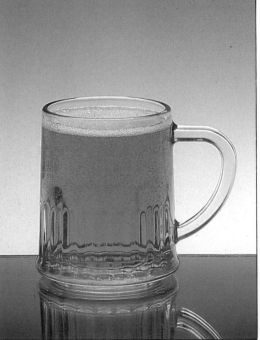

Cider *120 calories*
Dry ciders contain more alcohol than sweet so they tend to be slightly higher-calorie. Ordinary sweet and dry bottled ciders cost from 90 to 120 per 275ml/½ pint, but beware of specials. 'Vintage' and 'Triple' mean extra calories — up to 180 calories per 275ml/½ pint.

Campari Soda *115 calories*
The measure of Campari you get in most restaurants is ⅓ gill and the calories will cost twice as much as for a single spirit. Some pubs with concern for your pocket will serve a small $\frac{1}{6}$ gill measure. Top up a small Campari with no-calorie soda and this gives 60 calories.

Many a slimmer finds it all too easy to forget that liquids can pack enormous fattening power. See here the diet dangers in drinks. One sixth gill is 25ml or five 5ml teaspoons; ⅓ gill is approximately 50ml.

Stout *100 calories*
The calorie count for draught or bottled stout averages 100 per 275ml/½pint and for an 'extra' stout 110 calories. That is considerably less than most strong beers. Lowest you will pay is 90 calories; highest 115 calories.

Martini *100 calories*
Ask for a sweet martini in a pub and this what you can usually expect; ⅓ gill red vermouth costing 90 calories without the cherry. Classy bars may give you an American Martini: lots of gin to a little dry vermouth. Drink this and you will pay at least 150 calories.

Pernod with Lemonade *90 calories*
Stick to a single ⅙ gill measure of Pernod and top up with water for the lowest cost of 65 calories. Mixing Pernod with five parts lemonade adds 25 calories. People pour more at home and a double Pernod with lots of lemonade could cost 200 calories.

Beer *90 calories*
We show the average cost of an average draught 284ml/½pint. But 'better' bitters can soar over 100 and strong beers can top 200 calories per 275ml/½pint. Innocuous ales cost least: from 75 to 90 for a 275ml/½pint. Highest for a strong beer is around 225 calories.

Drinks *continued*

Lager *80 calories*
Lager costs from 70 to 95 calories per 275ml/ ½pint and the same amount of any lager labelled 'strong' or 'special' costs over 100. A dash of lime adds about 25 calories. 'Diabetic' lager may sound safe, but can cost 105 calories for a small bottle.

Cinzano Bianco *80 calories*
Few people pour more than the pub measure here (⅓ gill) but calories depend on how you drink it. Sweet white vermouths cost more than extra dry; but serve with lemonade and you add 30 calories. Lowest cost is 65 for extra dry vermouth — neat or iced.

Port *75 calories*
Port usually comes in special glasses holding the standard ⅓ gill measure. One small after-dinner glass will not cost more than 75 calories but a large port will double your calories. If you like your port with lemonade, remember to add an extra 15 to 30 calories.

Tia Maria *75 calories*
Liqueurs are very concentrated but they are traditionally served in ⅙ gill quantities usually from a tiny glass. Tia Maria is typical of the many liqueurs in the midway 75 to 80 calories per tiny glass mark. Kirsch is lowest at 50 calories; Green Chartreuse highest at 100.

Wine *75 calories*

This is the amount of wine (125ml/4floz) you will usually get in a bar. Sociable people fill the glass, though, giving twice as much at twice the calories. Dry wines are about 30 calories cheaper per 125ml/4floz than sweet, and the total here is the lowest you will pay.

Shandy *75 calories*

This is the traditional half-lemonade, half bitter pub shandy which costs about the same anywhere. Canned shandies come in variable sizes; the smallest can gives 70 calories and 110 for the 425ml/¾pint size. Low-calorie shandy is lowest at 15 calories per bottle.

Sherry *60 calories*

Sherry's virtue is that it usually comes in a genteel glass. Dry sherries come cheapest; a small ⅓ gill glass gives lowest count of 55 calories. A medium sherry costs just 5 calories more. Sweet sherries are highest at an average 90 calories per small glass.

Vodka *50 calories*

Most vodkas are standard 65-70°proof and cost 50 calories per single ⅙ gill measure. Higher proof varieties can cost twice as many calories. A double Polish vodka (140° proof) plus sweetened orange could cost 285 calories; an ordinary single plus low-calorie mixer just 50.

Whisky *50 calories*

All brands of whisky and gin cost 50 calories for a single ⅙ gill measure (⅕ gill, 65 calories in Scotland) but nobody pours a pub measure at home. Least you will pay is 50 calories for a pub single with soda. A double plus ordinary mixer could cost 130 calories.

Brandy *50 calories*

This single pub measure costs 50 calories for ⅙ gill, but any self-respecting host or wine waiter pours more. Small balloon glasses are safest. Even a treble measure looks tiny in a big balloon. If you add ginger ale, choose the low-calorie sort which adds no calories.

Maintenance meals

Here is an ideal maintenance menu for one day: **1**
*Grapefruit, Apple and Yoghurt (recipe page 72)
for breakfast;* **2** *Stuffed Courgettes (recipe page
173) for lunch;* **3** *Watercress Soup (recipe page
57) for lunch or dinner;* **4** *Chicken with Rice
(recipe page 162) for a main course;* **5** *Raspberry
Milkshake (recipe page 148) for a snack; and*
6 *Apricot Mousse (recipe page 112) for a
deliciously light dessert*

You've stepped on the scales and the needle
stops exactly where you want it. You are at
target weight, and it is just a matter of staying
there, so what do you do?

Your pre-diet 'normal' eating was what
got you overweight, so if you go back to it
you will get fat again. For you, 'normal'
must have a new meaning; at least a few of
your old eating habits must change for ever.
Shape control depends on 'balancing the
books'. You lost weight by limiting the
calories you took in each day so that they
added up to a total below the amount your
body was burning. Now you have to find the
total at which you easily keep in shape. The
average woman will maintain her weight on
around 2,000 calories a day, a man on 2,500
calories. But your calorie requirements
could be a little bit below average or, if you
are lucky, a little bit above average. In the
first week after reaching target weight do
not go mad — just allow yourself about an

extra 200 calories daily. Then weigh yourself
at the end of the week and, if you are still at
target, allow yourself a further 200 calories
daily over the next week. Eventually you
will settle down to a way of eating that suits
you and keeps you at target.

You may find that you prefer to continue
to stay on a fairly strict regime Monday to
Friday and reserve most of your indulgences
for the weekend. Or you may prefer to eat
very little during the day so that you can
afford a substantial meal with the family in
the evening. Whichever way you choose, it
is the week's grand total that counts. We
recommend a check up on the scales no
more often than once a week. This means
that everyday fluctuations, which are
perfectly natural, do not put you in a panic.
But if you find you have gained a pound,
see it off during the next seven days by
adjusting your calorie intake.

It makes sense to continue to control the

fats you consume — and if you have got used to a low-fat regime, you will probably find you do not want to return to a fatty way of eating. Even people without a surplus weight problem should cut their fat intake as a good health measure: continue to use skimmed or semi-skimmed milk, for instance, and use low-fat spreads instead of butter or margarine; keep the habits of your diet days regarding no fried foods, no pats of butter as a vegetable garnish, cream kept as a rare menu item. Enjoy special celebration meals or alcoholic parties in moderation, but realise that they may show on the scales unless you watch what you eat before or after in order to compensate.

If you have been following the low-fat method of dieting, you can increase your fat units by up to 5 when you reach target, but it is better if you eat more fat-free vegetables and fruit, wholemeal bread and cereals, instead. Whichever way you choose to control your weight, try to make sure that your fibre intake is between 30 and 40 grams a day.

The recipes in this chapter are four-portion meals that can be enjoyed by all the members of your family. If you eat alone you may like to cook a quarter portion or pick the recipes that will freeze. You can serve each meal with your own choice of vegetables. Many of the meals are old family favourites cooked in a new low-calorie, low-fat way. Although portions are reasonably substantial, many of the recipes are low enough in calories and fat units to include on days when you want to be a little more strict. It is a crying shame for anybody to have to deal with a sizeable weight problem more than once in a lifetime. Construct your weekly menus around these meals — there may be others that you have tried in other chapters that you would also like to include — and you will be a long way towards ensuring that this does not happen to you.

Beef

There are two things to remember when cooking beef. Firstly, always trim off any fat before cooking braising or stewing steak or before eating grilled steak. Secondly, always buy the leanest mince available and pre-fry it in a non-stick pan, discarding any fat that cooks out. Follow these rules and you will automatically reduce any beef dish's calories and fat units.

Beef and Pasta Casserole

The condensed soup used in this simple recipe will already be seasoned so there is no need to add extra salt and pepper. If the stewing steak you buy is not very lean, get a little extra so that you end up with 450g/1lb after all the fat has been discarded. This recipe freezes well.

450g/1lb lean stewing steak
225g/8oz carrots
298g/10½oz can condensed oxtail soup
225ml/8floz water
115g/4oz small pasta shapes or macaroni

Discard all visible fat from the meat and cut the lean into bite-sized cubes. Peel and slice the carrots. Place the meat and carrots in a casserole dish. Mix the soup with the water and add to the dish. Cover and cook at 150°C/300°F/gas mark 2 for 2½ hours. Stir in the pasta, making sure it is submerged in the liquid, and cook for another 30 minutes.

Serves 4/ per portion	cals.	fat units	grams fibre
white pasta	310	5	2.4
wholemeal pasta	300	5	4.1

Meat Loaf with Blue Cheese

A meat loaf is a very useful basic dish to add to your maintenance menus. It can be served hot with vegetables (jacket potatoes and broccoli are particularly good) or cold with salad. The cheese makes this loaf extra tasty, but if you are not fond of blue cheese you could substitute Leicester or Double Gloucester instead. This recipe freezes well.

450g/1lb very lean ground or minced beef
115g/4oz mushrooms
50g/2oz onion
1 egg, size 3
50g/2oz fresh wholemeal breadcrumbs
45ml/3 level tablespoons tomato ketchup
5ml/1 teaspoon Worcestershire sauce
Salt and pepper
75g/3oz Danish Blue cheese

Line a 450g/1lb loaf tin with foil. Finely chop the mushrooms and onion. If you have a food processor use it to chop them, if not do it by hand. Lightly beat the egg. Mix all the ingredients except the cheese together and season well with salt and pepper. Place half the mixture in the loaf tin and level the top. Grate the cheese and place on top of the meat. Cover with the remaining meat mixture. Cover with foil and bake at 180°C/350°F/gas mark 4 for 1 hour. Turn out and serve hot or cold.

Serves 4/325 calories
5 fat units/2.1 grams fibre per portion

Bobotie

This South African national dish consists of a curried meat and fruit mixture topped with a savoury custard.

40g/1½oz bread
250ml/9floz skimmed milk
450g/1lb very lean ground or minced beef
1 medium onion
1 medium cooking apple
20ml/4 level teaspoons curry powder
10ml/2 level teaspoons apricot jam
30ml/2 level tablespoons sultanas or raisins
15ml/1 tablespoon lemon juice
Salt and pepper
2 bay leaves
2 eggs, size 3

Place the bread in a bowl with 115ml/4floz milk and leave to soak. Brown the mince in a non-stick pan and drain off and discard the fat. Finely chop the onion. Peel, core and chop the apple. Add the onion, apple, curry powder, jam, sultanas and lemon juice to the meat. Stir in the bread and milk and season with salt and pepper. Mix well and turn into an ovenproof dish. Lay the bay leaves on top. Cover and cook at 180°C/350°F/gas mark 4 for 1 hour. Discard the bay leaves. Beat the eggs with the remaining milk and season with salt and pepper. Pour over the meat and return to the oven uncovered. Cook for another 30 minutes.

Serves 4/305 calories
3 fat units/1.8 grams fibre per portion

Beef and Spinach Bake

Spinach is a good source of fibre and makes this beef bake extra filling. Serve it hot with extra vegetables — potatoes mashed with a little skimmed milk would be good. This recipe freezes well.

350g/12oz frozen chopped spinach
350g/12oz very lean mince or ground beef
15ml/1 level tablespoon flour
115g/4oz mushrooms
5ml/1 level teaspoon mixed dried herbs
15ml/1 level tablespoon tomato purée
115g/4oz cottage cheese with chives and
  onion
150g/5oz carton low-fat natural yoghurt

Salt and pepper
115g/4oz Lancashire cheese

Cook the spinach as directed on the packet. Place in a sieve and press lightly with the back of a spoon to squeeze out any excess water. Brown the mince in a non-stick pan, then drain off and discard the fat. Stir the flour into the mince. Slice the mushrooms if small or chop roughly if large. Add to the meat with the spinach, herbs, tomato purée, cottage cheese and yoghurt. Season with salt and pepper and turn into an ovenproof dish. Level the top. Cover the dish and cook at 180°C/350°F/gas mark 4 for 35 minutes. Crumble the cheese and sprinkle on top. Cook uncovered for another 30 minutes. Brown the top under the grill.

Serves 4/315 calories
5 fat units/6 grams fibre per portion

Cheesey Mince Cobbler

You can use ready-grated Parmesan for this recipe if you wish, or buy a whole piece and grate it yourself. The cheesy cobbler gives a delicious topping to this beef casserole and makes a substantial and economical family meal.

450g/1lb lean minced or ground beef
15ml/1 level tablespoon flour
1 medium onion
225g/8oz can tomatoes
1 beef stock cube
150ml/¼ pint boiling water
Salt and pepper
115g/4oz self-raising flour
2.5ml/½ level teaspoon baking powder
2.5ml/½ level teaspoon dry mustard powder
25g/1oz butter or margarine
25g/1oz Parmesan cheese
25g/1oz mature Cheddar cheese
2.5ml/½ teaspoon mixed dried herbs
60ml-90ml/4-6 tablespoons skimmed milk

Brown the minced beef in a non-stick frying pan, then drain off all the fat. Stir in the flour and turn into a casserole dish. Finely chop the onion and roughly chop the tomatoes. Add to the meat with the juice from the tomatoes. Dissolve the stock cube in the water and then pour into the casserole. Season and stir to mix. Cover the dish and cook at 190°C/375°F/gas mark 5 for 40 minutes. Sieve together the flour, baking powder, dry mustard and a pinch of salt. Rub in the butter or margarine. Grate the cheeses and stir in with the herbs. Add enough milk to make a soft but not sticky dough. Knead very lightly for a few moments until smooth, then place on a lightly floured surface and pat into a square 5mm/¼in thick. Cut into 8 squares and place on the meat. Bake, uncovered, for another 20 minutes.

Serves 4/405 calories
5.5 fat units/1.8 grams fibre per portion

Beef Casserole with Wholemeal Dumplings

A lovely warming wintertime stew with dumplings that are extra filling because they are made with wholemeal flour. You will just need a few extra green vegetables to serve with this dish.

450g/1lb lean braising beef
30ml/2 level tablespoons flour for coating
1 medium onion
225g/8oz carrots
225g/8oz turnips
1 medium leek
1 beef stock cube
275ml/½ pint water
15ml/1 level tablespoon tomato purée
Bouquet garni
1.25ml/¼ teaspoon Worcestershire sauce
Salt and pepper
115g/4oz wholemeal flour
5ml/1 level teaspoon baking powder
50g/2oz shredded suet
Water

Discard all visible fat from the beef and cut the lean into cubes. Toss the meat in 30ml/2 tablespoons flour until all the pieces are coated. Place in a casserole dish with any excess flour. Chop the onion. Slice the carrots. Dice the turnips and white part of the leek. Add to the meat. Crumble the stock cube and add to the meat. Add the water, tomato purée, bouquet garni and Worcestershire sauce. Season with salt and pepper. Cover the dish and cook at 150°C/300°F/gas mark 2 for 2½ hours. Increase the oven temperature to 180°C/350°F, gas mark 4. Make the dumplings by mixing flour, baking powder, suet and a pinch of salt with enough water to make a soft but not sticky dough. Divide into 4 and shape into 4 balls. Place on top of the meat and vegetables and return to the oven for 15 minutes. Uncover the dish and cook for another 15 minutes.

Serves 4/410 calories
8.5 fat units/7.2 grams fibre per portion

Corned Beef Stew

It takes less than half an hour to make this easy stew. If you keep the ingredients in your store cupboard you can quickly prepare it when you arrive home later than expected and find the family clamouring for a meal. You could use drained canned new potatoes if you do not have fresh ones available. They will not need to be cooked — just place in a pan with the soup, corned beef and beans and heat through.

450g/1lb potatoes, weighed peeled
283g/10oz can low-calorie soup, Beef and Vegetable or Oxtail
350g/12oz can corned beef
454g/16oz can baked beans in tomato sauce

Cut the potatoes into small cubes and place

in a saucepan with the soup. Bring to the boil, cover the pan and simmer gently for 15 minutes until the potatoes are just tender. Cut the corned beef into bite-sized pieces and add to the saucepan with the baked beans. Stir gently, taking care not to break up the potatoes. Heat through, stirring occasionally.

Serves 4/385 calories
3.5 fat units/10.7 grams fibre per portion

Savoy Cabbage Special
(see picture page 161)

Low-fat spread and skimmed milk make a very acceptable cheese sauce and there really is no point in returning to butter and full cream milk sauces when you have reached your target weight. Small painless changes like this can make sure the weight does not go back on.

450g/1lb Savoy Cabbage
350g/12oz very lean mince or ground beef
1 medium onion
1 clove garlic, optional
425g/15oz can tomatoes
Salt and pepper
40g/1½oz low-fat spread
40g/1½oz plain flour
425ml/¾ pint skimmed milk
115g/4oz Edam cheese

Cut out any thick stalks, then boil the whole cabbage leaves in salted water for about 5 minutes. Drain thoroughly. Brown the mince in a non-stick frying pan, then drain off all the fat. Chop the onion and crush the garlic. Place the mince, onion, garlic and tomatoes in a saucepan and season. Cover the pan, bring to the boil and simmer gently for 20 minutes. While it is cooking make a cheese sauce. Place the low-fat spread, flour and milk in a saucepan and bring to the boil, whisking all the time. Grate the cheese and add most of it to the sauce. Season. Layer half the meat, cabbage and cheese sauce in an ovenproof dish. Repeat, finishing with cheese sauce. Sprinkle on the remaining cheese and cook at 190°C/375°F, gas mark 5 for 40 minutes.

Serves 4/365 calories
5.5 fat units/5.1 grams fibre per portion

Shepherd's Pie

This family favourite could be a great deal higher in calories and fat units if made the traditional way. Draining the fat from the mince and adding vegetables when this has been done, plus mashing potatoes without butter accounts for most of the saving. And we bet that the family never notices the difference. This recipe freezes well.

Chicken Curry (recipe page 163)

450g/1lb very lean mince or ground beef
30ml/2 level tablespoons flour
1 medium onion
15ml/1 level tablespoon tomato purée
2.5ml/½ teaspoon mixed dried herbs
1 beef stock cube
175ml/6floz water
Salt and pepper
675g/1½lb potatoes, weighed peeled
75ml/3floz skimmed milk

Brown the mince in a non-stick frying pan and drain off all the fat. Stir in the flour. Finely chop the onion and add to the meat with the tomato purée, herbs and crumbled stock cube. Place in an ovenproof dish and add the water. Season. Cover with a lid or foil and cook at 170°C/325°F/gas mark 3 for 50 minutes. While the meat is cooking, boil the potatoes until tender. Drain. Heat the milk and mash with the potatoes. Spread over the meat. Turn up the oven to 200°C/400°F/gas mark 6 and cook the pie for another 20 minutes.

Serves 4/345 calories
2 fat units/4.0 grams fibre per portion

Beefburger and Baked Bean Scone Pizza

A scone mixture makes an easy base for this very filling pizza. You can serve it hot with a few vegetables such as green beans or cold with a mixed salad. This recipe freezes well.

4 small beefburgers, 225g/8oz altogether
115g/4oz plain flour
10ml/2 level teaspoons baking powder
2.5ml/½ level teaspoon dry mustard
Good pinch salt
2.5ml/½ teaspoon mixed dried herbs
25g/1oz butter or margarine

Savoy Cabbage Special (recipe page 160)

1 medium onion
50-75ml/2-3floz skimmed milk
2 tomatoes
225g/8oz can baked beans with tomato
   sauce
75g/3oz Mozzarella cheese or Edam cheese

Grill the beefburgers really well, then cut each one into four strips. Sieve together the flour, baking powder, mustard and salt. Stir in the herbs, then rub in the butter or margarine. Peel and grate or finely chop the onion and add to the flour mixture. Stir in enough milk to make a soft but not sticky dough. Place on a baking tray and roll or pat out to a 20cm/8in round. Slice the tomatoes and place on top. Cover with the baked beans. Arrange the beefburger strips on top. Thinly slice the cheese and lay over the beefburgers. Bake at 200°C/400°F/gas mark 6 for 20-25 minutes.

Serves 4/ per portion	cals.	fat units	grams fibre
Mozzarella	375	6	6.0
Edam	365	6.5	6.0

Swiss Steak

Braising steak done this way is meltingly tender. You could also cook it in a slow cooker if you have one; just follow the manufacturer's instructions for cooking a casserole and heat the canned tomatoes before adding to the meat. Serve the steak with mashed potato and another vegetable if you wish. This recipe freezes well.

675g/1½1lb lean braising steak, cut in slices,
   about 1.2cm/½in thick
25g/1oz flour
Salt and pepper

1 large onion
1 clove garlic, optional
397g/14oz can chopped tomatoes
15ml/1 level tablespoon tomato purée
1 bay leaf

Discard any visible fat from the beef and divide into four steaks. Season the flour with salt and pepper and place in a plastic bag. Add the meat and shake until all the surfaces are coated. Place in a casserole dish, with any excess flour. Chop the onion and crush the garlic. Add to the dish with the tomatoes, tomato purée and bay leaf. Cover and cook at 150°C/300°F/gas mark 2 for 3 hours.

Serves 4/255 calories
6 fat units/1.6 grams fibre per portion

Steak and Kidney Casserole

If turnips are not available you can add extra carrots or onions to this casserole instead. Traditional casserole recipes pre-fry vegetables but this is not necessary and only adds unwanted fat and calories. This recipe freezes well.

450g/1lb lean stewing steak
225g/8oz pig's or lamb's kidneys
30ml/2 level tablespoons flour
115g/4oz mushrooms
175g/6oz carrots
1 medium onion
175g/6oz turnips
425ml/15floz boiling water
1 beef stock cube
1 bay leaf
15ml/1 level tablespoon tomato purée
5ml/1 level teaspoon Worcestershire sauce
Salt and pepper

Discard all visible fat from the beef and cut into bite-sized pieces. Core the kidneys and cut into fairly small pieces. Season the flour with salt and pepper. Toss the meats in the flour and place in a casserole dish with any excess flour. Quarter the mushrooms if large; leave whole if small. Slice the carrots. Chop the onion and dice the turnips. Add all the vegetables to the meat. Stir the crumbled stock cube into boiling water with the tomato purée and Worcestershire sauce. Pour over the meat and vegetables and add the bay leaf. Cover and cook at 150°C/300°F/gas mark 2 for 3 hours.

Serves 4/240 calories
4.5 fat units/3.5 grams fibre per portion

Curried Beef Pancakes

A delicious savoury pancake recipe that is good served with a few green beans. This recipe freezes well but put the filled pancakes and sauce in separate containers. Reheat the pancakes from frozen for 30 minutes. Reheat the sauce in a separate saucepan.

115g/4oz plain flour
Pinch salt
1 egg, size 3
275ml/½ pint skimmed milk
2.5ml/½ teaspoon oil
30ml/2 level tablespoons cornflour
10ml/2 level teaspoons curry powder
60ml/4 level tablespoons skimmed milk
  powder
575ml/1 pint water
30ml/2 level tablespoons apricot jam
60ml/4 level tablespoons mango chutney
1 beef stock cube
350g/12oz very lean mince or ground beef
1 medium onion
30ml/2 level tablespoons tomato purée
Salt and pepper

Follow the recipe for Smoked Haddock Pancakes (page...) to make a batter with the flour, salt, egg and milk. Cook 12 small or 8 medium pancakes using the oil to lightly grease a non-stick pan. Mix the cornflour, 5ml/1 level teaspoon curry powder and skimmed milk powder with a little of the water to make a smooth paste. Add the remaining water and pour into a saucepan. Add the apricot jam, mango chutney and stock cube. Bring to the boil, stirring all the time, then simmer for 1-2 minutes. Set aside. Brown the mince in a non-stick frying pan, then drain off all the fat. Turn the mince into a small saucepan. Finely chop the onion and add to the mince with the remaining 5ml/1 level teaspoon curry powder, tomato paste and one third of the curry sauce. Stir well and season with salt and pepper. Cover the pan and simmer gently for 15-20 minutes, stirring occasionally. If the mixture gets too dry add a little more water. Divide the minced beef mixture between the pancakes and roll up. Arrange in a single layer in an ovenproof dish. Cover with a lid or foil and reheat in the oven at 190°C/375°F/gas mark 5 for 10-15 minutes. Reheat the remaining sauce in a saucepan and serve with the pancakes.

Serves 4/385 calories
3 fat units/1.8 grams fibre per portion

Chicken and Turkey

Because of their low-fat content, chicken and turkey are the best meat buys you can continue to make to keep yourself in shape. They are so versatile, too. You can serve them plain roast — always remember to serve the skin to someone else — or make up any of the recipes that follow.

Chicken with Rice
(see picture page 157)

Chicken breast fillets are an excellent buy because they usually come skinless and are low in fat. Although they may appear a little expensive when compared to chicken joints, you need far less to make a satisfying meal as there are no wasted bones and you can eat every scrap. Turkey breast can also be used.

575g/1¼lb chicken breast fillets
1 small onion
275ml/½ pint water
1 chicken stock cube
2.5ml/½ level teaspoon dried thyme
225g/8oz button mushrooms
1 green or red pepper
30ml/2 level tablespoons cornflour
25g/1oz skimmed milk powder
Salt and pepper
175g/6oz long-grain rice

Cut the chicken breast fillets into bite-sized pieces. Chop the onion and place in a saucepan with the water, stock cube and thyme. Bring to the boil, cover the pan and simmer gently for 25 minutes. If the mushrooms are large, quarter them; if small, leave whole. Discard the pith and the seeds from the pepper and cut the flesh into strips. Add the mushrooms and the pepper to the saucepan and simmer for another 5 minutes. Mix the cornflour and skimmed milk powder with a little extra cold water to make a smooth paste. Add to the pan, stirring all the time, and simmer for 1-2 minutes. Season to taste. While the chicken is cooking, boil the rice. Drain and place on four plates. Serve the chicken on top with green beans.

Serves 4/ per portion:	cals.	fat units	grams fibre
white rice	390	2.5	2.6
brown rice	385	3	3.9

Sweet and Sour Aubergines
(see picture page 165)

This recipe uses up any left-over cooked chicken that you might have from a roast. Cooked chicken is very useful for all sorts of recipes and if you intend including some of these in your weekly menus it may be worth cooking a whole chicken and cutting it into portions to freeze. Discard any skin before freezing.

4 aubergines, 175g/6oz each
227g/8oz can pineapple in natural juice
1 small onion
1 small green or red pepper
15ml/1 level tablespoon tomato purée
10ml/2 teaspoons soya sauce
10ml/2 teaspoons vinegar
225g/8oz cooked chicken
175g/6oz Edam cheese
Salt and pepper

Cook the aubergines in boiling water for 10

Vegetable Hotpot (recipe page 172)

minutes. Drain and rinse in cold water until cool enough to handle. Cut in half lengthways and scoop out most of the flesh, leaving 13mm/½in shells. Chop the flesh. Drain the pineapple and reserve 75ml/3floz juice. Chop the pineapple. Pour the juice into a saucepan and add the aubergine flesh. Chop the onion and pepper and add to the pan with the soya sauce, tomato purée and vinegar. Bring to the boil, cover the pan and simmer gently until the pepper and onion are soft — about 5 minutes. Discard any skin from the chicken and chop the flesh. Add to the pan with the pineapple and season with salt and pepper. Pile into the aubergine shells. Slice the Edam thinly and place on top. Grill until melted and hot right through.

Serves 4/285 calories
5 fat units/5.2 grams fibre per portion

Chicken Curry
(see picture page 160)

This curry is excellent served with plain boiled rice. If you like your curry hot, add a little more curry powder, or if you like it mild cut the amount down to just one teaspoon. Curry powders vary in strength and it will usually say on the packet whether it is a hot or a mild mixture. Whatever sort you use, curry powder costs just 12 calories a teaspoon.

4 chicken leg joints, 225g/8oz each
1 small onion
1 bay leaf
1 chicken stock cube
275ml/½ pint water
15g/½oz butter or margarine
10ml/2 level teaspoons curry powder, mild or hot

15g/½oz flour
25g/1oz skimmed milk powder
225g/8oz peas, frozen
2 spring onions
Salt and pepper

Skin the chicken joints, then cut each one in half. Chop the onion and place in a saucepan with the chicken breasts, bay leaf, stock cube and water. Cover the pan, bring to the boil, then simmer gently for 30 minutes. Strain the stock into a measuring jug and if necessary make up to 275ml/½ pint with water. Discard the bay leaf. Keep the chicken warm. Melt the butter or margarine, then stir in the curry powder. Cook over a low heat for 1 minute. Remove from the heat and stir in the flour. Cook for a few moments. Whisk the skimmed milk powder into the reserved stock, then add to the curry mixture, whisking all the time. Bring back to the boil and simmer for 1-2 minutes. Boil the peas for 5 minutes. Drain and add a few to the sauce. Discard the roots and tough green leaves from the spring onions and chop the bulbs. Add to the sauce and simmer for 2 minutes. Season to taste with salt and pepper. Pour over the chicken and serve with the remaining peas.

Serves 4/275 calories
3 fat units/4.8 grams fibre per portion

Curried Chicken and Banana Salad

This is a very filling salad to which you will not need to add anything. It makes an excellent main meal for a hot day and would also be good served as a buffet dish when you are serving a selection of salads to guests.

115g/4oz long-grain rice
30ml/2 tablespoons oil-free French dressing

Cheese, Ham and Mushroom Soufflé (page 167)

Cheese Stuffed Trout (recipe page 168)

MAINTENANCE MEALS

450g/1lb boneless cooked chicken
275ml/½ pint natural low-fat yoghurt
60ml/4 level tablespoons mango chutney
5ml/1 level teaspoon curry paste or powder
Salt and pepper
1 green pepper
175g/6oz cucumber
2 medium bananas
30ml/2 tablespoons lemon juice
45ml/3 level tablespoons raisins or sultanas

Boil the rice until tender. Drain, rinse in cold water and drain again. Toss in the dressing. Arrange in a ring on a serving dish. Discard any skin from the chicken and cut the flesh into bite-sized pieces. Mix together the yoghurt, chutney and curry paste or powder. Season with salt and pepper. Discard the seeds from the pepper, then dice the flesh. Dice the cucumber. Peel and thickly slice the banana and toss in the lemon juice. Mix together the chicken, yoghurt dressing, pepper, cucumber, banana and raisins. Pile into the centre of the rice ring.

Serves 4/		fat	grams
per portion:	cals.	units	fibre
white rice	430	2.5	3.4
brown rice	425	2.5	4.2

Chicken Casserole

The skin from each 175g/6oz chicken breast will cost about 55 calories, if you decide not to discard it. Fat units would increase by 1.5 per portion. It makes sense, though, from a healthy eating viewpoint to continue to keep fats low even when you are down to your target weight. This recipe freezes well.

4 part-boned chicken breasts, 175g/6oz each
1 medium onion
1 green or red pepper
115g/4oz button mushrooms
397g/14oz can chopped tomatoes
½ chicken stock cube
1 bay leaf

2.5ml/½ level teaspoon dried basil or
  mixed herbs
Salt and pepper
15ml/1 level tablespoon cornflour

Discard the skin from the chicken breasts; place them in a casserole dish. Finely chop the onion. Discard the pith and seeds from the pepper and cut the flesh into strips. Slice the mushrooms. Arrange the prepared vegetables around the chicken breasts. Reserve 30ml/2 tablespoons tomato juice from the can and add the rest to the casserole. Add the bay leaf and basil or herbs and crumbled stock cube. Cover and cook at 180°C/350°F/ gas mark 4 for 50 minutes. Blend the reserved juice with the cornflour, then stir into the casserole. Return to the oven for another 20 minutes.

Serves 4/185 calories
1.5 fat units/2.4 grams fibre per portion

Sweet and Sour Chicken

This dish is very good served with boiled noodles or rice. Pineapple canned in natural juice is not only lower in calories than that canned in syrup, but it can also be used in this sort of savoury recipe where a syrupy fruit would not give a fresh-flavoured taste. This dish freezes well.

4 chicken leg joints, 250g/9oz each
1 small onion
275ml/½ pint water
1 chicken stock cube
30ml/2 tablespoons tomato ketchup
15ml/1 tablespoon vinegar
15ml/1 level tablespoon honey
15ml/1 tablespoon soya sauce
175g/6oz carrots
1 green pepper
227g/8oz can pineapple in natural juice
15ml/1 level tablespoon cornflour
Salt and pepper

Discard the skin from the chicken and place the joints in a large saucepan. Finely chop the onion and add to the chicken with the water, stock cube, tomato ketchup, vinegar, honey and soya sauce. Cover the pan, bring

Sweet and Sour Aubergines (recipe page 162)

Curried Seafood Eggs (recipe page 168)

to the boil and simmer gently for 25 minutes. Meanwhile, scrape the carrots and cut into matchstick-sized strips. Add to the pan for another 5 minutes. Discard the seeds and white pith from the pepper and cut into rings. Cut each ring into four pieces. Drain the pineapple and reserve the juice. If the pineapple is in rings, cut into small pieces. Add the pepper, pineapple and all but 30ml/2 tablespoons juice to the pan. Simmer for another 10 minutes. Blend the cornflour with the reserved juice and stir into the pan. Bring back to the boil, stirring continuously, then simmer for 1-2 minutes. Taste and season with salt and pepper.

Serves 4/275 calories
2 fat units/2.3 grams fibre per portion

Turkey and Sweetcorn Cobbler

Any raw, boneless turkey meat can be used for this recipe — packs labelled casserole turkey are often the cheapest if you can find them. Turkey is an ideal meat if you are watching your weight because it is very low in fat and only 30 calories per 25g/1oz. This thyme-flavoured cobbler topping goes deliciously with turkey and the wholemeal flour and sweetcorn make this recipe quite high in fibre. Chicken could be used instead of turkey.

450g/1lb boneless turkey meat
30ml/2 level tablespoons flour
2 medium carrots
1 small onion
1 chicken stock cube
275ml/½ pint boiling water
1 bay leaf
Salt and pepper
310g/11oz can sweetcorn kernels
115g/4oz wholemeal flour
10ml/2 level teaspoons baking powder
5ml/1 level teaspoon dried thyme
25g/1oz butter or margarine
60ml-90ml/4-6 tablespoons skimmed milk

Cut the turkey into small bite-sized pieces and toss in the flour. Place in a casserole dish with any excess flour. Slice the carrots and finely chop the onion. Add to the meat.

Dissolve the stock cube in the water and pour over the meat and vegetables. Add the bay leaf and season with salt and pepper. Cover the dish and cook at 180°C/350°F/gas mark 4 for 1 hour. Remove the bay leaf. Drain the corn and stir into the casserole. Raise the oven temperature to 190°C/375°F/gas mark 5. Make the cobbler. Place the flour, baking powder, thyme and a pinch of salt in a bowl and mix well. Rub in the butter or margarine. Add enough milk to make a soft but not sticky dough. Knead very lightly until smooth, then turn onto a lightly floured surface and pat out with your hands to form a square shape 5mm/¼in thick. Cut into 8 squares or oblongs and place on top of the casserole. Return to the oven for another 15-20 minutes or until the scones are risen and starting to brown.

Serves 6/365 calories
3 fat units/8.2 grams fibre per portion

Pork

The cut-off-all-fat rule applies to pork, too. There is a great deal of variation in calories between the different cuts of pork, depending on whether they are lean or fat. The lean tenderloin fillets, for example, are just 42 calories an ounce, but belly rashers with lean and fat shoot up to 108 calories an ounce.

Pork Stroganoff

Our version is lower in calories than most stroganoff recipes, even though we do use soured cream. Traditional recipes usually require you to add far more oil and butter. It is important to use pork fillet or tenderloin for this recipe as the meat must be very tender so that it cooks quickly. You can make the stroganoff even lower in calories if you use low-fat natural yoghurt instead of soured cream. This will save 30 calories/1.5 fat units per portion. Stroganoff is nicest served with boiled noodles or rice.

1 medium onion
10ml/2 teaspoons oil
5ml/1 level teaspoon butter

165

450g/1lb pork tenderloin or fillet
15ml/1 level tablespoon flour
Salt and pepper
150ml/¼ pint boiling water
½ chicken stock cube
15ml/1 level tablespoon tomato purée
90ml/6 level tablespoons cultured soured
  cream

Finely chop the onion. Heat the oil and butter in a deep non-stick frying pan with a lid. Add the onion and cook over a moderate heat until soft. Discard any fat from the pork, then cut the lean into strips — no bigger than your little finger. Season the flour with salt and pepper and place in a plastic bag. Add the meat and toss until all the pieces are coated. Add the pork to the pan with any remaining flour and cook over a fairly high heat until the meat changes colour on all sides. Dissolve the stock cube and tomato purée in the boiling water, then stir into the meat. Cover the pan and simmer gently for 15 minutes, stirring occasionally. Add the soured cream and mix well but do not allow to boil.

Serves 4/260 calories
6 fat units/0.3 grams fibre per portion

Pork and Fruit Coleslaw

A very nutritious family salad, this is delicious served with jacket potatoes. You can use other cold roast meats if you wish — beef will cost 25 calories/0.5 fat units less per portion, lamb 10 calories/0.5 fat units more.

350g/12oz cold roast pork
227g/8oz can pineapple in natural juice
1 medium eating apple
225g/8oz white cabbage
115g/4oz carrots
2 sticks celery
25g/1oz raisins
60ml/4 level tablespoons low-calorie salad
  cream
60ml/4 level tablespoons natural low-fat
  yoghurt
Salt and pepper

Discard all visible fat from the pork, then cut the lean into bite-sized pieces. Drain the pineapple and if in rings cut into small pieces. Core and dice the apple. Shred the cabbage; grate the carrots; slice the celery. Mix all the ingredients together and season.

Serves 4/265 calories
2 fat units/4.5 grams fibre per portion

Fruity Pork Steaks

Apple goes very well with pork and the fruity cider sauce you serve with these steaks makes it a rather special dish which is very

easy to make. It really is worthwhile cutting off all the fat from the pork even when you are not strictly dieting. A 150g/5oz pork leg steak with fat would come to 380 calories; without fat it goes down to 210 calories. That is a saving of 170 calories a portion for this recipe.

575g/1¼lb lean pork leg or shoulder steaks
1 medium onion
225g/8oz eating apples
30ml/2 level tablespoons raisins or sultanas
15ml/1 level tablespoon brown sugar
275ml/½ pint dry cider
Salt and pepper
30ml/2 level tablespoons cornflour
60ml/4 tablespoons water

Discard all visible fat from the pork, then place the lean steaks in a casserole dish. Chop the onion. Core and thickly slice the apples. Place the onion, apple slices and raisins or sultanas on top of the pork. Sprinkle on the sugar. Pour in the cider and season with salt and pepper. Cover the dish and cook at 170°C/325°F, gas mark 3 for 1½ hours. Divide the pork, onions and fruit between four plates. Pour the liquid into a saucepan. Blend the cornflour with the water until smooth. Stir into the liquid, then bring to the boil, stirring all the time. Simmer for 1-2 minutes, then pour over the pork.

Serves 4/300 calories
4 fat units/1.8 grams fibre per portion

Pork Goulash with Caraway Dumplings

Caraway goes well with goulash, but if your family do not like these flavoursome seeds, they can be omitted — the calories, fats and fibre will not be affected. The dumplings on their own come to 215 calories/1 fat unit/4 grams fibre each and can be served with other casserole recipes.

450g/1lb lean boneless pork
15ml/1 level tablespoon paprika
30ml/2 level tablespoons flour
1 large onion
2 caps canned pimento
1 beef stock cube
30ml/2 level tablespoons tomato purée
275ml/½ pint water
Salt and pepper
1 bay leaf
115g/4oz self-raising flour
5ml/1 level teaspoon caraway seeds
50g/2oz suet
Cold water
60ml/4 level tablespoons natural low-fat
  yoghurt

Discard all visible fat from the pork and cut the lean into bite-sized pieces. Mix together the flour and paprika and season with salt and pepper. Toss the meat in this mixture until well coated. Place in casserole with any remaining flour mixture. Chop the onion and cut the pimento into small squares. Add the bay leaf. Cover the dish and cook at 179°C/325°F/gas mark 3 for 1½ hours. Discard the bay leaf. Increase the oven temperature to 190°C/350°F/gas mark 4. Sieve the flour into a bowl with a good pinch of salt. Stir in the caraway seeds and suet, then add enough water to make a soft but not sticky dough. Lightly flour your hands, then shape the dough into four balls. Place on top of the meat for another 15 minutes. Uncover and cook for another 15 minutes. Remove the dumplings and place one on each plate. Stir the yoghurt into the goulash and serve with the dumplings.

Serves 4/435 calories
7.5 fat units/2.2 grams fibre per portion

Ham

The fat content of cooked ham varies enormously and you will find that some cuts come with a complete halo of fat, while others have the fat already trimmed off. When you buy ham, pick the leanest you can find, then there is less to discard. Watch out not only for the fat outside the ham, but also the fatty marbling. You will not be able to cut off any ingrained fat, so the less marbled your slices the better.

Cheese, Ham and Mushroom Soufflé
(see picture page 164)

Soufflés need to be served immediately they are taken from the oven so try this special recipe when you can guarantee the family can all be got to the dining table at the same time! You could serve the soufflé with a salad or with lightly boiled vegetables.

50g/2oz low-fat spread
50g/2oz plain flour
275ml/½ pint skimmed milk
75g/3oz lean cooked ham
115g/4oz mushrooms
150g/5oz Edam cheese
Salt and pepper
1 clove garlic
5ml/1 level teaspoon mustard
3 eggs, size 3

Preheat the oven to 190°C/375°F/gas mark 5. Lightly grease a 1 litre/2 pint soufflé dish with some of the low-fat spread. Place the remaining low-fat spread, flour and milk in a saucepan. Whisk over a low heat until smooth, thick and simmering. Set aside for a few minutes while you prepare the other ingredients. Discard all the visible fat from the ham and finely chop the lean. Finely chop the mushrooms. Grate the cheese. Crush the garlic and add to the sauce with the ham, mushrooms, cheese and mustard.

Separate the eggs and beat the yolks into the mixture. Season with salt and pepper. Whisk the egg whites until stiff but not dry. Gently fold into the soufflé mixture, then turn into the greased dish. Bake for 40-45 minutes. Serve immediately.

Serves 4/340 calories
7 fat units/1.2 grams fibre per portion

Ham and Egg Mornay

This dish is easy to prepare and would be very nice served with a baked potato or with green beans.

6 eggs, size 3
115g/4oz lean cooked ham
198g/7oz can sweetcorn
30ml/2 level tablespoons cornflour
275ml/½ pint skimmed milk
75g/3oz mature Cheddar cheese
Salt, pepper and a little mustard
15g/½oz fresh breadcrumbs

Hard-boil the eggs for 8 minutes. Cool in cold water. Shell, halve and arrange in an ovenproof dish, cut side down. Discard all visible fat from the ham and chop the lean. Drain the sweetcorn and mix with the ham. Place around and in between the eggs. Blend the cornflour with a little milk. Heat the remaining milk and then pour onto the cornflour, stirring all the time. Return to the pan and bring to the boil, stirring continuously. Simmer for 1 minute. Grate the cheese and add two-thirds to the sauce. Season with salt, pepper and mustard. Pour over the eggs. Mix the remaining cheese with the crumbs and sprinkle on top. Bake at 190°C/375°F/gas mark 5 for 15-20 minutes.

Serves 4/345 calories
6 fat units/3.2 grams fibre per portion

Spaghetti with Spinach and Ham Sauce

This is a very filling meal and the spinach makes a tasty change from the usual tomatoey spaghetti sauces. Using skimmed milk powder in sauces is another keep-slim habit that is worth adopting.

1 medium onion
227g/8oz frozen chopped spinach
275ml/½ pint boiling water
1 chicken stock cube
2.5ml/½ level teaspoon mixed dried herbs
50g/2oz skimmed milk powder
15ml/1 level tablespoon cornflour
75ml/3floz cold water
115g/4oz lean cooked ham
Salt and pepper
115g/4oz spaghetti
50g/2oz Leicester or Gouda cheese

Chop the onion and place in a saucepan with the frozen spinach, boiling water, stock cube and herbs. Heat until the spinach thaws. Cover the pan and simmer gently for

5 minutes. Purée in a liquidiser or food processor. Blend the skimmed milk powder and cornflour with cold water. Place in a saucepan with the spinach purée and bring to the boil, stirring all the time. Simmer for 1-2 minutes. Discard all visible fat from the ham and chop the lean. Add to the sauce. Taste and season with salt and pepper. Boil the spaghetti until just tender for 12-15 minutes. Drain and divide between four plates. Serve the sauce on the spaghetti. Grate the cheese and sprinkle on top.

Serves 4/ per portion:	cals.	fat units	grams fibre
white spaghetti	285	2.5	4.7
wholewheat spaghetti	275	2.5	6.7

Fish

All sorts of fish make excellent stay-slim meals. Shellfish and white fish are low in fat and as long as you do not fry or add buttery sauces you really cannot go wrong if you choose them. Oily fish is higher in fat and calories but can be plain grilled without anything added or can be baked with a low-calorie stuffing to make an excellent meal which is very reasonable in calories.

Crab and Bread Pudding

If you like bread and butter pudding, you will enjoy this rather special savoury version. Serve it as a light meal with baked tomatoes or a small mixed salad.

150g/5oz sliced bread
2 x 42g/1½oz cans dressed crab
2 eggs, size 3
275ml/½ pint skimmed milk
Salt and pepper
50g/2oz mature Cheddar cheese

Spread the bread with the dressed crab, then cut into fingers. Arrange, crab side up, in an ovenproof dish. Lightly beat the eggs and milk together and season well with salt and pepper. Pour over the bread and leave to soak for 15 minutes. Sprinkle the cheese on top and bake at 180°C/350°F/gas mark 4 for 30-40 minutes.

Serves 4/ per portion:	cals.	fat units	grams fibre
white bread	240	3.5	1.0
brown bread	235	3.5	1.8
wholemeal bread	230	3.5	3.0

Cheese Stuffed Trout
(see picture page 164)

Boning trout is very easy if you follow the instructions given in this recipe. If you buy your trout frozen it will come slit and gutted, but if you buy it fresh you may have to ask your fishmonger to gut it for you if you prefer not to do this yourself.

4 trout, 175g/6oz each, fresh or frozen
1 small onion
150g/5oz Edam cheese
2 small lemons
50g/2oz fresh breadcrumbs
60ml/4 level tablespoons chopped parsley
Salt and pepper
4 slices lemon to garnish, optional
4 sprigs parsley to garnish, optional

Gut the fish if this has not already been done. Make sure that the cut in the belly extends the length of the fish, then place the trout on a board, cut side down. Press firmly along the backbone to loosen it. Turn fish over and ease out the bone using a small sharp knife to free any pieces of fish that stick. Finely chop the onion and grate the cheese. Finely grate the rind from both lemons and squeeze out the juice. Mix together the onion, cheese, rind of both lemons and juice of one, breadcrumbs and parsley. Season with salt and pepper and stuff into the trout cavities. Lay side by side in an ovenproof dish and pour over the juice of the second lemon. Cover with a lid or foil and bake at 170°C/325°F/gas mark 3 for 30 minutes. Garnish with extra lemon slices and parsley before serving.

Serves 4/ per portion:	cals.	fat units	grams fibre
white bread	295	5	0.6
brown bread	295	5	0.9
wholemeal bread	295	5	1.4

Curried Seafood Eggs
(see picture page 165)

This unusual cheesy curry sauce is very tasty and the curried eggs could be served without prawns for a more economical dish. That would bring calories down to 285. Fat units and fibre would be the same.

8 eggs, size 3
225g/8oz peeled prawns
5ml/1 level teaspoon paprika
400ml/¾ pint skimmed milk
30ml/2 level tablespoons cornflour
5-10ml/1-2 level teaspoons curry powder
75g/3oz Edam cheese
Salt and pepper
4 whole prawns in shells, optional
4 sprigs parsley, optional

Hard-boil the eggs, then cool in cold water. Shell, halve and arrange in an ovenproof dish with the prawns. Sprinkle with paprika. Blend a little of the milk with the cornflour and curry powder until smooth. Heat the remaining milk to boiling point, then pour onto the cornflour mixture stirring all the time. Return to the pan and bring to boiling point, stirring all the time. Simmer for a minute. Grate the cheese and add to the sauce. Season with salt and pepper. Pour over the eggs and bake at 180°C/350°F/gas mark 4 for about 15 minutes. Garnish with parsley and prawns.

Serves 4/345 calories
6 fat units/0.1 grams fibre per portion

Salmon and Macaroni Bake

If you thought canned salmon was only suitable for serving cold with salad, try this recipe. The macaroni and sweetcorn mixture makes it a particularly filling meal which you could serve with a few extra vegetables if you wish. This dish freezes well.

115g/4oz macaroni
425g/15oz can salmon
30ml/2 level tablespoons cornflour
25g/1oz skimmed milk powder
115g/4oz canned sweetcorn
Salt and pepper
2 tomatoes
50g/2oz Edam cheese
25g/1oz fresh wholemeal breadcrumbs

Boil the macaroni until just tender. Drain, rinse under cold water and drain again. Drain the salmon and reserve the liquid. Flake the fish. Make the liquid up to 275ml/½ pint with water. Blend a little of this liquid with the cornflour and milk powder until smooth. Heat the remaining liquid to boiling point. Pour onto the blended mixture, stirring all the time, then return to the pan. Bring back to the boil stirring all the time and simmer for a minute. Stir in the macaroni, salmon and sweetcorn. Season with salt and pepper. Turn into an ovenproof dish. Slice the tomato and arrange on top. Grate the cheese and mix with the breadcrumbs. Sprinkle over the dish and bake at 190°C/375°F/gas mark 5 for 20 minutes.

Serves 4/ per portion:	cals.	fat units	grams fibre
white macaroni	400	5	3.6
wholewheat macaroni	390	5	5.5

Smoked Haddock Pancakes

Bland-tasting pancakes are best filled with some strong-tasting mixture, and smoked haddock is ideal for fish pancakes. Make sure you use only one teaspoon of oil for greasing your pan when frying the pancakes. Although the oil is not included in the basic mixture, the pancakes will absorb it when cooking.

Pancakes:
115g/4oz plain flour
1 egg, size 3
275ml/½ pint skimmed milk
5ml/1 teaspoon oil
Filling:
450g/1lb smoked haddock fillet

250ml/9floz skimmed milk
1 bay leaf
1 slice onion
Sprig of parsley, optional
115g/4oz peas, frozen
1 egg, size 3
30ml/2 level tablespoons cornflour
30ml/2 tablespoons water
Salt and pepper
1 lemon

Mix together the flour, egg and milk to make a batter. Grease a small non-stick pan with the oil and make 12 very small or 8 small pancakes. Place the smoked haddock in a saucepan with the milk, bay leaf, onion and parsley. Bring to the boil, cover the pan and poach gently for about 10 minutes or until it flakes easily. Meanwhile, boil the peas for 2-3 minutes. Drain, rinse in cold water and drain again. Hard-boil the egg for 8 minutes, then cool in cold water. Shell and chop. Strain the milk from the haddock into a measuring jug. You should have 250ml/9floz. If necessary make up with water. Discard the bay leaf, onion and parsley. Skin and bone the fish and flake. Blend the cornflour with the water until smooth. Heat the fish milk to boiling point and then pour onto the cornflour mixture, stirring all the time. Return to the pan and bring to the boil, stirring continuously. Simmer for 1 minute. Stir in the haddock, egg and peas. Season with salt and pepper. Divide between the pancakes and roll up. Place in an ovenproof dish in a single layer and reheat at 190°C/375°F/gas mark 5 for 15 minutes. Cut the lemon into wedges and serve with the pancakes.

Serves 4/345 calories
2 fat units/3.3 grams fibre per portion

Tuna French Bread Pizzas

French bread makes a crunchy, thick pizza base and this recipe is quick to put together. Serve the pizzas with a salad or just on their own. You can freeze the pizzas made up ready to pop into the oven for baking. Allow an extra 10 minutes if baking from frozen.

1 medium onion
5ml/1 teaspoon oil
5ml/1 level teaspoon butter
45ml/3 tablespoons tomato ketchup
5ml/1 level teaspoon mixed dried herbs
200g/7oz can tuna in brine
1 small French loaf, 250g/9oz
4 tomatoes
115g/4oz Edam cheese

Finely chop the onion, then cook in the oil and butter until soft. Stir in the tomato ketchup and herbs. Set aside. Drain and flake the tuna. Cut the French stick in half lengthways and cut each piece in half. Spread the cut surfaces with tomato ketchup and onion mixture. Slice the tomatoes and arrange on top. Cover with flaked tuna. Grate the cheese and sprinkle on top. Place the pizzas on a baking tray and bake at 200°C/400°F/gas mark 6 for 15 minutes.

Serves 4/335 calories
4 fat units/2.8 grams fibre per portion

Curried Fish and Cheese Salad
(see picture page 173)

Serve this salad with lettuce which will add just a few more calories; you could also eat it with a slice of bread. If you prefer you can use Cheddar or Cheshire cheese instead of Caerphilly — or reduce calories and fat units by using one of the low-fat Tendale cheeses. With Tendale, calories would come down to 275 per portion and fat units to 4.

450g/1lb cod or haddock fillet
275ml/½ pint skimmed milk
1 bay leaf
25g/1oz salted peanuts
4 tomatoes
175g/6oz Caerphilly cheese
10ml/2 level teaspoons curry paste
30ml/2 tablespoons oil-free French dressing
Salt and pepper

Place the fish in a shallow pan with the milk and bay leaf. Season. Cover the pan and simmer gently for 10 minutes. Drain and reserve the milk. Discard the bay leaf. Skin and bone the fish and break into large flakes. Skin the tomatoes and squeeze out and discard the seeds. Cut into small pieces. Cut the cheese into small cubes. Whisk together the oil-free French dressing, curry paste and half of the reserved milk. Stir in the fish, tomatoes, peanuts and cheese and serve.

Serves 4/350 calories
6 fat units/1.4 grams fibre per portion

Fish and Asparagus Bake

Cod or haddock frozen steaks are a very useful food to keep in the freezer. An average steak weighing just under 115g/4oz will cost 80 calories. You can serve them grilled with a tiny amount of low-fat spread, or bake them in a tasty sauce or a condensed soup as in this recipe. You can make up this dish and freeze ready for baking. If you use frozen fish, however, do not allow it to thaw before re-freezing.

450g/1lb cod, haddock or coley steaks,
*   fresh or frozen*
30ml/2 level tablespoons cornflour
60ml/4 tablespoons skimmed milk
298g/10½oz can condensed asparagus soup
25g/1oz fresh wholemeal breadcrumbs
25g/1oz mature Cheddar cheese

Place the fish steaks in a single layer in an ovenproof dish. Blend together the cornflour and milk, then mix with the condensed soup. Spread over the fish. Grate the cheese and mix with breadcrumbs. Sprinkle on top of the fish. Bake at 180°C/350°F/gas mark 4 for 30 minutes for fresh fish, or 45 minutes for frozen fish. Brown the top under the grill.

Serves 4/200 calories
2 fat units/0.7 grams fibre per portion

Liver and Kidney

Liver and kidney are good low-fat nutritious foods from which you can make very economical family meals. A small quantity actually cooks up to look a lot on your plate.

Savoury Liver Bake

Many traditional recipes fry liver before adding it to a dish but this is not necesary as liver cooks very quickly. This dish can be served with vegetables of your choice.

450g/1lb lamb's liver, cut into 1.2cm/½in
*   thick slices*
75g/3oz fresh wholemeal breadcrumbs
15ml/1 level tablespoon chopped parsley
15ml/1 level tablespoon chopped fresh
*   mixed herbs or*
5ml/1 level teaspoon dried mixed herbs
5ml/1 level teaspoon grated orange rind
30ml/2 tablespoons unsweetened orange
*   juice*
Salt and pepper
50g/2oz streaky bacon rashers
150ml/¼ pint boiling water
½ beef stock cube

Place the liver in a single layer in an oven-proof dish. Mix together the breadcrumbs, parsley, mixed herbs, orange rind and juice. Season and spread over the liver. Discard the rind from the bacon and stretch out the rashers using the back of a knife. Cut into pieces 2.5cm/1in long. Arrange on top of the stuffing. Dissolve the stock cube in the boiling water and pour into the dish. Cover with a lid or foil and bake at 180°C/350°F/gas mark 4 for 45 minutes, removing the lid for the last 15 minutes to crisp the bacon.

Serves 4/310 calories
6 fat units/1.8 grams fibre per portion

Liver and Prune Casserole

This combination of liver and prunes is much nicer than you may imagine before you try it. You could use ready-to-eat prunes if you wish but would need to use 165g/5½oz. This recipe freezes well.

115g/4oz dried prunes
2 medium onions
450g/1lb lamb's liver

2.5ml/½ teaspoon dried mixed herbs
Salt and pepper
30ml/2 level tablespoons cornflour
25g/1oz skimmed milk powder

Soak the prunes overnight in cold water. Drain and place in a small pan with 275ml/ ½ pint fresh water. Cover and simmer for 10 minutes. Drain and reserve the liquid. Chop the onions and place in the dish with the liver and prune liquid. Add the herbs and season with salt and pepper. Cover and bake at 170°C/325°F/gas mark 3 for 1½ hours. Blend the cornflour and skimmed milk powder together with an extra 150ml/ ¼ pint water. Add to the casserole with the prunes and cook for another 20 minutes.

Serves 4/300 calories
4.5 fat units/4.4 grams fibre

Liver and Bacon Casserole

Pig's liver has a slightly stronger taste than lamb's and is about 7 calories and 0.5 fat units an ounce cheaper. The calories for this recipe are based on lamb's liver, so if you choose pig's liver, calories per portion will come down to 270 and fat units to 3. This recipe freezes well.

450g/1lb lamb's or pig's liver
30ml/2 level tablespoons flour
Salt and pepper
2 medium onions
2 ham or bacon steaks, 115g/4oz each
397g/14oz can chopped tomatoes
10ml/2 teaspoons Worcestershire sauce
5ml/1 level teaspoon mixed dried herbs

Thinly slice the liver. Rinse and pat dry with kitchen paper. Season the flour with salt and pepper, then toss the liver in it. Place the liver in a casserole dish with any excess flour. Finely chop the onions. Discard any fat from the bacon steaks and cut the lean into small pieces. Add the onion, ham or bacon, tomatoes, Worcestershire sauce and herbs to the liver. Cover and cook at 170°C/ 325°F/gas mark 3 for 1 hour.

Serves 4/300 calories
5 fat units/1.5 grams fibre

Spaghetti with Kidney Sauce

If the family is particularly fond of spaghetti, you could cook up a little more. An extra 25g/1oz weighed dry comes to 107 calories for white and 97 calories for wholewheat. There is little fat in spaghetti but each ounce of white contains 0.8 grams fibre and wholewheat 2.8 grams.

4 rashers streaky bacon
450g/1lb lamb's kidneys
225g/8oz button mushrooms
1 medium onion
60ml/4 level tablespoons tomato purée
2.5ml/½ level teaspoon mixed dried herbs
275ml/½ pint water

1 beef stock cube
Salt and pepper
15ml/1 level tablespoon cornflour
175g/6oz spaghetti, white or wholemeal

Grill the bacon well, then cut into small pieces. Halve, core and slice the kidneys. Slice the mushrooms and chop the onion. Place the bacon, mushrooms, onion, tomato purée, herbs, water and stock cube in a saucepan. Season. Bring to the boil, add the kidneys, cover the pan and simmer very gently for 15 minutes. While the kidney sauce is cooking boil the spaghetti for 12-15 minutes. Blend the cornflour with a little cold water until smooth, then stir into the kidney sauce. Simmer for 1-2 minutes, stirring all the time. Drain the spaghetti and divide between four serving plates. Serve the sauce on top.

Serves 4/ per portion	cals.	fat units	grams fibre
white spaghetti	350	2.5	3.0
wholewheat spaghetti	335	2.5	6.0

Sausages

Sausages are a reasonable food to use as long as you grill them well allowing the fat to drip away into your grill pan. A pork chipolata before it is grilled will be 105 calories; after it has been well grilled it comes down to 65 calories.

Sausage and Bacon Casserole

An economical family meal that is a bit more special than the normal mixed grill. Serve it with mashed potatoes or your favourite choice of cooked vegetables.

225g/8oz pork chipolata sausages
200g/7oz bacon or ham steak
225g/8oz eating apples, preferably Cox's
175g/6oz tomatoes
30ml/2 level tablespoons tomato chutney
45ml/3 tablespoons water
Salt and pepper

Grill the sausages and bacon or ham steak until cooked through. Discard any fat from the steak and cut the lean into strips the width of the sausages. Place all the meat in an ovenproof dish. Peel, core and slice the apples. Skin and slice the tomatoes. Layer the apple and tomatoes on top of the sausages and bacon. Mix the water with the tomato chutney and spoon on top. Season with salt and pepper. Cover the dish and bake at 190°C/375°F/gas mark 5 for 40 minutes.

Serves 4/220 calories
5 fat units/1.8 grams fibre per portion

Toad in the Hole

A low-calorie version of a recipe which is a great favourite with many families. It is lower in calories because we use skimmed milk and just a little oil for cooking. The nicest accompaniment is baked beans.

225g/8oz pork chipolata sausages
115g/4oz plain flour
2.5ml/½ teaspoon salt
1 egg, size 3
275ml/½ pint skimmed milk
15ml/1 tablespoon cooking oil

Preheat the oven to 220°C/425°F, gas mark 7. Grill the sausages. Sieve the flour and salt together. Make a well in the centre and add the egg and half of the milk. Gradually beat together to make a smooth thick batter. Beat in the remaining milk. Alternatively place the flour, salt, egg and milk in a liquidiser or food processor and blend until smooth. Place the oil in a small roasting tin and brush all over the surface. Arrange the sausages in the tin and heat in the oven for 5 minutes. Pour in the batter and cook for 35-40 minutes until puffed up and golden. Serve hot.

Serves 4/305 calories
6 fat units/1.2 grams fibre per portion

Potato and Sausage Salad

This salad is tastiest made with new potatoes — if you leave the skins on it will give the dish a slightly nutty flavour. You could make the salad with old potatoes, but if you do, make sure they are the ones that stay firm when boiled — some varieties tend to disintegrate in the water.

575g/1¼lb new potatoes
30ml/2 tablespoons oil-free French dressing
225g/8oz pork chipolata sausages
2 sticks celery
8 radishes
4 spring onions
60ml/4 level tablespoons low-calorie salad
  cream
60ml/4 level tablespoons low-fat yoghurt
2.5ml-5ml/½-1 level teaspoon mustard
Salt and pepper

Scrub the potatoes, then boil until tender. Drain and remove the skins if liked. Cut into cubes and toss in the oil-free French dressing while still hot. Grill the sausages well, then cut into short pieces. Slice the celery, radishes and spring onions. Mix together the low-calorie salad cream, yoghurt and mustard. Season. Add the vegetables and sausages and mix gently.

Serves 4/305 calories
4.5 fat units/4.2 grams fibre per portion

Cheese

Most hard cheeses are high in calories so always treat them with respect even when you are down to target weight. If you have any left-over cheese from these recipes grate it and pop it in the freezer immediately so you will not be tempted to tidy up any small pieces straight into your mouth.

Farmers' Pancakes
(see picture page 143)

These cheesy pancakes make a tasty supper dish which is good served with a crunchy coleslaw.

115g/4oz plain flour
Pinch salt
1 egg, size 3
275ml/½ pint skimmed milk
5ml/1 teaspoon oil
1 large onion
175g/6oz mushrooms
1 green pepper
425g/15oz can tomatoes
5ml/1 level teaspoon mixed dried herbs
Salt and pepper
175g/6oz Edam cheese

Make a batter by mixing together the flour, salt, egg and milk. Lightly grease a small non-stick omelet pan with some of the oil and cook 12 very small or 8 small pancakes. Stack together and keep warm on a plate standing over a pan of simmering water. Slice the onion and mushrooms. Cut the pepper into strips. Roughly chop the tomatoes and place in a saucepan with the onion, mushrooms and pepper. Add the herbs and season with salt and pepper. Simmer, uncovered, over a low heat for 15 minutes or until the vegetables are tender. Drain off any liquid. Spread the filling on the pancakes and fold into four. Arrange on a heatproof plate. Grate the cheese and sprinkle on top. Grill until melted.

Serves 4/295 calories
5 fat units/3.8 grams fibre per portion

Vegetable Hotpot
(see picture page 163)

A good warming hotpot is a firm family favourite and our cheesy version gives you lots of filling power for a very reasonable number of calories — you will not need to add anything else. You can freeze the hotpot without the cheese if you wish. Sprinkle on the cheese before you reheat the hotpot in the oven — it will take about 45 minutes from frozen.

1 medium onion
1 medium leek
225g/8oz carrots, weighed peeled
225g/8oz parsnips, weighed peeled
275ml/½ pint boiling water
1 chicken stock cube

10ml/2 teaspoons Worcestershire sauce
15ml/1 level tablespoon tomato purée
Salt and pepper
425ml/¾ pint tomato juice
450g/1lb potatoes, weighed peeled
225g/8oz Lancashire cheese

Slice the onion, leek, carrots and parsnips. Place in a 1.1 litre/2 pint ovenproof dish. Dissolve the stock cube in boiling water, then stir in Worcestershire sauce and tomato purée. Season and add half the tomato juice. Pour over the vegetables. Slice the potatoes and arrange in an overlapping pattern on top. Pour on the remaining tomato juice. Cover and bake at 200°C/400°F/gas mark 6 for 1½ hours, occasionally basting with the juices. Crumble the cheese and sprinkle on top. Brown under the grill.

Serves 4/400 calories
6 fat units/7.4 grams fibre per portion

Stuffed Courgettes
(see picture page 156)

6/5g/1½lb courgettes
175g/6oz tomatoes
2.5ml/½ level teaspoon mixed dried herbs
175g/6oz peeled prawns
15ml/1 level tablespoon tomato ketchup
Salt and pepper

25g/1oz skimmed milk powder
275ml/½ pint water
25g/1oz low-fat spread
25g/1oz flour
75g/3oz mature Cheddar cheese
25g/1oz fresh breadcrumbs

Trim the ends from the courgettes, then boil them in salted water for just 5 minutes. Drain into a colander and rinse in cold water until cold. Carefully cut a lengthwise slice off the top of each and scoop out the flesh, leaving the shells intact. Chop the flesh. Skin and chop the tomatoes and mix with the herbs, prawns, tomato ketchup and chopped tomatoes. Season with salt and pepper. Arrange the courgettes in a shallow ovenproof dish in a single layer and fill with the stuffing. Mix the skimmed milk powder with the water, then place in a saucepan with the low-fat spread and flour. Bring to the boil, whisking all the time, then simmer for 1 minute. Grate the cheese and stir into the sauce. Season and pour over the courgettes. Sprinkle the breadcrumbs on top and bake at 190°C/375°F/gas mark 5 for 15-20 minutes or until hot right through.

Serves 4/235 calories
4 fat units/4.1 grams fibre

Curried Fish and Cheese Salad (recipe page 170)

Chart of basic foods

Below you will find the calories, fibre and fat units in most basic foods. Where no figure is given, this means information on this food is presently unavailable. Some sweet foods and drinks do not contain fat but are still high in calories and could severely hamper your weight loss if you consume too much. We have, therefore, accorded them an equivalent fat unit count.

Abbreviations: C=calories; GF=grams fibre; FU=fat units

A

	C	GF	FU
ALMONDS			
Shelled, per 28g/1oz	160	4.1	5.5
Ground,			
per 15ml/1 level tablespoon	30	0.8	1
per 20ml (Australian tablespoon)	40	1.0	1
Per almond, whole	10	0.2	0.5
Per sugared almond	15	0.2	0.5
ANCHOVIES			
Per 28g/1oz	40	0	
Per anchovy fillet	5	0	
ANCHOVY ESSENCE			
Per 5ml/1 level teaspoon	5	0	0
ANGELICA			
Per 28g/1oz	90	0	1
Per average stick	10	0	0
APPLES			
Eating, per 28g/1oz, flesh only	13	0.6	0
Cooking, per 28g/1oz, fresh only	11	0.7	0
Medium whole eating, 142g/5oz	50	2.7	0
Medium whole cooking, 227g/8oz	80	4.3	0
Apple sauce, sweetened, per 15ml/			
1 level tablespoon	20	0	0
per 20ml (Australian tablespoon)	25	0	0
Apple sauce, unsweetened, per 15ml/			
1 level tablespoon	10	0	0
per 20ml (Australian tablespoon)	15	0	0
APRICOTS			
Canned in natural juice, per 28g/1oz	13	0.4	0
Canned in syrup, per 28g/1oz	30	0.4	0
Dried, per 28g/1oz	52	6.8	0.5
Fresh with stone, per 28g/1oz	7	0.5	0
Per dried apricot	10	1.3	0
ARROWROOT			
Per 28g/1oz	101	0.8	0
Per 5ml/level teaspoon	10	0	0
ARTICHOKES			
Globe, boiled, per 28g/1oz	4		0
Jerusalem, boiled, per 28g/1oz	5		0
ASPARAGUS			
Raw or boiled, soft tips, per 28g/1oz	5	0.4	0
Per asparagus spear	5	0.4	0
AUBERGINES (Eggplants)			
Raw, per 28g/1oz	4	0.7	0
Sliced, fried, 28g/1oz raw weight	60	0.7	2
Whole aubergine, 198g/7oz	28	5.0	0
Whole aubergine, sliced, fried, 198g/7oz			
raw weight	405	5.0	14
AVOCADO			
Flesh only, per 28g/1oz	63	0.6	2.5
Per half avocado, 106g/3¾oz	235	2.1	8.5

B

	C	GF	FU
BACON (see also gammon)			
Per 28g/1oz			
Back rasher, raw	122	0	4
Collar joint, raw, lean and fat	91	0	3
Collar joint, boiled, lean only	54	0	1
Collar joint, boiled, lean and fat	92	0	2.5
Streaky rashers, raw	118	0	4
1 streaky rasher, well grilled or fried,			
21g/¾oz raw weight	50	0	1
1 back rasher, well grilled or fried, 35g/			
1¼oz raw weight	80	0	1.5
1 bacon steak, well grilled, 99g/3½oz			
average raw weight	105	0	1.5
BAKING POWDER			
Per 28g/1oz	46	0	0
Per 5ml/1 level teaspoon	5	0	0
BAMBOO SHOOTS			
Canned, per 28g/1oz	5	0.1	0
BANANAS			
Small whole fruit, 115g/4oz	55	2.3	0
Medium whole fruit, 170g/6oz	80	3.4	0
Large whole fruit, 198g/7oz	95	4.0	0
BARCELONA NUTS			
Shelled, per 28g/1oz	181	2.9	6.5
BARLEY			
Pearl, raw, per 28g/1oz	102	1.8	0
Pearl, boiled, per 28g/1oz	34	0.6	0
Per 15ml/1 level tablespoon raw	45	0.8	0
Per 20ml (Australian tablespoon)	60	1.0	0
BASS			
Fillet, steamed, per 28g/1oz	35	0	0
BEAN SPROUTS			
Raw, per 28g/1oz	8	0.3	0
Boiled, per 28g/1oz	7	0.3	0
BEANS			
Per 28g/1oz			
Baked, canned in tomato sauce	20	2.1	0
Black eye beans, raw weight	93	7.2	0
Broad, boiled	14	1.2	0
Butter, boiled	27	1.4	0
Butter, raw, dry weight	77	6.1	0
French, boiled	10	0.9	0
Haricot, boiled	26	2.1	0
Haricot, raw weight	77	7.2	0
Red kidney, canned	25	2.3	0
Red kidney, raw, dry weight	77	7.0	0
Mung, raw, dry weight	92	6.2	0
Runner, boiled	5	0.9	0
Runner, raw, green	10	0.9	0
Soya, dry weight	108	1.2	1.5
BEECH NUTS			
Shelled, per 28g/1oz	160		5
BEEF			
Per 28g/1oz			
Brisket, boiled, lean and fat	92	0	2.5
Brisket, raw, lean and fat	71		2
Ground beef, very lean, raw	45	0	0.5
Ground beef, very lean, fried and			
drained of fat	55	0	0.5
Ground beef, lean, fried and drained of			
fat, per 28g/1oz raw weight	40	0	0.5
Minced beef, raw	74	0	1.5
Minced beef, well fried and drained of			
fat	82	0	1
Minced beef, well fried and drained of			
fat per 28g/1oz raw weight	60	0	0.5

174

	C	GF	FU
Rump steak, fried, lean only	54	0	1
Rump steak, raw, lean and fat	56	0	1
Rump steak, grilled lean only, 28g/1oz	48	0	0.5
Rump steak, medium grilled, 170g/6oz raw	260	0	4
Rump steak, well grilled, 170g/6oz raw	290	0	5.5
Rump steak, rare grilled, 170g/6oz raw	310	0	6
Silverside, salted, boiled, lean and fat	69	0	1.5
Silverside, salted, boiled, lean only	49	0	0.5
Sirloin, roast, lean and fat	80	0	2
Sirloin, roast, lean only	55	0	1
Stewing steak, raw, lean only	35	0	1
Stewing steak, raw, lean and fat	50	0	0
Topside, raw, lean only	35	0	0.5
Topside, raw, lean and fat	51	0	1
Topside, roast, lean and fat	61	0	
Topside, roast, lean only	44	0	0.5
BEEFBURGERS			
Beefburger, fresh or frozen, well grilled, 57g/2oz raw weight	115	0.2	3
Beefburger, fresh or frozen, grilled 113g/4oz raw weight	240	0.4	6
BEETROOT			
Raw, per 28g/1oz	8	0.9	0
Boiled, per 28g/1oz	12	0.7	0
Per baby beet, boiled	5	0.4	0
BILBERRIES			
Raw or frozen, per 28g/1oz	16		0
BISCUITS			
Per average biscuit			
Chocolate chip cookie	60		1.5
Digestive, large	70	0.8	0.5
Digestive, medium	55	0.6	0.5
Digestive, small	45	0.4	0.5
Fig roll	65	0.7	0.5
Garibaldi, per finger	30	0.2	0.25
Ginger nut	40	0.2	0.5
Ginger snap	35	0.2	0.25
Jaffa cake	50		0.5
Lincoln	40	0.1	0.5
Malted milk	40		0.5
Marie	30	0.2	0.25
Morning coffee	25	0.2	0.25
Nice	45		0.5
Osborne	35	0.2	0.25
Petit Beurre	30		0.25
Rich tea finger	25	0.2	0.25
Rich tea, round	45	0.2	0.5
Sponge finger	20		0.25
BLACKBERRIES			
Raw or frozen, 28g/1oz	8	2.4	0
Stewed, without sugar, per 28g/1oz	7	1.8	0
BLACKCURRANTS			
Raw or frozen, per 28g/1oz	8	24	0
Stewed without sugar, per 28g/1oz	7	2.1	0
BLOATERS			
Fillet, grilled, per 28g/1oz	71	0	1.5
On the bone, grilled per 28g/1oz	53	0	1.5
BRAINS			
Per 28g/1oz			
Calves' or lamb's, raw	31	0	1
Calves', boiled	43	0	1
Lamb's boiled	36	0	1
BRAN			
Per 28g/1oz	58	12.5	0.5
Per 15ml/level tablespoon	10	1.2	0
Per 20ml (Australian tablespoon)	15	1.6	0
BRAWN			
Per 28g/1oz	43	0	1.5

	C	GF	FU
BRAZIL NUTS			
Shelled, per 28g/1oz	175	2.5	6
Per nut, shelled	20	0.3	0.5
Per buttered brazil	40	0.3	0.5
Per chocolate brazil	55	0.3	0.5
BREAD			
Per 28g/1oz slice			
Black rye	90		0.5
Brown or wheatmeal	63	1.5	0.25
Currant	70	0.5	0.5
Enriched, eg. cholla	110	0.8	0.25
French	85	0.8	0.5
Fruit sesame	120		0.5
Granary	70		0.25
Light rye	70		0.25
Malt	70	1.4	0.5
Milk	80		0.5
Soda	75	0.65	0.25
Vogel	65		0.25
Wheatgerm, eg. Hovis and Vitbe	65	1.3	0.25
White	66	0.8	0.25
Wholemeal (100%)	61	2.4	0.25
Rolls, buns etc., each			
Baby bridge roll, 14g/½oz	35	0.4	0.25
Bagel, 42g/1½oz	150		1.5
Bap, 42g/1½oz	130	1.2	1.5
Bath bun, 42g/1½oz	120	1.1	0.5
Brioche roll, 45g/1⅝oz	215		2
Chelsea bun, 92g/3¼oz	255	2.3	2.5
Croissant, 71g/2½oz	280		5.5
Crumpet, 42g/1½oz	75		0.5
Crusty roll, brown or white, 50g/1¾oz	145	2.9	0.5
Currant bun, 50g/1¾oz	150	0.9	1.5
Devonshire split, with cream, 71g/2½oz	195		4
Dinner roll, soft, 42g/1½oz	130	1.2	0.5
Hot cross bun, 57g/2oz	180		1.5
Muffin, 64g/2¼oz	125		0.5
Pitta, 71g/2½oz	205		0.5
Scone, plain white, 57g/2oz	210	1.2	3
Soft brown roll, 50g/1¾oz	140	2.7	1
Soft white roll, 50g/1¾oz	150	1.4	1
Tea cake, 57g/2oz	155	1.2	1.5
Per 15ml/level tablespoon			
Breadcrumbs, dried	30	0.7	0
Breadcrumbs, white, fresh	8	0.1	0
Bread sauce	15	0.1	0.5
Per 20ml (Australian tablespoon)			
Breadcrumbs, dried	40	0.9	0
Breadcrumbs, white, fresh	10	0.1	0
Bread sauce	20	0.1	0.5
BREAKFAST CEREALS			
Per 28g/1oz			
All Bran cereal	70	8.0	0.25
Bran flakes	85	4.2	0
Cornflakes	100	0.5	0
Muesli or Swiss style	105	2.1	0.5
Porridge oats	115	4.3	0.5
Puffed wheat	100	4.3	0.5
Sultana bran	85	3.6	0.25
Weetabix or whole wheat biscuits, per biscuit	65	2.4	0.25
BROCCOLI			
Raw, per 28g/1oz	7	1.0	0
Boiled, per 28g/1oz	5	1.1	0
BRUSSELS SPROUTS			
Raw, per 28g/1oz	7	1.2	0
Boiled, per 28g/1oz	5	0.8	0
BUTTER			
All brands, per 28g/1oz	210	0	8

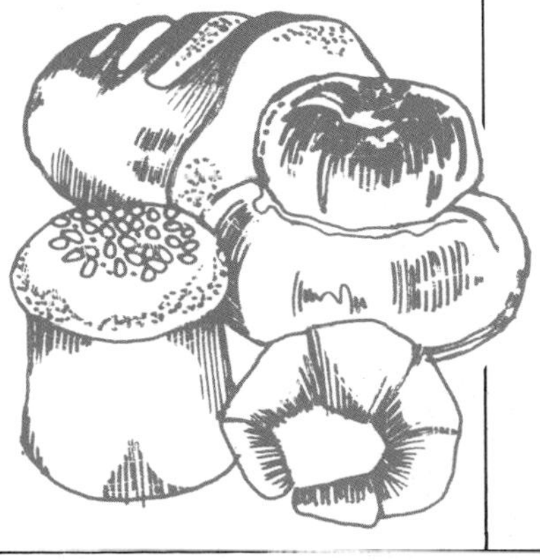

C

	C	GF	FU
CABBAGE			
Per 28g/1oz			
Raw	6	0.7	0
Boiled	4	0.7	0
Pickled red	3	0.9	0
CANDIED PEEL			
Per 28g/1oz	90	0	1
Per 15ml/level tablespoon	45	0	0.5
Per 20ml (Australian tablespoon)	60	0	0.5
CAPERS			
Per 28g/1oz	5		0
CARROTS			
Raw, per 28g/1oz	6	0.8	0
Boiled, per 28g/1oz	5	0.8	0
Per average carrot, 57g/2oz	12	1.6	0
CASHEW NUTS			
Shelled, per 28g/1oz	160	4.0	4
Per nut	15	0.3	0.5
CASSAVA			
Fresh, per 28g/1oz	43	0.3	0
CAULIFLOWER			
Raw, per 28g/1oz	4	0.6	0
Boiled, per 28g/1oz	3	0.5	0
CAVIAR			
Per 28g/1oz	75	0	
CELERIAC			
Boiled, per 28g/1oz	4	1.4	0
CELERY			
Raw, per 28g/1oz	2	0.4	0
Boiled, per 28g/1oz	1	0.6	0
Per stick of celery	5	1.0	0
CHEESE			
Per 28g/1oz			
Austrian smoked	78	0	2.5
Babybel	97	0	2
Bavarian smoked	80	0	2
Bel Paese	96	0	3.5
Blue Stilton	131	0	4
Bonbel	102	0	3.5
Boursin	116	0	4
Bresse bleu	80	0	2
Brie	88	0	2.5
Caerphilly	120	0	3
Caithness Morven	110	0	3
Caithness full fat soft	110	0	3
Camembert	88	0	2.5
Cheddar	120	0	3.5
Cheese spread	80	0	3.5
Cheshire	110	0	3
Cheviot	120	0	3.5
Cotswold	105	0	3

	C	GF	FU
Cottage cheese, plain or with chives, onion, pepper or pineapple	27	0	0.5
Cream cheese	125	0	4.5
Curd cheese	54	0	1
Danbo	98	0	2
Danish Blue	103	0	3
Danish Elbo	98	0	3
Danish Esrom	98	0	3
Danish Fynbo	100	0	3
Danish Havarti	117	0	3.5
Danish Maribo	100	0	3
Danish Molbo	100	0	3
Danish Mozzarella	98	0	3
Danish Mycella	99	0	3
Danish Samsoe	98	0	3.5
Derby	110	0	3
Dolcellata	100	0	3
Double Gloucester	105	0	3
Edam	88	0	2.5
Emmental	115	0	3
Fetta	54	0	1.5
Gorgonzola	112	0	2.5
Gouda	100	0	3
Gruyère	117	0	3.5
Ilchester Cheddar and beer	112	0	3.5
Jarlsberg	95	0	2.5
Lancashire	109	0	3
Leicester	105	0	3
Norwegian blue	100	0	3
Norwegian Gjeost	133	0	4
Orangerulle	92	0	3
Orkney Claymore	111	0	3
Parmesan	118	0	3
Philadelphia	90	0	3.5
Port Salut	94	0	3
Processed	88	0	2.5
Rambol, with walnuts	117	0	3
Red Windsor	119	0	3.5
Riccotta	55	0	2
Roquefort	88	0	3
Sage Derby	112	0	3
Skimmed milk soft cheese (quark)	25	0	0.5
St Paulin	98	0	2.5
Tôme au raisin	74	0	2
Wensleydale	115	0	3
White Stilton	108	0	4
Per 15ml/level tablespoon			
Cottage cheese	15	0	0
Cream cheese	60	0	4.5
Curd cheese	25	0	1
Parmesan cheese	30	0	3
Per 20ml (Australian tablespoon)			
Cottage cheese	20	0	0
Cream cheese	75	0	6
Curd cheese	35	0	1
Parmesan cheese	40	0	4

CHERRIES	C	GF	FU
Fresh, with stones, per 28g/1oz	12	0.4	0
Glacé, per 28g/1oz	60		0
Per glacé cherry	10		0
CHESTNUTS			
Per 28g/1oz			
Shelled	48	1.9	0.25
With shells	40	1.6	
Unsweetened chestnut purée	30		
CHICKEN			
Per 28g/1oz			
On bone, raw, no skin	25	0	0.25
Meat only, raw	34	0	0.5
Meat only, boiled	52	0	0.5
Meat only, roast	42	0	0.5
Meat and skin, roast	61	0	1.5
Chicken drumstick, raw, 99g/3½oz average raw weight	90	0	1.5
Chicken drumstick, grilled and skin removed, 99g/3½oz average raw weight	65	0	1
Chicken drumstick, grilled, 99g/3½oz raw weight	85	0	1.5
Chicken joint, raw 227g/8oz average weight	410	0	0.3
Chicken joint, grilled and skin removed, 227g/8oz average raw weight	165	0	2
Chicken joint, grilled, with skin, 227g/8oz	250	0	5
CHICORY			
Raw, per 28g/1oz	3	0.4	0
CHILLIES			
Dried, per 28g/1oz	85	7.1	0
CHIVES			
Per 28g/1oz	10		0
CHINESE LEAVES			
Raw, per 28g/1oz	3	0.6	0
CHOCOLATE			
Per 28g1/1oz			
Milk or plain	150	0	1.5
Cooking	155	0	1.5
Filled chocolates	130	0	1.5
Vermicelli	135	0	1.5
Per 5ml/level teaspoon			
Chocolate spread	20	0	0.25
Drinking chocolate	10	0	0
Vermicelli	20	0	0.25
CLAMS			
With shells, raw, per 28g/1oz	15	0	0
Without shells, raw, per 28g/1oz	25	0	
COB NUTS			
With shells, per 28g/1oz	39	1.7	1.5
Shelled, per 28g/1oz	108	0.6	3.5
Per nut	5	0	0
COCKLES			
Without shells, boiled, per 28g/1oz	14	0	0
COCOA POWDER			
Per 28g/1oz	88		2
Per 5ml/level teaspoon	10		0.5
COCONUT			
Per 28g/1oz			
Fresh	100	3.8	3.5
Desiccated	171	6.6	6
Fresh coconut milk, per 28ml/1floz	6	0	0
Creamed coconut	218		8
Desiccated, per 15ml/level tablespoon	30	1.1	1
Per 20ml (Australian tablespoon)	40	1.4	1
COD			
Per 28g/1oz			
Fillet, raw	22	0	0
Fillet, baked or grilled with a little fat	27	0	0.5
Fillet, poached in water or steamed	24	0	0
Frozen steaks, raw	19	0	0
On the bone, raw	15	0	0
COD LIVER OIL			
Per 5ml/teaspoon	40	0	1.5
COD ROE			
Raw, hard roe, per 28g/1oz	32	0	0.25
COFFEE			
Coffee beans, roasted and ground infusion	0	0	0
Instant, per 5ml/teaspoon	0	0	0
COLEY			
Per 28g/1oz			
Raw	21	0	0
On the bone, steamed	24	0	0
Fillet, steamed	28	0	0
COOKING OR SALAD OIL			
Per 28g/1oz	255	0	10
Per 15ml/1 level tablespoon	120	0	5
Per 20ml (Australian tablespoon)	160	0	6
CORNED BEEF, CANNED			
Per 28g/1oz	62	0	1
CORNFLOUR			
Per 28g/1oz	100	0.8	0
Per 15ml/1 level tablespoon	33	0.3	0
Per 20ml (Australian tablespoon)	44	0.4	0
CORN OIL			
Per 28g/1oz	255	0	10
Per 15ml/1 level tablespoon	120	0	5
Per 20ml (Australian tablespoon)	160	0	6
CORN ON THE COB			
Average whole cob	155	4.5	0
COURGETTES (Zucchini)			
Raw per 28g/1oz	4	0.5	0
Per courgette, 70g/2½oz	10	1.3	0
CRAB			
With shell, per 28g/1oz boiled	7	0	0
Meat only, per 28g/1oz boiled	36	0	0.5
Average crab with shell	95	0	1.5
CRANBERRIES			
Per 28g/1oz	4	1.2	0
CRANBERRY SAUCE			
Per 28g/1oz	65		0.5
Per 15ml/1 level tablespoon	45		0.5
Per 20ml (Australian tablespoon)	60		0.5
CREAM			
Per 28g/1oz			
Clotted	165	0	5.5
Double	127	0	5
Half cream	35	0	1
Imitation	85	0	3
Single	60	0	2
Soured	60	0	2
Sterilised, canned	65	0	2.5
Whipping	94	0	3.5
Per 15ml/1 level tablespoon			
Clotted	105	0	3.5
Double	55	0	2
Half cream	20	0	0.5
Imitation	55	0	2
Single	30	0	1
Soured	30	0	1
Sterilised, canned	35	0	1
Whipping	45	0	1.5
Per 20ml (Australian tablespoon)			
Clotted	140	0	4.5
Double	75	0	3
Half cream	25	0	0.5
Imitation	75	0	2.5
Single	40	0	1.5
Soured	40	0	1.5
Sterilised, canned	45	0	1.5
Whipping	60	0	2
CRISPS (potato)			
All flavours per 28g/1oz	150	3	3
CUCUMBER			
Raw, per 28g/1oz	3	0.1	0

177

	C	GF	FU
CURRANTS			
Per 28g/1oz	69	2.2	1
Per 15ml/1 level tablespoon	20	0.6	0.25
Per 20ml (Australian tablespoon)	28	0.9	0.25
CURRY PASTE OR CONCENTRATE			
Per 28g/1oz	40	0	1
CURRY POWDER			
Per 28g/1oz	66		0
Per 5ml/1 level teaspoon	12		0
CUSTARD APPLE			
Flesh only, per 28g/1oz	25		0
CUSTARD POWDER			
Per 28g/1oz	100	0.8	0
Per 15ml/1 level tablespoon	33	0.2	0
Per 20ml (Australian tablespoon)	44	0.3	0

	C	GF	FU
DAMSONS			
Fresh, with stones per 28g/1oz	11	1.0	0
Stewed, no sugar, per 28g/1oz	8	0.9	0
DATES			
Per 28g/1oz			
Dried, with stones	60	2.1	0.5
Dried, without stones	70	2.4	0.5
Fresh, with stones	30		0
Per date, fresh	15		0
DELICATESSEN SAUSAGES			
Per 28g/1oz			
Belgian liver sausage	90	0.1	2.5
Bierwurst	75	0	2.5
Bockwurst	180	0	5
Cervelat	140	0	4
Chorizo	140		3
Continental liver sausage	85	0.1	3
Frankfurter	78	0.3	2.5
French garlic sausage	90	0	3
Garlic sausage	70	0	2.5
Ham sausage	50	0	0.5
Kabanos	115	0	3.5
Krakowska	80	0	2.5
Liver sausage	88	0.1	2.5
Mettwurst	120		3.5
Mortadella, Italian	105	0	3
Polish country sausage	60		1
Polony	80	0.2	2
Pork boiling ring, coarse	110	0	3.5
Salami, Belgian	130	0	4
Salami, Danish	160	0	4.5
Salami, Hungarian	130	0	4
Salami, German	120	0	3.5
Saveloy	74	0.1	2
Smoked Dutch sausage	105	0	3
Smoked pork sausage	130	0	3.5
Smoked ham sausage	65	0	2
DRIPPING			
Per 28g/1oz	253	0	10
Per 15ml/1 level tablespoon	125	0	5
Per 20ml (Australian tablespoon)	165	0	6

	C	GF	FU
DUCK			
Per 28g/1oz			
Raw, meat only	35	0	0.5
Raw, meat, fat and skin	122	0	4.5
Roast, meat only	54	0	1
Roast, meat, fat and skin	96	0	3
DUCK EGGS			
99g/3½oz egg	170	0	4

	C	GF	FU
EEL			
Meat only, raw per 28g/1oz	48	0	1
Meat only, stewed in water, per 28g/1oz	57	0	1.5
Jellied eels plus some jelly, 85g/3oz	180	0	4
EGGS, each			
Size 1	95	0	2.5
Size 2	90	0	2.5
Size 3	80	0	2
Size 4	75	0	2
Size 5	70	0	2
Size 6	60	0	1.5
Yolk of size 3 egg	65	0	2
White of size 3 egg	15	0	0
EGG PLANTS			
see aubergines			
ENDIVE			
Raw, per 28g/1oz	3	0.6	0

	C	GF	FU
FAGGOTS			
Per 28g/1oz	76	0	2
FIGS			
Dried, per 28g/1oz	60	5.2	0.5
Fresh, green, per 28g/1oz	12	0.7	0
Per dried fig	30	2.6	0.25
FLOUNDER			
On the bone, raw, per 28g/1oz	20	0	
On the bone, steamed, per 28g/1oz	15	0	
FLOUR			
Per 28g/1oz			
Wheatmeal	93	2.1	0.25
White, plain	99	1.0	0
White, self-raising	96	1.0	0
White, strong	96	0.8	0
Wholemeal	90	2.7	0.25
Buckwheat	99	0.3	0.25
Cassava	97	0.4	0
Granary	99		0
Maizemeal (96%)	103	0.4	0.5
Maizemeal (60%)	100	0.2	0
Rice	100	0.7	0
Rye (100%)	95	3.3	0.25
Soya, low fat	100	4.0	0.5
Soya, full fat	127	3.4	2.5
Yam	90	0.4	0

Per 15ml/1 level tablespoon	C	GF	FU
White	32	0.3	0
Wholemeal	29	0.9	0
Per 20ml (Australian tablespoon)			
White	43	0.4	0
Wholemeal	39	1.1	0
FRENCH DRESSING			
Per 15ml/tablespoon	75	0	3
Per 20ml (Australian tablespoon)	100	0	4
Oil-free, per 15ml/tablespoon	5	0	0
per 20ml (Australian tablespoon)	6	0	0
FRUIT			
Crystallised, per 28g/1oz	75	0	1

GAMMON	C	GF	FU
Per 28g/1oz			
Gammon joint, raw, lean and fat	67	0	2
Gammon joint, boiled, lean and fat	76	0	2
Gammon joint, boiled, lean only	47	0	0.5
Gammon rashers, grilled, lean and fat	65	0	1
Gammon rashers, grilled, lean only	49	0	0.5
GARLIC			
One clove	0	0	0
GELATINE, powdered			
Per 15ml/1 level tablespoon	30	0	0
Per 28g/1oz	96	0	0
Per 20ml (Australian tablespoon)	40	0	0
Per 10g envelope	35	0	0
GHEE			
Per 28g/1oz	235	0	10
GHERKINS			
Per 28g/1oz	5		0
GINGER			
Ground, per 28g/1oz	73		0.5
Ground, 5ml/1 level teaspoon	8		0
Root, raw, peeled, 28g/1oz	18		0
Stem in syrup, strained, per 28g/1oz	60		0.5
GOOSE			
Roast, on bone, per 28g/1oz	55	0	2
Roast, meat only (without skin), per 28g/1oz	90	0	2
GOOSEBERRIES			
Fresh, ripe dessert, per 28g/1oz	10	1	0
Fresh, cooking, per 28g/1oz	5	0.9	0
GRAPEFRUIT			
Per 28g/1oz			
Canned in syrup	17	0.2	0
Canned in natural juice	11	0.2	0
Flesh only	6	0.2	0
Flesh and skin	3	0.1	0
Juice, unsweetened, per 28ml/1floz	9	0	0
Juice, sweetened, per 28ml/1floz	11	0	0
Medium whole fruit, 340g/12oz	35	1.0	0
GRAPES			
Black, per 28g/1oz	14	0.1	0
White, per 28g/1oz	17	0.2	0

	C	GF	FU
GREENGAGES			
Fresh, with stones, per 28g/1oz	13	0.7	0
Stewed, with stones, no sugar, per 28g/1oz	11	0.6	0
GRENADINE SYRUP			
Per 28g/1oz	72	0	1
GROUSE			
Roast, meat only, per 28g/1oz	50	0	0.5
GROUND RICE			
Per 28g/1oz	100	0.7	0
Per 15ml/1 level tablespoon	33	0.2	0
Per 20ml (Australian tablespoon)	44	0.3	0
GUAVAS			
Canned, per 28g/1oz	17	1.0	0
GUINEA FOWL			
Roast, on bone, per 28g/1oz	30	0	0
Roast, meat only, per 28g/1oz	60	0	0

HADDOCK	C	GF	FU
Per 28g/1oz			
Fillet, raw	21	0	0
Fillet in breadcrumbs, fried	50	0.1	1
On the bone, raw	15	0	0
Smoked fillet, raw	25	0	0
HAGGIS			
Cooked, per 28g/1oz	88	0	2
HAKE			
Per 28g/1oz			
Fillet, raw	20	0	0
Fillet, steamed	30	0	0
Fillet, fried	60	0	1
On the bone, raw	10	0	0
HALIBUT			
Per 28g/1oz			
Fillet, steamed	37	0	0.25
On the bone, raw	26	0	0
On the bone, steamed	28	0	0
Steak, 170g/6oz	155	0	2
HAM			
Per 28g/1oz			
Chopped ham roll or loaf	75	0	1.5
Ham, boiled, lean	47	0	0.5
Ham, boiled, fatty	90	0	2
Honey roast ham	50	0	0.5
Old smokey ham	65	0	1
Maryland ham	55	0	0.25
Virginia ham	40	0	0.25
Ham steak, well grilled, 99g/3½oz, average raw weight	105	0	1
HARE			
Stewed, meat only per 28g/1oz raw	55	0	1
Stewed, on bone, per 28g/1oz	39	0	0.5
HASLET			
Per 28g/1oz	80	0	1.5
HAZELNUTS			
Shelled, per 28g/1oz	108	1.7	3.5
Per nut	5	0	0
Chocolate hazelnut whirl, each	40	0	0
HEART			
Per 28g/1oz			
Lamb's raw	34	0	0.5
Ox, raw	31	0	0.5
Pig's, raw	26	0	0.5

HERRING	C	GF	FU
Per 28g/1oz			
Fillet, raw	66	0	2
Fillet, grilled	56	0	1.5
On the bone, grilled	38	0	1
Rollmop herring	47	0	1
Rollmop herring, 70g/2½oz average weight	120	0	3
Whole herring, grilled, 128g/4½oz average weight	170	0	3.5
HERRING ROE			
Fried, per 28g/1oz	69	0	1.5
Raw, soft roe	23	0	0.5
HONEY			
Per 15ml/level tablespoon	60		0.5
Per 20ml (Australian tablespoon)	80		1
Per 5ml/1 teaspoon	20		0
HORSERADISH			
Fresh root, per 28g/1oz	17	2.4	0
Horseradish sauce, per 15ml/1 level tablespoon	13		0
per 20ml (Australian tablespoon)	17		0
HUMUS			
Per 28g/1oz	50		0.5

I

ICE-CREAM	C	GF	FU
Per 28g/1oz			
Chocolate	55	0	1
Coffee	50	0	1
Cornish dairy	50	0	1
Raspberry ripple	50	0	1
Soft ice-cream	45	0	1
Strawberry	50	0	1
Vanilla	45	0	1

J

JAM	C	GF	FU
Per 15ml/level tablespoon	45	0.2	0.5
Per 5ml/level teaspoon	15	0	0
Per 20ml (Australian tablespoon)	60	0.2	0.5
JELLY			
Cubes as sold, per 28g/1oz	73	0	0
Made up with water, per 142ml/¼ pint	85	0	0
Per cube	29	0	0

K

KIDNEY	C	GF	FU
All types, raw, per 28g/1oz	25	0	0.25
Lamb's kidney, grilled, without fat, 57g/2oz average raw weight	50	0	0.5
KIPPERS			
Fillet, baked or grilled, without fat, per 28g/1oz	58	0	1
On the bone, baked, per 28g/1oz	31	0	0.5
Whole kipper, grilled, without fat, 170g/6oz	280	0	3.5

L

LAMB	C	GF	FU
Per 28g/1oz			
Breast, boned, raw, lean and fat	107	0	3.5
Breast, boned, roast, lean and fat	116	0	3.5
Breast, boned roast, lean only	71	0	1.5
Leg, raw, lean and fat, without bone	68	0	2
Leg, roast, lean and fat, without bone	75	0	2
Leg, roast, lean only, without bone	54	0	1
Scrag and neck, raw, lean and fat, weighed with bone	54	0	3
Scrag and neck, raw lean and fat, weighed without bone	90	0	4
Scrag and neck, stewed, lean only, weighed with bone	38	0	1
Scrag and neck, stewed, lean only. weighed without bone	72	0	1.5
Shoulder, boned, roast, lean and fat	89	0	2.5
Shoulder, boned, roast, lean only	56	0	1
Chump chop, well grilled, 142g/5oz raw weight	205	0	6
Leg steak, boneless, well grilled, 227g/8oz raw weight	370	0	7
Loin chop, well grilled, 142g/5oz raw weight	175	0	6.5
LARD			
Per 28g/1oz	253	0	10
LAVERBREAD			
Per 28g/1oz	15		0
LEEKS			
Raw, per 28g/1oz	9	0.8	0
Average whole leek, raw	25	2.2	0
LEMON			
Flesh and skin, per 28g/1oz	4	1.5	0
Whole lemon, 142g/5oz	20	7.4	0
Lemon juice, per 15-20ml/1 tablespoon	0	0	0
LEMON CURD			
Per 28g/1oz	80	0	0
Per 5ml/1 level teaspoon	15	0	0
LEMON SOLE			
Per 28g/1oz			
Fillet, steamed or poached	26	0	0
On the bone, raw	23	0	0
On the bone, steamed or poached	18	0	0
LENTILS			
Raw, per 28g/1oz	86	3.3	0
Split, boiled, per 28g/1oz	28	1.0	0
LETTUCE			
Fresh, per 28g/1oz	3	0.4	0
LIVER			
Per 28g/1oz			
Calves, raw	43	0	1

	C	GF	FU
Chicken's, raw	38	0	0.5
Chicken's, fried	55	0	1
Lamb's, raw	51	0	1
Lamb's, fried	66	0	1.5
Ox, raw	46	0	1
Pig's, raw	44	0	0.5
LOBSTER			
With shell, boiled, per 28g/1oz	12	0	0.25
Meat only, boiled, per 28g/1oz	34	0	0.5
LOGANBERRIES			
Fresh, per 28g/1oz	5	1.8	0
Canned in natural juice, per 28g/1oz	9	1	0
LOW-FAT SPREAD			
All brands, per 28g/1oz	105	0	4
Per 5ml/level teaspoon	15	0	0.5
LUNCHEON MEAT			
Per 28g/1oz	89	0	2.5

M

	C	GF	FU
MACARONI			
Per 28g/1oz			
White, raw	105	0.8	0.25
Wholewheat, raw	95	2.8	0.25
White, boiled	33	0.3	0
Wholewheat, boiled	30	0.9	0
MACEDONIA NUTS			
Per 28g/1oz	188		6.5
MACKEREL			
Per 28g/1oz			
Fillet, raw	63	0	1.5
Kippered mackerel	62	0	1.5
Smoked mackerel fillet	70	0	2.5
Whole raw mackerel, 227g/8oz	320	0	7.5
MAIZE			
Whole grain, per 28g/1oz	103	0.6	0
MANDARINS			
Canned in natural juice, per 28g/1oz	11	0.1	0
Fresh, weighed with skin, per 28g/1oz	7	0.4	0
Medium whole fruit, 70g/2½oz	20	0.9	0
MANGO			
Raw, per 28g/1oz	17	0.4	0
Canned in syrup, per 28g/1oz	22	0.3	0
Mango chutney, per 15ml/1 level tablespoon	40		0
per 20ml (Australian tablespoon)	55		0
MAPLE SYRUP			
Per 15ml/tablespoon	50	0	0.5
MARGARINE			
All brands including those labelled 'high in polyunsaturates', per 28g/1oz	210	0	8
MARMALADE			
Per 28g/1oz			
Per 15ml/1 level tablespoon	74	0.2	1.0
	45	0.1	0.5
Per 20ml (Australian tablespoon)	60	0.1	0.5
MARRON GLACE			
Per 28g/1oz	74	0	1
MARROW			
Raw, flesh only, per 28g/1oz	5	0.5	0
Boiled, per 28g/1oz	2	0.2	0

	C	GF	FU
MARZIPAN (Almond Paste)			
Per 28g/1oz	126	1.8	2.5
Petit fours	126		2.5
MAYONNAISE			
Per 28g/1oz	205	0	6.0
Per 15ml/l level tablespoon	120	0	3.5
Per 20ml (Australian tablespoon)	160	0	4.5
MEDLARS			
Flesh only, per 28g/1oz	12	2.9	0
MELON			
Per 28g/1oz			
Cantaloupe, with skin	4	0.1	0
Honeydew or Yellow, with skin	4	0.1	0
Ogen, with skin	5	0.2	0
Watermelon, with skin	3	0.1	0
Slice of Cantaloupe, Honeydew or Yellow, with skin, 227g/8oz	30	1.3	0
MILK			
Per 568ml/1 pint			
Buttermilk	232	0	0
Channel Island or gold top	445	0	10
Evaporated milk, full cream, reconstituted	360	0	10
Goat's	415	0	9.5
Homogenised or red top	380	0	8
Instant dried skimmed milk with vegetable fat, reconstituted	280	0	6
Longlife or UHT	380	0	8
Pasteurised or silver top	380	0	8
Pasteurised or silver top with cream removed, 510ml/18floz	240	0	0.5
Skimmed or separated	200	0	0
Soya milk, diluted as directed	370	0	12
Sterilised	380	0	8
Untreated farm milk or green top	380	0	8
Per 15ml/1 level tablespoon			
Channel Island or gold top	15	0	0.5
Condensed full cream, sweetened	50	0	0.5
Condensed, skimmed, sweetened	40	0	0.5
Evaporated full cream	23	0	0.5
Homogenised, pasteurised, green top, silver top and sterilised	10	0	0
Instant low fat milk, dry	18	0	0
Instant low fat milk, reconstituted	5	0	0
Skimmed or separated	5	0	0
Canned milk, per 28g/1oz			
Evaporated full cream	45	0	1
Condensed, skimmed, sweetened	76	0	0.5
Condensed full cream, sweetened	91	0	1
Condensed, unsweetened	40	0	0.5
MINCEMEAT			
Per 28g/1oz	67	0.9	0.5
Per 15ml/1 level tablespoon	40	0.5	0.5
Per 20ml (Australian tablespoon)	55	0.7	0.5
MINT			
Fresh, per 28g/1oz	3		0
MINT SAUCE			
Per 15ml/1 level tablespoon	5		0
Per 20ml (Australian tablespoon)	7		0
MOLASSES			
Per 28g/1oz	78	0	1
Per 15ml/1 level tablespoon	45	0	0.5
Per 20ml (Australian tablespoon)	60	0	0.5

	C	GF	FU
MUESLI			
Per 28g/1oz	105	2.1	0.5
Per 15ml/1 level tablespoon	30	0.5	0
Per 20ml (Australian tablespoon)	40	0.7	0
MULBERRIES			
Raw, per 28g/1oz	10	0.4	0
MULLET			
Raw, flesh only, per 28g/1oz	40	0	0.5
MUSHROOMS			
Raw, per 28g/1oz	4	0.7	0
Sliced and fried, per 28g/1oz	60	1.1	3.5
MUSSELS			
With shells, boiled, per 28g/1oz	7	0	0
Without shells, boiled, per 28g/1oz	25	0	0.25
Per mussel	10	0	0
MUSTARD AND CRESS			
Raw, per 28g/1oz	3	1	0
Whole carton	5	1.6	0
MUSTARD			
Dry, per 28g/1oz	128		0
Made mustard, English, per 5ml/1 level teaspoon	10		0

N

	C	GF	FU
NECTARINES			
Whole fruit, medium	50	2.5	0
NOODLES			
Cooked, per 28g/1oz	33		0
NUTMEG			
Powdered, per 2.5ml/½ level teaspoon	0	0	0

O

	C	GF	FU
OATMEAL			
Raw, per 28g/1oz	114	2	1
Per 15ml/1 level tablespoon, raw	40	0.7	0
Per 20ml (Australian tablespoon), raw	55	0.8	0
OCTOPUS			
Raw, per 28g/1oz	20	0	0
OKRA (ladies' fingers)			
Raw, per 28g/1oz	5	0.9	0

	C	GF	FU
OLIVE OIL			
Per 28ml/1floz	255	0	10
Per 15ml/1 level tablespoon	120	0	5
OLIVES			
Stoned, in brine, per 28g/1oz	29	1.2	1
With stones, in brine, per 28g/1oz	23	1	1
Per stuffed olive	5	0.2	0
ONIONS			
Per 28g/1oz			
Raw	7	0.4	0
Boiled	4	0.3	0
Fried, sliced	98	1.3	3.5
Dried, per 15ml/1 level tablespoon	10	0.6	0
Whole onion, raw, 85g/3oz	20	1.2	0
Pickled onion, each	5	0.2	0
Cocktail onion, each	1	0	0
ORANGES			
Flesh only, per 28g/1oz	10	0.6	0
Flesh with skin, per 28g/1oz	7	0.4	0
Whole fruit, small, 142g/5oz	35	2.1	0
Whole fruit, medium, 227g/8oz	60	3.4	0
Whole fruit, large, 284g/10oz	75	4.2	0
ORANGE JUICE			
Per 28ml/1floz			
Canned, sweetened	15	0	0
Unsweetened	11	0	0
OXTAIL			
Stewed, without bone, per 28g/1oz	69	0	1.5
On the bone, stewed and skimmed of fat, per 28g/1oz	26	0	0.5
OYSTERS			
With shells, raw, per 28g/1oz	2	0	0
Without shells, raw, per 28g/1oz	14	0	0
Per oyster	5	0	0

P

	C	GF	FU
PARSLEY			
Fresh, per 28g/1oz	6	2.6	0
Parsley sauce, per 15ml/1 level tablespoon	45	0	0
per 20ml (Australian tablespoon)	60	0	0
PARSNIPS			
Per 28g/1oz			
Raw	14	1.1	0
Boiled	16	0.7	0
Roast	30		0.5
PARTRIDGE			
Roast, on bone, per 28g/1oz	36	0	0.5
Roast, meat only, per 28g/1oz	60	0	0.5
PASSION FRUIT			
Flesh only, per 28g/1oz	10	4.5	0
PASTA			
White, all shapes, raw, per 28g/1oz	105	0.8	0
White, boiled, per 28g/1oz	33	0.3	0
Wholewheat, raw	95	2.8	0.25
Wholewheat, boiled	30	0.9	0
PASTRY			
Per 28g/1oz			
Choux, raw	60	0.2	1.5
Choux, baked	95	0.4	2
Flaky, raw	120	0.4	3
Flaky, baked	160	0.6	4
Shortcrust, raw	130	0.6	3
Shortcrust, baked	150	0.7	3
PAW PAW (Papaya)			
Canned, per 28g/1oz	18	0.1	0
Fresh, flesh only, per 28g/1oz	11	0.2	0
PEACHES			
Canned in natural juice, per 28g/1oz	13	0.2	0
Canned in syrup, per 28g/1oz	25	0.2	0.25
Fresh, with stones, per 28g/1oz	9	0.3	0
Whole fruit, 115g/4oz	35	1.4	0
PEANUTS			
Per 28g/1oz			
Shelled, fresh	162	2.3	5
Dry roasted	160	2.3	5

	C	GF	FU
Roasted and salted	162	2.3	5
Peanut butter	177	2.1	5.5
Per peanut	5	0	0
PEARS			
Per 28g/1oz			
Cooking pears, raw, peeled	10	0.8	0
Dessert pears	8	0.5	0
Canned in syrup	22	0.5	0.25
Whole fruit, medium, 142g/5oz	40	2.4	0
PEAS			
Per 28g/1oz			
Frozen	15	2.2	0
Canned, garden	13	1.8	0
Canned, processed	23	2.2	0
Dried, raw	81	4.7	0
Dried, boiled	29	1.3	0
Split, raw	88	3.4	0
Split, boiled	33	1.4	0
Per 30ml/1 rounded tablespoon			
Dried, boiled	30	1.3	0
Fresh, boiled	10	1.1	0
Pease pudding	35		0
Per 40ml (Australian rounded tablespoon)			
Dried, boiled	40	1.8	0
Frozen, boiled	13	1.1	0
Pease pudding	45		0
PECANS			
Per nut	15	0	1
PEPPER			
Powdered, per pinch	0	0	0
PEPPERS (capsicums)			
Red or green, per 28g/1oz	4	0.3	0
Average pepper, 142g/5oz	20	1.3	0
PERCH			
White, raw, per 28g/1oz	35	0	0.5
Yellow, raw, per 28g/1oz	25	0	0.5
PHEASANT			
Meat only, roast, per 28g/1oz	60	0	1
On the bone, roast, per 28g/1oz	38	0	0.5
PICKLES AND RELISHES			
Mixed pickles, per 28g/1oz	5	0.5	0
Per 15ml/1 level tablespoon			
Piccalilli	15	0.3	0
Ploughmans	35	0.3	0
Sweet pickle	35	0.3	0
Per 20ml (Australian tablespoon)			
Piccalilli	20	0.4	0
Ploughmans	45	0.4	0
Sweet pickle	45	0.4	0
PIGEON			
Meat only, roast, per 28g/1oz	65	0	1.5
On the bone, roast, per 28g/1oz	29	0	0.5
PIKE			
Raw fillet, per 28g/1oz	25	0	0
PILCHARDS			
Canned in tomato sauce, per 28g/1oz	36	0	0.5
PIMENTOS			
Canned in brine, per 28g/1oz	6		0

	C	GF	FU
PINEAPPLES			
Canned in natural juice, weighed with juice, per 28g/1oz	15	0.2	0
Canned in syrup, per 28g/1oz	22	0.2	0.25
Fresh, weighed without skin and core, per 28g/1oz	13	0.3	0
Ring of canned, drained pineapple in syrup	35	0.5	0.25
Ring of canned, drained pineapple in natural juice	20	0.5	0
PISTACHIO NUTS			
Shelled, per 28g/1oz	180		5.5
Per nut	5		0
PLAICE			
Per 28g/1oz			
Fillet, raw or steamed	26	0	0.25
Fillet, in batter, fried	79	0.2	2
Fillet, in breadcrumbs, fried	65	0.1	1.5
PLANTAIN			
Per 28g/1oz			
Green, raw	32	1.6	0
Green, boiled	35	1.8	0
Ripe, fried	76	1.6	1
PLUMS			
Per 28g/1oz			
Cooking plums with stones, stewed without sugar	6	0.6	0
Fresh dessert plums, with stones	10	0.6	0
Cooking plums, with stones	7	0.7	0
Victoria dessert plum, medium, each	15	0.6	0
POLLACK			
On the bone, raw, per 28g/1oz	25	0	0
POLONY			
On the bone, raw, per 28g/1oz	80	0.2	2
POMEGRANATE			
Flesh only, per 28g/1oz	20		0
Whole pomegranate, 205g/7¼oz	65		0
POPCORN			
Per 28g/1oz	110		1
PORK			
Per 28g/1oz			
Belly rashers, raw, lean and fat	108	0	3.5
Belly rashers, grilled, lean and fat	113	0	3.5
Fillet, raw, lean only	42	0	1
Leg, raw, lean and fat, weighed without bone	76	0	2.5
Leg, raw, lean only, weighed without bone	42	0	1
Leg, roast, lean and fat	81	0	2
Leg, roast, lean only	52	0	0.5
Crackling	190	0	4

	C	GF	FU
Scratchings	185	0	4
Pork chop, well grilled, 184g/6½oz raw weight, fat removed	240	0	4
POTATOES			
Per 28g/1oz			
Raw	25	0.6	0
Old, baked, weighed with skin	24	0.7	0
Boiled, old potatoes	23	0.3	0
Boiled, new potatoes	22	0.5	0
Canned, new potatoes drained	15	0.7	0
Chips (average thickness)	70	0.6	7.5
Crisps	150	3.4	3.5
Roast, large chunks	40	0.6	0.5
Sauté	40	0.6	0.5
Instant mashed potato powder, per 15ml/level tablespoon, dry	40	1.0	0
Per 20ml (Australian tablespoon)	55	0.3	0
Jacket-baked potato, 198g/7oz raw weight	170	4.9	0
PRAWNS			
With shells, per 28g/1oz	12	0	0
Without shells, per 28g/1oz	30	0	0.25
Per shelled prawn	2	0	0
PRUNES			
Per 28g/1oz			
Dried, no stones	46	4.6	0.5
Stewed, without sugar, fruit and juice without stones	21	2.1	0
Prune juice	25	0	0
Per prune	10	0	0
PUMPKIN			
Raw, flesh only per 28g/1oz	4	0.1	0

Q

	C	GF	FU
QUINCES			
Raw, per 28g/1oz	7	1.8	0

R

	C	GF	FU
RABBIT			
Per 28g/1oz			
Meat only, raw	35	0	0.5
Meat only, stewed	51	0	1.5
On the bone, stewed	26	0	0.5
RADISHES			
Fresh, per 28g/1oz	4	0.5	0
Per radish	2	0.2	0
RAISINS			
Dried, per 28g/1oz	70	2.8	1
Per 15ml/1 level tablespoon	25	0.7	0.25
Per 20ml (Australian tablespoon)	35	0.9	0.25
RASPBERRIES			
Fresh or frozen, per 28g/1oz	7	2.1	0
Canned, drained, per 28g/1oz	25		0
REDCURRANTS			
Fresh, per 28g/1oz	6	2.3	0
Redcurrant jelly, per 5ml/1 level teaspoon	15		0
RHUBARB			
Raw, per 28g/1oz	2	0.7	0
Stewed without sugar, per 28g/1oz	2	0.6	0
RICE			
Per 28g/1oz			
Brown, raw	99	1.2	0.25
White, raw	102	0.3	0
White, boiled	35	0.1	0
Brown, boiled	33	0.4	0
ROCK			
Seaside rock, per 28g/1oz	95	0	1

S

	C	GF	FU
SAGO			
Raw, per 28g/1oz	101	0.8	0
SAITHE (Coley)			
Per 28g/1oz			
Fillet, raw	21	0	0
Fillet, steamed	28	0	0
On the bone, steamed	24	0	0
SALAD CREAM			
Per 15ml/1 level tablespoon	50	0	1.5
Per 20ml (Australian tablespoon)	65	0	2
Low-calorie salad cream, per 15ml/1 level tablespoon	25	0	0.5
per 20ml (Australian tablespoon)	35	1	1
SALMON			
Per 28g/1oz			
Canned	44	0	1
Fillet, steamed	56	0	1.5
Fresh, raw, flesh only	52	0	1
On the bone, steamed	45	0	1
Smoked	40	0	0.5
SALSIFY			
Boiled, per 28g/1oz	5	0.1	0
SALT			
Per 28g/1oz	0	0	0
SARDINES			
Per 28g/1oz			
Canned in oil, drained	62	0	1.5
Canned in tomato sauce	50	0	1
SAUSAGES, each			
Beef chipolata, well grilled	50	0	1.5
Beef, large, well grilled	120	0	3
Beef, skinless, well grilled	65	0	1.5
Pork chipolata, well grilled	65	0.1	2
Pork, large, well grilled	125	0.2	3.5
Pork, skinless, well grilled	95	0	2
Pork and beef chipolata, well grilled	60	0	1.5
Pork and beef, large, well grilled	125	0	3
SCALLOPS			
Steamed, without shells per 28g/1oz	30	0	0
SCAMPI			
Fried in breadcrumbs, per 28g/1oz	90	0.3	2
SEAKALE			
Boiled, per 28g/1oz	2	0.3	0
SEMOLINA			
Raw, per 28g/1oz dry	99	0.8	0
Per 15ml/1 level tablespoon	35	0.2	0
SESAME SEEDS			
Per 28g/1oz	168		5
SHRIMPS			
Per 28g/1oz			
Canned, drained	27	0	0
Fresh, with shells	11	0	0
Fresh, without shells	33	0	0

SKATE	C	GF	FU
Fillet, in batter, fried, per 28g/1oz	57	0.1	1
SMELTS			
Without bones, fried, per 28g/1oz	115	0	1
SNAILS			
Flesh only, per 28g/1oz	25	0	0
SOLE			
Per 28g/1oz			
Fillet, raw	23	0	0
Fillet, steamed or poached	26	0	0
On the bone, steamed or poached	18	0	0
SPAGHETTI			
Per 28g/1oz			
White, raw	107	0.8	0.25
Wholewheat, raw	97	2.8	0.25
White, boiled	33	0.3	0
Wholewheat, boiled	30	0.9	0
Canned in tomato sauce	17	0.1	0
SPINACH			
Boiled, per 28g/1oz	9	1.7	0
SPRATS			
Fried without heads, per 28g/1oz	110	0	4
SPRING GREENS			
Boiled, per 28g/1oz	3	1.1	0
SPRING ONIONS (scallions)			
Raw, per 28g/1oz	10	0.4	0
Per onion	3	0.1	0
SQUID			
Flesh only, raw per 28g/1oz	25	0	0
STRAWBERRIES			
Fresh or frozen, per 28g/1oz	7	0.6	0
Canned, drained, per 28g/1oz	23		0
Per fresh strawberry	2	0.1	0
STURGEON			
On the bone, raw, per 28g/1oz	25	0	0
SUET			
Shredded, per 28g/1oz	235	0	8.5
Per 15ml/1 level tablespoon	85	0	3
Per 20ml (Australian tablespoon)	115	0	4
SUGAR			
White, brown, caster,			
Demerara, granulated,			
icing, per 28g/1oz	112	0	1
Per 15ml/1 level tablespoon	50	0	0.5
Per 20ml (Australian tablespoon)	70	0	0.5
SULTANAS			
Dried, per 28g/1oz	71	1.9	0.5
Per 15ml/1 level tablespoon	25	0.7	0.25
Per 20ml (Australian tablespoon)	35	0.9	0.25
SUNFLOWER SEED OIL			
Per 28g/1oz	255	0	10
Per 15ml/1 tablespoon	120	0	5
Per 20ml (Australian tablespoon)	160	0	6
SWEDES			
Raw, per 28g/1oz	6	0.7	0
Boiled, per 28g/1oz	5	0.8	0
SWEETBREADS			
Lamb's, raw, per 28g/1oz	37	0	1
SWEETCORN			
Canned in brine, per 28g/1oz	22	1.6	0
Fresh, kernels only, boiled, per 28g/1oz	25	1.3	0
Frozen, per 28g/1oz	25	1.3	0
Whole medium cob	155	4.5	0

SWEETS	C	GF	FU
Per 28g/1oz			
Barley sugar	100	0	1
Boiled sweets	93	0	1
Butterscotch	115	0	1
Filled chocolates	130		1.5
Fudge	111	0	1.5
Liquorice allsorts	105		1
Marshmallows	90	0	1
Nougat	110		1
Nut brittle or crunch	120		1
Peppermints	110	0	1
Toffees	122		1

T

TANGERINES	C	GF	FU
Flesh only, per 28g/1oz	10	0.5	0
Flesh with skin, per 28g/1oz	7	1.8	0
Whole fruit, 70g/2½oz	20	0.9	0
TAPIOCA			
Dry per 28g/1oz	102	0.8	0
TARAMASALATA			
Per 28g/1oz	135	0	5
TARTARE SAUCE			
Per 15ml/1 level tablespoon	35		1
Per 20ml (Australian tablespoon)	45		1
TEA			
All brands, per cup, no milk	0	0	0
TOMATOES			
Per 28g, 1oz			
Raw	4	0.4	0
Canned	3	0.2	0
Fried, halved	20	0.8	0.5
Fried, sliced	30	0.8	0.5
Ketchup	28	0	0
Purée	19	0	0
Whole medium tomato, 57g/2oz	8	0.8	0
Per 15ml/1 level tablespoon			
Chutney	45	0.3	0
Ketchup	15		0
Purée	10		0
Per 20ml (Australian tablespoon)			
Chutney	60	0.4	0
Ketchup	20		0
Purée	13		0
TONGUE			
Per 28g/1oz			
Lamb's, raw	55	0	1.5
Lamb's, lean only, stewed	82	0	2.5
Ox, lean only, boiled	83	0	2.5
TREACLE			
Black, per 28g/1oz	73	0	1
Per 15ml/1 level tablespoon	50	0	0.5
Per 20ml (Australian tablespoon)	65	0	0.5
TRIPE			
Dressed, per 28g/1oz	17	0	0.25
Stewed, per 28g/1oz	28	0	0.5

185

TROUT	C	GF	FU
Fillet, smoked, per 28g/1oz	38	0	0.5
Whole trout, poached or grilled without fat, 170g/6oz	150	0	2
Whole smoked trout, 156g/5½oz	150	0	2
TUNA			
Per 28g/1oz			
Canned in brine, drained	30	0	0
Canned in oil	82	0	2
Canned in oil, drained	60	0	1.5
TURKEY			
Per 28g/1oz			
Meat only, raw	30	0	0.25
Meat only, roast	40	0	0.25
Meat and skin, roast	48	0	0.5
TURNIPS			
Raw, per 28g/1oz	6	0.8	0
Boiled, per 28g/1oz	4	0.6	0

V

VEAL	C	GF	FU
Per 28g/1oz			
Fillet, raw	31	0	0.25
Fillet, roast	65	0	1
Jellied veal, canned	35	0	0
VENISON			
Roast meat only, per 28g/1oz	56	0	0.5
VINEGAR			
Per 28ml/1floz	1	0	0

W

WALNUTS	C	GF	FU
Shelled, per 28g/1oz	149	1.5	5
Per walnut half	15	0.1	0.5
WATERCHESTNUTS			
Per 28g/1oz	10		0
WATERCRESS			
Per 28g/1oz	4	0.9	0
WATERMELON			
Flesh only, per 28g/1oz	6		0
Flesh with skin, per 285g/10oz slice	30	0.8	0

WHEATGERM	C	GF	FU
Per 28g/1oz	100	0.6	1
Per 15ml/1 level tablespoon	18	0.1	0.25
Per 20ml (Australian tablespoon)	24	0.1	0.25
WHELKS			
With shells, boiled, per 28g/1oz	4	0	0
Without shells, boiled, per 28g/1oz	26	0	0
WHITEBAIT			
Fried coated in flour, per 28g/1oz	149	0	5
WHITE PUDDING			
As sold, per 28g/1oz	128	0	3
WHITING			
Per 28g/1oz			
Fillet, fried in breadcrumbs	54	0	1
Fillet, steamed	26	0	0
On the bone, fried in breadcrumbs	49	0	1
On the bone, steamed	18	0	0
WINKLES			
With shells, boiled, per 28g/1oz	4	0	0
Without shells, boiled, per 28g/1oz	21	0	0
WORCESTERSHIRE SAUCE			
Per 28ml/1floz	20	0	0
Per 15ml/1 level tablespoon	13	0	0
Per 20ml (Australian tablespoon)	17	0	0

Y

YAMS	C	GF	FU
Raw, per 28g/1oz	37	1.2	0
Boiled, per 28g/1oz	34	1.1	0
YEAST			
Fresh, per 28g/1oz	15	1.9	0
Dried, per 28g/1oz	48	6.1	0
Dried, per 5ml/1 level teaspoon	8	1.0	0
YOGHURT			
Per 150g/5oz carton			
Low fat, natural	75	0	0.5
Low fat, flavoured	115	0	0.5
Low fat, fruit	135	0	0.5
Low fat, nut	150	2.5	1.5
YORKSHIRE PUDDING			
Cooked, per 28g/1oz	60	0.3	1

Index

Numbers in *italics* refer to illustrations

191

Picture credits
All photographs are the property of Slimming Magazine
except for the following:
Hermes Sweeteners Ltd: pages 118-119, 124, 125, 127, 146
Cadbury Typhoo Ltd: pages 160, 161